BASIC LAW FOR THE LAW ENFORCEMENT OFFICER

PAUL W. WELLS

Legal officer, Mississippi Highway Safety Patrol; Staff Instructor, Mississippi Law Enforcement Officers' Training Academy, Jackson, Mississippi

ILLUSTRATED BY

H. MAURICE HOOKS

1976

W. B. SAUNDERS COMPANY
Philadelphia • London • Toronto

W. B. Saunders Company: West Washington Square
Philadelphia, Pa. 19105

12 Dyott Street
London, WC1A 1DB

833 Oxford Street
Toronto, Ontario M8Z 5T9, Canada

Library of Congress Cataloging in Publication Data

Wells, Paul W

Basic law for the law enforcement officer.

Includes index.

1. Criminal procedure—United States. 2. Criminal law—United States. 3. Police—United States. I. Title.

KF9619.W4 345′.73′052 75–8190

ISBN 0–7216–9205–2

Basic Law: For the Law Enforcement Officer ISBN 0-7216-9205-2

Last digit is the print number: 9 8 7 6 5 4 3 2 1

To my wife, PAT

FOREWORD

In terms of personnel, the police are by far the largest segment of the criminal justice system. For many years, these dedicated persons have directed their efforts toward protecting the lives and property of the public while attempting to acquire the professional status they deserve. Often these officers have been discouraged by seemingly adverse court decisions in their attempt to accomplish this task. The increasing complexity of the criminal law has created many problems for the courts as well as the police. It would be foolish to suggest that requiring all law enforcement officers to be lawyers, or all judges to first be police officers would be a solution to the difficulty—an understanding of the criminal law is needed.

From my experience as a supreme court justice, it is my observation that too often the officer of today places a great deal of emphasis on the major criminal issues and neglects many minor but important ones. Possibly because of emphasis created by the courts, the basics of criminal law have been somewhat overlooked. Writings and texts in this area have been relatively few, since most books have been written primarily for law schools or universities.

This book, *Basic Law for the Law Enforcement Officer,* is greatly needed. Those who are currently engaged in police work cry out for assistance in their efforts to improve their activities. Colleges and universities offering curricula in law enforcement are hampered by the lack of up-to-date and suitable texts in the specific area. The author has taken a giant step toward providing a valuable tool for both education and training in basic criminal law. One who studies this text will gain a great deal of worthwhile knowledge which cannot be found in any other single publication.

To say the least, the author should not be described as a "neutral observer" or an academician in an "ivory tower." For over 12 years, he has been personally involved in the enforcement of laws and the training of law enforcement personnel. However, the fact that he works in the field of law enforcement should not make this writing any less informative or objective. He has coupled on-the-street experience with formal legal education to bring the reader a book on basic criminal law written in a positive, concise, and easy-to-understand language. Law enforcement officers have, for many years, been trained and educated in a negative manner; thus they often are only aware of what *cannot* be done legally. The positive approach with which

Basic Law for the Law Enforcement Officer is written, in my opinion, will be of value to every law enforcement officer in the nation as well as to the student of law enforcement.

NEVILLE PATTERSON

Associate Justice

Mississippi Supreme Court

PREFACE

For several years, law enforcement officers, educators, and students have searched for legal textbooks that deal with the practical applications of the law and that are written in language that is clear and easily understood. Many writers have considered this an impossible objective, primarily because the study of law is, in itself, so technical in nature. In addition, many writers of legal texts have had no actual experience in law enforcement that would give them greater insight into the problems facing the law enforcement officer today.

This book is written by a law enforcement officer for law enforcement officers, using terms and language that are easily understood. It provides both easy and interesting reading for the officer who wants to learn about the laws that affect him in the performance of his duties. Factual situations are used as examples throughout the book, many of which are derived from actual experiences of the author, as an aid to the reader in applying the theory presented. The idea of what an officer *must* know, as opposed to what it would be *nice* to know, is emphasized throughout each chapter. Law enforcement officers from every jurisdiction have become disenchanted with having the courts, their superiors, their legal instructors, and others tell them the many things they cannot do because of the legal issues involved. By far, the majority would like to be told what they *can* do for a change. *Basic Law* is written with a positive approach and is specifically aimed at this very important objective.

Chapter I presents an overview of the law enforcement officer's place in the criminal justice system. This chapter examines the relationship and interdependence of the three main segments of the system, the police, the courts, and corrections. It also gives the officer a solid foundation for understanding the legal issues discussed in the following chapters.

Basic concepts of the laws of arrest are presented in Chapter II, along with positive suggestions and ideas for their application to actual situations facing the officer. Chapter III is concerned with the most important types of criminal evidence and the rules that govern their admissibility. However, a more detailed discussion of Fifth and Sixth Amendment rights that apply to the taking of confessions from accused persons is given in this chapter because of the emphasis the courts have placed on this issue since the *Miranda* decision in 1966.

An entire chapter is devoted to the complex legal issues involved in searches and seizures because of their importance in the field of criminal law today. In addition to discussing the application of the exclusionary rule, which regulates the admissibility of evidence gained in searches and seizures, Chapter IV gives the officer many positive directives for effectively employing the legal means available to him for searching for and seizing evidence.

Major felony crimes and the more frequently committed misdemeanors are discussed in Chapter V. The basic common law elements of each crime are explained, so that the officer can recognize which crime, if any, has been committed when he is confronted by a particular situation.

Because the procedures for handling juvenile offenders vary from state to state, Chapter VI gives a general discussion of the rules of law relevant to juveniles. Quotations from various sources have been cited that explore the causes of and possible solutions to the problem of juvenile delinquency in our society. It is hoped that this material will help the officer to devise and implement procedures and programs for preventing juvenile delinquency in his own community.

Chapter VII discusses the civil and criminal liability of law enforcement officers and how it can be avoided. Examples are given of improper or illegal actions that can result in lawsuits against the officer for such crimes and torts as deprivation of civil rights, assault and battery, false arrest, and malicious prosecution. Even though the officer has legal authority to control others in many instances, he must know the limits of that authority and the probable consequences of abusing it.

It is hoped that this text will help the officer to better understand the rules of law and court decisions that are relevant to law enforcement and to deal more effectively and professionally with the complex problems that he faces daily in the performance of his duties.

Paul W. Wells

CONTENTS

TABLE OF CASES

BASIC LAW:

For the Law Enforcement Officer

42972

CHAPTER I

THE CRIMINAL JUSTICE SYSTEM

For all practical purposes, the criminal justice system is divided into three separately organized parts: law enforcement agencies, the courts and prosecutors, and penal institutions. These three entities are referred to more simply as the police, the courts, and corrections. The actions of a single part of the system have a direct effect on each of the other parts. A court can only deal with those whom the police arrest, and only if the court sees fit to sentence an offender would he be dealt with by a correctional institution.

Many people are unfamiliar with the criminal justice system or have only a superficial understanding of it. Indeed many civic-minded citizens have more knowledge and understanding of the system than an officer who is directly involved in it. The average officer has many misconceptions about the duties and responsibilities of the various agencies which make up the system. For example, many officers tend to get irritated when they have worked long hours solving a particular case only to have it thrown out of court on a "mere technicality" of law. This aspect of criminal justice is not easily understood by most officers. If asked the question, "Who enforces the law?" the officer would surely answer, "I do." However, if he really understood the system he would know that this is not true. The courts enforce the laws and the officer apprehends the offender and appears as a witness for the state at the trial of the offender. Later in this chapter, an attempt will be made to define the duties and responsibilities of each class of officer as they relate to his specific law enforcement agency.

This chapter will provide the officer with a general introduction to the criminal justice system, which will be discussed in more detail in the chapters that follow.

AGENCIES EXERCISING POLICE POWER

THE MUNICIPAL POLICE

Almost every city, town, or municipality in the United States has some type of police agency. The officers of these agencies have (with certain exceptions) jurisdiction over violations of city ordinances and state statutes which occur within the boundaries of their municipality. These officers are primarily responsible to the municipality rather than to the state or any other governmental entity. In terms of manpower (police officers and auxiliary personnel), these municipal law enforcement agencies make up the largest part of the police segment of the criminal justice system.

COUNTY-LEVEL LAW ENFORCEMENT AGENCIES

The Sheriff. Most states have a county sheriff's department. While some sheriffs act as tax collectors and have few or no law enforcement duties, others have what is generally recognized to be a most effective and efficient law enforcement department. Sheriffs having police power are usually recognized as the chief law enforcement officers of their county. Although their jurisdiction is usually county wide, extending to incorporated as well as unincorporated areas within the county, most sheriffs leave policing in the incorporated areas to the municipal police force. In some areas, the sheriff will handle all felonies and the municipal police agency will handle all misdemeanors occurring within the municipality. Depending on the state, other functions of the county sheriff may include acting as executive officer of the courts in his county and operating or administering the county jail.

County Police and Metro Police. The county and metro police agencies usually operate under a separate charter from the municipality or sheriff's department. However, they are very similar since the officers of these agencies have jurisdiction over violations of state law and specially enacted ordinances within their respective boundaries. These agencies are usually found in the nation's larger metropolitan areas.

The Constable. In many states, each district within a county will have one or more constables who usually function as process-servers for the courts of limited criminal jurisdiction (sometimes known as inferior courts). In most states, these constables are elected by the voters in their district and are paid through a fee system based on the processes they serve. Unfortunately these methods of selection and payment have often resulted in a lack of continuity and professionalism in this office; however, the mandatory training laws of many states have improved this situation. In addition to acting as process-server, the constable has jurisdiction over violations of state statutes within his district, except in the case where he is also a deputy sheriff and would then have county-wide authority.

STATE-LEVEL LAW ENFORCEMENT AGENCIES

Highway Patrol vs. State Police. Since state governments have a great effect on the conduct of the local police, we will take a close look at law enforcement agencies at the state level. The basic difference between a state highway patrol and a state police force is that the former generally is restricted in its jurisdiction to violations of traffic laws and related statutes, while the latter usually has full police power with state-wide authority. However, in some states, the governor has statutory authority to issue a proclamation whereby a highway patrol force with traffic enforcement authority becomes a state police force with full police power. This extension of power usually lasts only for a statutory period and must be regranted when the need arises. For a better understanding of state-level police agencies, the following quotes are offered from the Commission Report of the Advisory Commission on Intergovernmental Relations (ACIR) on State-Local Relations in the Criminal Justice System:[1]

> States not only prescribe conditions under which the local police function is exercised, they also provide direct police services in all the states except Hawaii. State police forces range from North Dakota's 112 man unit to California's 8,000 man force.
>
> The 49 state police forces exhibit a wide variety of assigned tasks. Thus, state forces in Alabama, Oklahoma, and North Carolina devoted more than 90% of their time to general highway patrol duty while those in New York and Delaware spent 40% of their time in statewide criminal investigation. Another indication of the different scope of police work in the various state forces is reflected in the fact that 23 such agencies do not have statewide crime control responsibilities but are mainly highway patrol agencies. Moreover, seven states restrict state police patrol solely to unincorporated areas, and only 26 states give their police forces statewide investigative responsibilities.
>
> Of course, the limited character of many state police departments is due to the manner in which states organize their public safety responsibilities. Certain states have chosen to vest their police agencies with a full range of police responsibilities. Some separate their police and investigative agencies and both report to a common public safety director (e.g., Idaho, Illinois, Oklahoma, and Utah). Others vest criminal identification, criminalistics, and investigation responsibilities in 'special' police agencies, apart from state police (e.g., Colorado, South Carolina, South Dakota, and Wyoming). Overall, it appears that only a relatively small number of state police agencies have a full range of police responsibilities (e.g., Alaska, Delaware, Michigan, New Jersey, New York, Pennsylvania, and Vermont).

As an example of one type of state police agency, let us examine the structure of Mississippi's Department of Public Safety. A commissioner of public safety is appointed by the governor and has control over the following subdivisions:

State Highway Patrol. The uniformed officers of the Enforcement Division of the Mississippi Highway Safety Patrol have jurisdiction to apprehend violators of traffic laws on state and federal highways within the state, and upon proclamation of the governor, these officers may be vested with full police power whereby they would have authority and jurisdiction to apprehend *any* law violators anywhere in the state.

An Identification Bureau is manned by highway patrol investigators who have, by statute, full police power. This bureau, upon request from other agencies on both the state and local level, provides assistance in investigation and identification to any municipal, county, state, or federal agency. This bureau also maintains a central criminal records system which is available to any bona fide law enforcement agency.

The state Automobile Theft and Livestock Theft Bureaus are likewise a part of the highway patrol; they are manned by highway patrol investigators and are under the supervision of the commissioner of public safety. These two bureaus also maintain record systems relating to their respective fields; all livestock brands, for example, must be registered and kept on record in the Brands Division of the Livestock Theft Bureau. Officers from these bureaus will assist any law enforcement agency upon request.

Mississippi is fortunate in having a centrally located, statewide Crime Laboratory. This laboratory, which is a division of the Department of Public Safety, provides laboratory services and expertise in the field of evidence.

There is a state Narcotics Bureau which is also a division of the Department of Public Safety. This bureau furnishes manpower to any law enforcement agency desiring help with a drug problem and in addition to works on many cases of its own. The identity of most of the agents working for this bureau is kept secret for a two-year period, since they are required to work undercover. This agency works very closely with local, state, and federal agencies inside and outside the state.

The Mississippi Law Enforcement Officer's Training Academy is the central training center for all local, county, and state law enforcement officers. Although Mississippi has no mandatory training law, the academy is operated year round and is always filled to capacity. The academy is staffed by uniformed members of the highway patrol and its administrator is under the direct supervision of the commissioner of public safety. In addition to the law enforcement training, any officer-student who meets certain requirements and successfully completes the prescribed courses of study can gain college credit for his attendance.

In addition to the aforementioned divisions and bureaus, the highway patrol administers the state's driver licensing laws through the Driver Control Division (which maintains a computerized file of all licensed drivers within the state) and the motor vehicle inspection laws through the Motor Vehicle Inspection Division.

Since the foregoing discussion dealt with only one state of the 50, the officer should examine the statutes of his own municipality, township, county, parish, or state in order to gain a working knowledge of the structure of the law enforcement agencies. Although many states have different agencies, or perhaps merely different names for the same agencies, the general structure would be similar to that of Mississippi.

In the Mississippi example, only the most important agencies exercising police authority were mentioned. However, in most states, there are many other agencies that are primarily regulatory in nature and have no real criminal jurisdiction. These may include the Motor Vehicle Comptroller's Office, which enforces all the laws concerning the levying and collection of motor vehicle license privilege taxes; the Alcoholic Beverage Control Bureau, which is usually a division of the state Tax Commission since this agency is primarily concerned with enforcement of tax laws; the state Conservation Commission or, as it is sometimes called, the Game and Fish Bureau, which enforces all laws and regulations pertaining to wild animals, birds, and fish; the Boat and Water Safety Commission, which is sometimes part of a local or county agency and which is mainly concerned with safety rather than crime; and the state Fire Marshal's Office, which might be a part of the state Insurance Commission since fire insurers endeavor to prevent arson.

The foregoing discussion has been designed to acquaint the law enforcement officer with the state structure of the police segment of the criminal justice system. The officer who desires to be effective and proficient must first understand his position within his own department and his department's position within the state structure, because understanding leads to good communication and good communication leads to a more professional and competent officer.

FEDERAL-LEVEL AGENCIES

Since this text deals mainly with the education and training of officers in state- and local-level police agencies, federal-level agencies will be only briefly mentioned. Working in most states are officers of the Federal Bureau of Investigation, the Alcohol, Tobacco and Firearms Division of the Internal Revenue Service, and the United States Bureau of Narcotics and Dangerous Drugs in addition to the United States marshals who are officers of the federal district courts. If there is a federal park or recreational area in the state, members of the National Park Service (an agency of the Department of Interior) will be employed there. In a state located on a national border, there will be members of the United States Border Patrol.

RELATED AGENCIES

In every state there are several related or associated agencies, clubs, and organizations that work for the benefit of the criminal justice system. Among these may be a state crime commission, a fraternal order of police, a law enforcement association, or a research and development center.

COURTS: THEIR JURISDICTION AND PROCEDURE

Although the structure of the court system varies somewhat from state to state, the following classification of courts is generally applicable to most states.

COURTS OF LIMITED JURISDICTION

In this category are the justice of the peace, the municipal, police, and traffic courts and, in some states, the county, family, small claims, juvenile, probate, and magistrate's courts. Normally, these courts have both civil and criminal jurisdiction in matters which occur within their venue; however, their criminal jurisdiction is limited to misdemeanors. Usually the judge of this type of court will have, by statute, certain extended powers that allow him to sit as a committing judge in criminal cases that are beyond the scope of his jurisdiction. He cannot try these cases, but he has the power to bind an accused person over to appear before the proper court, or he may refuse bail and commit the accused to jail in cases in which the offense is not bailable. In any case, he can *try* only misdemeanors.

Since this court is used most by all law enforcement officers, an understanding of the court's procedure is most important. The officer should also understand that it is not only his evidence which wins the case for him, but also the manner in which he presents that evidence. A good understanding and application of procedure will enhance the possibility of a successful outcome. An officer familiar with court procedure will be more at ease on the witness stand and can concentrate more on what is going on around him. This relaxed mental attitude will also allow him to give serious consideration to each question asked of him so he can formulate an effective answer, and, if he is being examined by the defense counsel, will give him time to think before answering and offer the prosecutor time to object to the question if necessary. Therefore, the following step-by-step procedure for a misdemeanor case should become as familiar to the officer as his badge and gun.

The Affidavit. An affidavit is a written or printed declaration of fact, sworn to by a law enforcement officer or other proper person, stating that the affiant has personal knowledge or sufficient probable cause to believe that there has been a violation of the law and that the person or persons named or described therein committed the crime charged. The affidavit must set forth enough information to permit the judge to make an independent assessment of the probability that the accused committed the crime charged. An affidavit must be on file, charging the commission of the misdemeanor, before a trial may be had—it is the foundation for establishing jurisdiction in the lower courts. After the affidavit is made, the judge may then issue an arrest warrant or a subpoena, whichever the case requires.

The Warrant. An arrest warrant is a legal process, issued by competent authority, directing a law enforcement officer to arrest a person upon grounds stated therein. (See Chapter II for a detailed description of the arrest warrant.) Once the arrest warrant is issued, it is delivered to the proper person for service. The officer, upon finding the person named or described therein, then makes the arrest. Remember, the arrest warrant only allows the officer one alternative: to make the arrest. He is not allowed to accept money or payment of a fine in lieu thereof nor can the officer legally allow the defendant to remain free (i.e., the officer cannot un-arrest a person). He must, upon arrest, put the subject in jail or present the subject to the judge for a preliminary hearing of his case.

The Preliminary Hearing. Almost all states have statutory provisions that make it mandatory for the officer to provide the defendant with a preliminary hearing. Compare the wording in the following statute with the statute in your state: "Every person making an arrest shall take the offender before the proper officer, without unnecessary delay, for examination of his case." Note that the statute specifies who shall take the person before the judge, and by using the word "shall," leaves the officer no alternative but to do as the statute commands. Also, the phrase "without unnecessary delay" makes it mandatory that the officer act promptly.

The basic purpose of a preliminary hearing is to prevent an arresting officer from detaining a person for an unreasonable length of time without affording him an opportunity to have a hearing on the merits of the accusations against him. An accused is entitled to have a determination made, as soon after arrest as possible, of whether or not the state's evidence presents a strong enough case to warrant holding the accused to await action of the grand jury or to proceed to trial and, in bailable cases, if he is entitled to bail. In accordance with the general principle that an accused may waive his rights, he may waive his right to a preliminary hearing, in which case he would be held to await either the action of a grand jury or the trial itself.

There are certain advantages for an accused person in having a preliminary hearing. After hearing its evidence, the judge may decide that the state has not presented a strong enough case to warrant holding the accused, and he will be released immediately. A preliminary hearing forces the state to reveal some of its evidence against the accused. The accused is entitled to cross-examine the prosecution witnesses and may obtain information which will be of value in preparing his defense. Testimony of the defense witnesses is preserved; should a key defense witness die prior to trial, an exception to the hearsay rule allows the use of the deceased's testimony given under oath at the preliminary hearing.

There are also some disadvantages in having a preliminary hearing. For example, a key prosecution witness may also die prior to the trial and his testimony at the preliminary hearing will have been preserved and will be admissible at the trial. Publicity resulting from a preliminary hearing may be detrimental to the accused. Damaging testimony may be given by the prosecution witnesses at a time when the matter is fresh in their minds and will thus be saved for the trial. Generally, rules of evidence do not apply at the preliminary hearing and the prosecution may be able to introduce certain evidence that may not be admissible at trial. If, however, the judge violates any substantive rights of the accused, the resulting commitment may be set aside. At the preliminary hearing, the standard of proof required of the prosecution is only that there be probable cause to believe that the accused committed the crime charged; however, at trial he would have to be found guilty beyond a reasonable doubt.

The Trial in the Lower Court. Although in trying a misdemeanor case there is not much uniformity in procedure among the many different lower courts, the following description will give an indication of what takes place at the trial. If, at the trial of a criminal case, the judge discovers that the crime charged is a felony, he cannot render any judgment finally disposing of the case, but must require the accused to give bail, in bailable cases, or commit him to jail to await action of a grand jury. However, if the crime is a misdemeanor, the trial judge may release the accused on his own recognizance or may authorize an appearance bond in whatever sum he may set, but bond cannot be excessive. As a general rule of thumb, many lower courts set bond at twice the amount of the fine which may be assessed for that particular violation.

On or before the return day of process, a person accused of a crime may demand a trial by jury in certain lower courts, and in those cases, the judge will order the statutory number of persons to be summoned to serve as jurors. In some courts, if the jury fails to reach a verdict it may be dismissed and another summoned, and so on until a verdict is obtained.

A trial in the lower court is usually informal in nature, possibly because of the heavy case load of traffic offenses and other petty misdemeanors. The judge will usually open court and immediately swear in any witness who may be present and the officer who has made the charge. He next will ask, after reading the affidavit and advising the defendant of the formal charge, how he would plead. The defendant may generally plead in one of three ways: guilty, not guilty, or nolo contendere, which means "no contest." After the plea is entered, the judge will usually ask questions of each side and subsequently issue his final decision. In many instances, these trials are conducted without a prosecuting or defense attorney being present; however, in a few lower courts, the trial is conducted in strict accordance with the general rules of criminal procedure, which will be discussed in detail later in this chapter. The same rules of evidence which apply in higher courts are equally applicable in the lower courts (these will be discussed in detail in Chapter III). After a decision has been rendered, the defendant has a right to appeal. He might post an appeal bond with the judge or other proper person as provided for in the state statutes. Upon the perfecting of an appeal, there would be a trial de novo (a new trial from the beginning), because these lower courts are not technically courts of record since no transcript of the proceeding is made. However, they are courts of record in the sense that affidavits, warrants, and other copies of process are kept on file.

COURTS OF ORIGINAL AND GENERAL JURISDICTION

The cases that the courts in this general category usually handle include civil suits (usually with no statutory limitation), criminal prosecutions on all levels, equity suits, probate matters, and land suits. Courts of this type which try all kinds of criminal cases are called district courts (Nebraska, Nevada, Iowa, Colorado, Idaho, Kansas, Louisiana, Minnesota, Montana, New Mexico), superior courts (Alaska, Arizona, Connecticut, Georgia), circuit courts (Alabama, Hawaii, Kentucky, Michigan, Mississippi), and common pleas courts (Ohio, Pennsylvania). Although courts at this level may be called by various names, they all have one thing in common—they are the trial courts of general jurisdiction and all may try felony cases.

Trial procedure at this level is of major importance to the law enforcement officer, because the rules of procedure are applied more strictly here than in most lower courts. Therefore, the following step-by-step description of a criminal trial from indictment to appeal, although general, should help the officer to understand the trial procedure in his own state.

Preliminaries to a Criminal Trial

First, we must consider the fact that a criminal trial may be instituted in several ways (the filing of an affidavit was discussed previously). The United States Constitution and most state constitutions have provisions concerning the institution of a trial in a felony case. In a majority of states, there must first be an indictment from a lawfully empanelled grand jury before a person accused of committing a felony can legally be tried. A state grand jury is composed of 16 to 23 persons who are usually qualified electors or resident freeholders of the district in which the particular court sits. Twelve of these jurors must agree before an indictment may be had.

The Indictment. An accused can be formally charged with a crime in several ways. One method is by a bill of information, which is a written accusation against a person for a criminal offense made to the court by a prosecuting officer. It differs from the indictment in that the indictment issues from the grand jury rather than the prosecutor. Another way is by a bill of presentment which is an informal written statement, signed by the required number of grand jury members, representing to the court that a public offense has been committed which is triable in that particular district, and that there is probable cause for believing that a particular individual named or described therein has committed it. A bill of presentment is not always sufficient to charge an accused with a capital crime; an indictment is required in a majority of states.

An accused can also be formally charged by a grand jury indictment. If a private citizen were seeking an indictment, he would make a formal complaint to the prosecutor. The prosecutor would then present the matter to the grand jury and would procure all necessary witnesses and evidence. If an officer wished to obtain an indictment, he normally would contact the prosecutor and would present the evidence that had been gathered. The prosecutor would then decide whether there was sufficient evidence to present the matter to the grand jury. If so, the officer would be called to testify before the grand jury. After hearing the witnesses and examining the evidence, the required number of grand jury members must concur before an indictment is returned. At that point, the indictment would be delivered to the judge for continuation of process.

"John Doe" indictments are permitted where there is insufficient information to enable the magistrate to identify the defendant in a warrant. Where the grand jury fails to indict the result is called simply "No Bill." After an indictment is had, it is returned, usually in open court, and passes from the grand jury foreman to the judge. The judge will then issue an order (called a fiat) to the clerk of the court who will issue the warrant. The clerk of the court has no general authority to issue arrest warrants. Even though he does the actual paper work much of the time, he can issue process from the court only on direction of the court.

Upon issuance of the arrest warrant, it is delivered to the proper person for service. In most states there is a two-year statute of limitations for prosecution of all crimes except murder, manslaughter, arson, burglary, forgery, counterfeiting, robbery, larceny, rape, embezzlement, and obtaining money or property under false pretense. These crimes are sometimes referred to as "infamous crimes" (a term derived from the common law). The statute of limitations on a crime does not begin to run while the accused is outside the jurisdiction of the court or cannot be found so that process can be served. In different states, different persons have the power or authority to serve the arrest warrant. Usually the warrant is delivered to an officer of the court for service, but any officer having full police power can make an arrest under the provisions of the warrant if it is made within his jurisdiction. If the defendant is located in another state, an officer of the other state possessing arrest power may make the arrest. In this instance, there must be an extradition agreement with the other state in order for the defendant to be returned to the original jurisdiction of issuance. Extradition is necessary in all felony cases except where the accused waives his extradition rights, in which case the accused can be immediately returned to the court of original jurisdiction.

The Preliminary Hearing. Once the accused is taken into custody he must be granted a preliminary hearing within a reasonable time; in other words, the officer may not put the accused in jail and completely forget about him, allowing the accused to remain incarcerated for an indefinite period without affording him some type of relief. In some states preliminary hearings are not granted when the arrest stems from a grand jury indictment, but in this instance, the accused has a constitutional right to petition the court for a writ of habeas corpus. This is an order from the court to the person holding the accused to present himself and the accused to the court to show cause why the accused is being held without bail. The preliminary hearing and the habeas corpus hearing are very similar, and both most often result in the accused's being allowed bail. Other motions are also heard during the preliminary hearing, such as a motion to quash an indictment.

Trial of a Felony Case in State Court

After a person is indicted and arrested, his case is placed on the criminal docket of the particular court having jurisdiction to try the case. Generally, particular terms of the court or parts of terms are set aside for hearing criminal matters. During the term set for trial, the defendant is first arraigned. He is directed to stand, along with his counsel, before the bench while the judge reads the formal charge. After the charge is read, the defendant is called upon to plead thereto; he must plead guilty or not guilty (the nolo contendere plea is not allowed in felony cases). If the defendant pleads guilty, the judge may sentence him at that time or may set a future date for sentencing. If the defendant pleads not guilty and there is no other delay, the judge will ask both the prosecutor and defense attorney if they are ready for trial; if the answers are in the affirmative the trial begins. The defense attorney decides whether or not to have a trial by jury. He may choose to let the judge hear the case without a jury, but this does not happen often.

The first major step in the trial is the selection of the jury, which is accomplished by voir dire examination. Both at common law and by statute, litigants are permitted to interrogate prospective jurors to determine their freedom from partiality or prejudice. The voir dire examination is designed to produce a petit jury of 12 persons who are acceptable to both the prosecutor and defense counsel. The principal purpose of the voir dire examination is to test the qualifications of prospective jurors and to permit counsel for both sides to obtain information about the jurors which will enable them to eliminate those who are unlikely to be completely fair in their consideration of the case. During voir dire examination, the attorneys make their initial contact with those who will be selected as jurors and have an opportunity to impress upon them the theory of law which they will use. For the defense attorney, this provides an additional opportunity to attempt to eliminate any prejudice toward his client.

A prospective juror can be excused for cause, but since it is often difficult, if not impossible, to determine partiality or prejudice, each side is allowed a certain number of peremptory challenges. By a peremptory challenge, the prosecutor or defense counsel can dismiss a juror without giving any reason. In a number of states, both sides are allowed 12 peremptory challenges in capital cases and four or six in all other criminal cases. There are two basic ways in which the challenges are exercised. In the first, the entire jury selection procedure is done in open court. As a juror is dismissed, another is called, and so on until all peremptory challenges are used, resulting in the seating of 12 jurors and one or two alternate jurors (sometimes called talesmen). The alternates hear the case as the regular jurors do but are not permitted to vote on any issue except when a regular juror is unable to perform because of sickness, or some other reason, in which case the alternate would take his place.

The other method also begins in open court, but not all challenges are used there. Initially, in open court, all jurors who show cause are dismissed and all challenges for cause are used, leaving a sufficient number of jurors so that each side can use the total number of peremptory challenges allowed by statute. The attorneys for each side then meet privately with the judge at which time 21 jurors are seated. Each side then exercises all four challenges, resulting in seating of 12 jurors and one alternate. Some of the "causes" often used for dismissing a prospective juror are prior involvement in a similar litigation; relationship to the accused or one of the attorneys; incompetency; previous jury service; an unfounded interest in the case; open prejudice or bias; or a fixed opinion of the case.

Preliminary or Opening Statements. Following the seating of the jury, opening statements are normally made by both the prosecution and defense. These statements are designed to acquaint the members of the jury with the nature of the case and the issues involved. Opening statements are usually presented in narrative style to give the jurors a clear picture of the case from the beginning. In criminal cases, the prosecution will make the first opening statement, setting forth the crime charged, those involved, and other facts. If the defense counsel so chooses, he may make a statement in which he attempts to show the defendant in the best possible light. It would also be most proper and ethical for the prosecutor and defense attorney to caution the jury not to form a premature opinion of the case or to reach a conclusion as to guilt after hearing only one or two witnesses.

Presentation of the Case. Although this part of the trial is described only briefly here, it is often the most time-consuming part of the actual trial. The prosecution will call its witnesses and present their testimony and any documentary, real, or other evidence which it may have. Remember that in a criminal case the defendant must be found guilty beyond a reasonable doubt, and in cases based solely on circumstantial evidence, the proof must exclude every other reasonable hypothesis except that of guilt. Each prosecution witness is subject to cross-examination by the defense counsel, and there may be re-direct and re-cross examination by either side. Upon completion of its case, the prosecution rests. At this point, there may be motions made by either or both parties (e.g., motions to dismiss, for a directed verdict, and so forth), but these motions are not often sustained.

After the prosecution rests its case, the defense follows with its witnesses and evidence. The defense witnesses are, in turn, subject to cross-examination by the prosecution. After the defense rests its case, the prosecution is entitled to present evidence in rebuttal and the defense may then reply to the rebuttal.

Submission of the Case to the Jury. After both sides have presented their cases, the court recesses and the attorneys meet with the judge in his chambers in order to submit written jury instructions which they deem necessary or appropriate. A copy of each instruction is given to the opposing counsel who follows along as the judge examines them. The judge then approves or rejects each instruction, which is usually stamped "given" or "denied" by the judge and then delivered to the clerk of the court. The clerk files the denied instructions in the case file so that a copy is available for appeal purposes. The given instructions are returned to the judge or the submitting attorney, depending on whether the attorneys or the court itself will instruct the jury. When the court reconvenes, the jury is instructed (the given instructions are read to the jury). After the instruction of the jury, each attorney gives his final argument. In their arguments, the attorneys attempt to organize and summarize the evidence presented during the trial so that the jury can draw the logical inferences from the evidence. This final gathering together of the evidence might be called a "word picture" of the facts presented during the trial. The party having the burden of proof (always the prosecution in a criminal case) has the right to open and close with his final argument. For example, the prosecutor might begin his final argument, speak for only five minutes, and then allow the defense attorney to present his entire argument before completing his own.

Reversible error may occur at any time during the trial, including final argument, if the prosecutor or judge comments on the defendant's failure to take the stand in his own behalf. Under the Supreme Court's interpretation of the Fifth Amendment to the Constitution, an accused is not required to testify, and the courts have consistently held that if a defendant does not take the stand, there can be no comment on his failure to so do.

Verdict of the Jury. Upon completion of final arguments, the written instructions which were allowed and all desired tangible evidence is presented to the jury foreman and the jury is sent to a secluded room to deliberate. At this time the court will usually recess. After reaching a verdict, which often may take hours, the foreman notifies the bailiff who reconvenes the court. The jury is then brought back in, and in open court, the foreman hands the written verdict of the jury to the clerk of the court. He passes it to the judge, who reads it and passes it back to the clerk, who then reads the verdict aloud.

In most states, the jury may be polled at this point to determine that a sufficient number of jurors concurred in the verdict announced. Most states require that in a criminal case all twelve jurors must agree in order for the defendant to be found guilty of the crime charged. When a jury fails to reach a verdict the judge will declare a mistrial, and the state then decides whether to proceed with a new trial. This new trial would not violate the constitutional prohibition against double jeopardy, since in the first trial there was no final disposition of the case.

Appeals

In a majority of the states, appeals from the trial court of general jurisdiction go to the court of last resort in the state, which is usually called the state supreme court. However, in 20 states, there is an intermediate appellate court. These intermediate courts were established because of the increasing caseloads of the supreme courts. All state constitutions, except that of New Hampshire, provide for a court of last resort. A state's court of last resort is a creature of that state's constitution, and so the rules governing the appeal procedure vary somewhat from state to state. Since the following general discussion is based on the appeal procedure in Mississippi, the officer should acquaint himself with the specific appeal procedure in his state.

The Mississippi Rules of Appellate Procedure provide that "an appeal must be taken within 90 days after a judgment is rendered. The appellant [one who is pursuing the appeal] must file a Suggestion of Error and a Brief of the case within 40 days after the record of the trial is filed with the Supreme Court. The appellant may pre-pay the costs or post an appeal bond. After the appeal is perfected, the appellee's [one who would defend on appeal] brief is due not later than 60 days from the time the record is filed with the Supreme Court." While many states have no statutory provision for it, the United States Supreme Court has held that an indigent defendant must be provided with a transcript of the case for the purpose of appeal, with the cost of the transcript to be borne by the state. Of course, all states now abide by this decision.

An appellate court will review only the errors claimed by the appellant and will not usually rule on those which are not claimed. A state may appeal in criminal cases from a lower court judgment sustaining a demurrer, from a sustained motion to quash an indictment, from the actual quashing of an affidavit charging a crime, or from a judgment of acquittal when a determination of a question of law is sought. However, in the latter instance, the judgment of the lower court is not reversed, nor can the defendant be retried; the appeal goes only to the question of law to be determined. Quite often the attorney general of a state will pursue an appeal of this type in order to set a legal precedent on which to base future opinions from his office. In most states, a defendant who intelligently pleads guilty in a lower court would be estopped from appealing to the state's court of last resort.

After a defendant has exhausted all his appeals and is sentenced, he can petition the appropriate court for a writ of error coram nobis. This writ is restricted to cases where new, material evidence is discovered after a final decision has been rendered. If granted, the defendant would be allowed a new trial.

Another post-conviction remedy quite often used by those incarcerated is the writ of habeas corpus. "This writ has for centuries been esteemed the best and only sufficient defense of personal freedom, a high prerogative common law writ, having for its object the speedy release by judicial decree of persons who are illegally restrained of their liberty, or illegally detained from the control of those who are entitled to the custody of them. It is essentially a writ of inquiry, and on matters in which the state itself is concerned, in aid of right and liberty. The writ is directed to the person in whose custody the person is detained, and requires the body of the person alleged to be unlawfully held in custody or restrained of his liberty to be brought before the court that appropriate judgment may be rendered upon judicial inquiry into the alleged unlawful restraint."[2]

Appeals to the United States Supreme Court. Since there is no automatic right of appeal to the United States Supreme Court, a party wishing to appeal a decision rendered by a state court of last resort must petition the Supreme Court for a writ of certiorari. If the Court finds that the case merits review, it will issue the writ, commanding the state court to deliver up the record so that the aggrieved party may have a review of the proceedings. If certiorari is denied, the sentence imposed by the state court goes into effect.

THE PROSECUTION

A prosecuting officer conducts, on behalf of the state, criminal proceedings against those persons accused of committing crimes. It is within his power to decide whether or not to carry a particular case to trial and in certain instances he may decide which crime or crimes the accused should be formally charged with. He often works very closely with the police officer in the investigation and preparation of cases that may have a serious impact on the community. In these instances, every officer should avail himself of the prosecutor's legal knowledge, for it is the prosecutor who must plan trial strategy, effectively use all admissible evidence, and help the officer to prepare to testify as a witness. In the same way, the prosecutor relies on the cooperation and legwork of the police officer. Teamwork between the officer and prosecutor is very important; the work of one should enhance the work of the other.

> The systems of prosecutions are different across the nation and range from centralized, appointive ones where the state attorney general has charge of all local prosecutions to the multitiered systems where local prosecutors are elected by county and judicial district.
>
> The local prosecutor is elected in 45 states and appointed in five—Alaska, Connecticut, Delaware, New Jersey, and Rhode Island. The constitutions of Colorado, California, New York, and Washington permit appointment, but in New York and Washington only where there is a charter form of county government. The local prosecutor's office is a constitutional one in 36 states, though the constitutions of Idaho, Kentucky, Nevada, and North Carolina provide that the office may be abolished or the number of prosecutors be reduced by action of the legislature.
>
> The prosecutor is elected by county in 29 states and by judicial district in another 12. Most of their districts are multi-county in nature. In four states prosecutors are elected both from counties and judicial districts. In these states, county prosecutors usually handle misdemeanors and preliminary felony work, while the district prosecutors handle all other criminal matters.[3]

As one can see from these statistics, the method of prosecutor selection is varied. However, the manner of prosecuting a criminal case is fairly uniform as far as general procedures are concerned. Any officer desiring to proceed to trial with an important case should, after the arrest, visit the prosecutor and seek his assistance. The officer should explain the case in minute detail, being very careful not to overlook issues which are seemingly insignificant, since they may be of major importance in the trial. In addition, the officer should explain the procedures and theories of law used in the investigation and arrest, since he may be more familiar with criminal law than a newly elected or appointed prosecutor might be. In many instances, an attorney may have practiced law for five or ten years or even longer without ever working on a criminal case, and since during that period, he was primarily concerned with other fields of law, he probably would not have kept abreast of current criminal decisions. On the other hand, the officer, who is directing his efforts and thoughts toward the apprehension of criminals, would avail himself of the many educational and training programs offered through colleges, training academies, seminars, and police departments. This is one reason why communication between the officer and prosecutor is so essential. Through the professional cooperation extended to one from the other, they may be able to build what every attorney desires—an unassailable case.

CORRECTIONS

> A system is an arrangement of working parts or organizations that together make up a whole. For example, the automobile and the human body are systems with parts (or subsystems) that must

work together if the whole is to operate. Criminal Justice is also a system, and its parts are organizations such as the police, the courts, and corrections. The system of criminal justice will not work at all if any of the parts are missing; it will work at a low level of efficiency if any of the parts are not operating well.

In examining the main functions of each part of the system, it is possible to see their inter-relationships. For example, the police force has the responsibility for criminal investigations and apprehension, the courts for determination of guilt, and corrections for confinement and rehabilitation. These are greatly simplified descriptions of the individual functions of each part of the system, but they illustrate what each part does.[4]

CORRECTIONAL OBJECTIVES

The general underlying premise for the new directions in corrections is that crime and delinquency are symptoms of failures and disorganization of the community as well as of individual offenders. In particular, these failures are seen as depriving offenders of contact with the institutions that are basically responsible for assuring development of law-abiding conduct: sound family life, good schools, employment, recreational opportunities, and desirable occupations, to name only some of the more direct influences. The substitution of deleterious habits, standards, and associates for these strengthening influences contributes to crime and delinquency.

The task of corrections therefore includes building or rebuilding solid ties between the offender and the community, integrating and reintegrating the offender into community life, restoring family ties, obtaining employment and education, and securing in the larger sense a place for the offender in the routine functioning of society.[5]

THE JAIL

On the correctional continuum, jails are at the beginning of the penal or institutional segment. They are, in fact, the reception units for a greater variety and number of offenders than will be found in any other segment of the correctional process, and it is at this point that the greatest opportunity is offered to make sound decisions on the offender's next step in the correctional process. Indeed, the availability of qualified services at this point could result in promptly removing many from the correctional process who have been swept in unnoticed and undetected and who are more in need of protective, medical, and dental care from welfare and health agencies than they are in need of custodial care in penal and correctional institutions. In a broad sense, the jails and local correctional institutions are reception centers for the major institutions.[6]

Relationship of Jails and Police

Not only is the jail located strategically in terms of numbers of persons that come in contact with it and influence it has on them, it also performs a service function for the agencies within the system. The relationship of the jail to the police is one of accommodation and cooperation. The jail has the responsibility to accept any prisoner who is legally detained and who can be legally received by the jail. It should be noted, for example, that in some jurisdictions the jail cannot admit juveniles even when the arrest is legal. The jail plays a passive role, and to some extent the jail population will reflect this. For example, if the police are concerned with drunks and have periodic cleanup campaigns, the jail will hold a number of these persons. In some jurisdictions, drunks and homeless men are handled by methods other than arrest—for example, detoxification stations where the drunk can be sobered up and private agencies such as the Salvation Army where vagrants may be housed.

Obviously, the number of persons arrested for other crimes will depend more on the amount of crime than on police arrest policy. The important point is that the jail feels the effects of community and police policy. The jail is not an independent unit in the community, uninfluenced by events around it. It is a part of a larger system, and what the rest of the system does will affect the jail. The way the jail operates will also affect the community and the criminal justice system.

The jail holds the accused until the formal machinery of criminal justice begins to move. While the accused is in jail, coordination between the police and the jail personnel may be required. Some exchange of information between police and jail personnel will be necessary, particularly where there is a need to keep accomplices separated. When a long-term investigation is required, the police and the jail may need to coordinate their efforts in scheduling investigation interviews or in otherwise making the accused available to the police, the prosecuting attorney, and defense counsel. The need for information exchange and coordination is of equal importance when the jail is holding a material witness whereby the jail performs a service function for police.[7]

Admitting a Prisoner

The officer assigned to the admissions desk is responsible for the legal admission of all prisoners brought to the jail. He must therefore be thoroughly familiar with confinement orders and court commitment papers and be capable of determining their legality. Each jurisdiction has different forms and laws, but certain basic requirements are the same for all jurisdictions. The confinement order should contain a legal charge. Such statements as "Hold for investigation," or "Will see Dr. Smith in the morning" are not legal charges and should not be accepted. In some jurisdictions the county attorney has approved the booking of prisoners on "suspicion of" charges. This does not make it legal.

There is no statute in any jurisdiction that makes it an offense to be under suspicion of having committed an offense. A person can be suspected of committing a crime and if the evidence is sufficient can be arrested and jailed. But when he is booked he must be booked for the *offense,* and not the suspicion of having committed it. Each admissions officer should know what a valid charge is or have a list of valid charges available for reference. Care in admitting prisoners to jail will minimize the possibility of civil suits.

The prisoner must be admitted by the arresting officer. When the arresting officer cannot be present, the officer bringing the prisoner to the jail must have a citation that originated with and is signed by the arresting officer. This will eliminate the "hold for Joe" charges that sometimes appear on confinement orders.

Persons admitted to the jail for probation or parole violation should be accompanied by papers. The probation violator should be admitted with papers from the court; the parole violator should have papers signed by the parole board or the parole officer.

Prisoners sentenced to the jail are legally confined by the commitment order issued by the court. Some jurisdictions require that all commitment orders be signed by the judge, not his clerk. Generally, however, the signature or initial of the clerk is sufficient. Only rarely is a prisoner committed in error. Should this occur, however, the only protection the admissions officer has is a commitment order signed by the proper authority. Obviously, the name of the prisoner and the charge should be given correctly in the order.

The identity of the person bringing the prisoner to jail should be known. In many instances, he may be a member of another law enforcement agency. Prisoners in transit may be brought in by police or federal marshals. All these persons should be required to furnish proof of identity and to show papers that give them legal custody of the prisoner.

The admissions officer must also be familiar with the laws of the state regarding confinement of juveniles. In some states, juveniles cannot be admitted to a jail under any circumstances; other states permit juveniles in jails only upon written order of a judge or under special circumstances.

Often the admissions officer is faced with an injured, sick, or unconscious prisoner. If medical care is available in the jail this is no problem. Most jails, however, even though they are not prepared to accept such prisoners, must do so under law. The statutes of some jurisdictions provide no clear instructions about what the jail must do. In any case, the admissions officer can make one assumption: if he admits an injured, sick, or unconscious prisoner, the jail is responsible for providing medical treatment.

At the time of commitment, preferably at the booking desk, all personal property should be taken from the prisoner and listed item by item. Care should be taken in listing personal property to describe properly such items as watches, rings, and other kinds of jewelry. A ring, for example, should be identified by color of metal and color of stone. The inside band should be examined for initials and other identifying marks. A platinum ring will contain a notation such as the following: .900 Plat. 100 Irid. A gold ring will be inscribed with "24 (or 10 or 14) carat." A watch can be described by color and kind of band and color of face. The make should always be listed. All clothing should be described by color and by labels, if there are any. The fact that clothing has no labels should be noted; otherwise a Salvation Army handout becomes a Brooks Brothers suit. The condition of clothing should also be recorded, as for example, "one blue suit, Bonds label, tear inside pocket and at the elbow, two buttons missing from jacket front." The wallet should be described and its contents inventoried. Money should be counted while the prisoner watches, and the amount entered on a separate slip and signed by the prisoner.

All personal items received from an inmate at the time of booking should be placed in a sealed envelope signed by both the receiving officer and the prisoner, and the prisoner should receive a carbon copy of the receipt.[8]

The Enforcement Officer's Role

The preceding excerpts were selected to acquaint the police officer with some of the current ideas, concepts, theories, and suggestions concerning the correctional system of today. Normally the enforcement officer would not have any direct dealings with a person after he was incarcerated, except when the officer is obligated to afford the defendant a preliminary hearing, when the officer is acting as jailer (in many police departments the officer serves in a dual capacity), and when the officer is required to present the defendant in court. However, in general, once the arresting officer presents the defendant to the admissions officer at the jail, he has fulfilled his obligations to the department and to the defendant. Later, at the trial of the case, the arresting officer would appear as a witness for the state. The arresting officer is not responsible for the defendant during incarceration, nor is he normally responsible for presenting the defendant at trial.

In many instances, an officer will arrest a person who needs psychiatric care or examination. In some states, the psychiatric examination of arrested persons is done at the jail; however, in other states, facilities and personnel are not available at the jail for this type of care, and the arresting officer may be obligated to transport the prisoner to a state mental hospital. Almost every state has statutes providing for the admission of a person to a state mental hospital by court order. However, very often the officer will need to have a person admitted at night, on weekends, and at other times when court is not in session. For this reason, some state statutes allow the officer to admit a person for mental care upon the written advice of two licensed physicians, thus eliminating the need for a court order.

When a person is arrested and charged with a felony, a psychiatric examination is often needed in order to determine his mental state at the time the crime was committed or to determine if he is mentally capable of giving a free and voluntary waiver of his constitutional rights. The prosecutor or defense counsel may request or petition the court to order the examination, which may be done by private or state-employed physicians. If the court so orders, a defendant may be sent to a state mental institution for an examination to determine if he is mentally competent to stand trial. These institutions usually have a maximum security complex where the accused is housed until examination is completed. Other persons who have been adjudged criminally insane are also incarcerated in the maximum security complex for indefinite periods which often are, by necessity, for life.

STATE PENITENTIARIES

Every state has some type of state prison or penitentiary. These institutions are primarily for adults who have been convicted of and sentenced for committing felonies. Many state prisons were originally organized as plantation systems, some occupying more than 20,000 acres of land, where the prisoners were required to farm or work the land; hence, most were self supporting and some that sold their agricultural products made a profit in their operations. These profits were directed back into the system and used for improvements and upkeep of prison facilities. However, today only a few of these prison farms remain, but they are still found in Arkansas, Georgia, and Mississippi. In other states, the prisoner is kept in a central prison facility and is often required to do very little except keep his cell clean. Much argument and many books have centered on the subject of incarceration and rehabilitation of prisoners, and the federal courts deal with the controversy through litigation almost daily.

LOCAL JAILS AND PRISONS

Some states, by statute, allow individual counties and municipalities to construct, maintain, and operate jails, prisons, and prison farms. Other statutes allow the governmental entity to employ prisoners on road construction on state and county roads and similar projects (however, these statutes specifically prohibit the leasing or hiring of a prisoner to any individual or corporation for any purpose whatsoever). Other statutes also provide that several governmental entities may operate consolidated jails or prisons or that a governmental entity can allow its prisoners to work in another contiguous entity, provided that both are in the same judicial district. There are also statutory provisions which allow municipalities to operate their own jails and to hold county prisoners and others in them, and municipal prisoners may likewise be kept in the county jail or work on the county prison farm. A county and a municipality located within that county may also jointly construct, own, and use one jail. In any case, the enforcement officer should make himself familiar with what type of local facility he will be dealing with and also with the local guidelines he must follow in admitting the arrestee.

JUVENILE DETENTION

> Juvenile detention involves holding delinquent children of juvenile court age in secure temporary custody pending court disposition or transfer to another jurisdiction or agency. A unique feature of juvenile court law is the authorization for a child to be taken into custody in order to protect his health and welfare.
>
> Two different types of temporary care can serve this purpose: detention and shelter. Detention is providing care for a child who has committed a delinquent act and requires secure custody. Shelter is providing care for dependent and neglected children or those apprehended for delinquency whose homes are unfit for their return. It is provided in a physically unrestricting facility such as boarding or group homes or temporary care institutions, pending the child's return to his own home or placement for longer term care. Detention serves the juvenile court exclusively, while shelter serves both the court and child and family welfare agencies. Detention, however, is sometimes used punitively or resorted to because of the lack of other community services and facilities. In some jurisdictions, it is routine to detain all arrested children whether or not they are subsequently referred to court. In addition, detention may be extended following court disposition when space in a juvenile institution is not available.[9]

Since dealing with juvenile offenders, the juvenile courts, and juvenile detention is an important part of the officer's daily activities, a later chapter (Chapter VI) is devoted to the subject of juvenile offenders. For this reason, a discussion of juvenile courts is not included in this chapter, and juvenile detention is discussed only briefly here.

PROBATION AND PAROLE

The probation and parole component of the correctional system is usually the responsibility of a state probation and parole board. State statutes generally provide for the appointment of a number of officers to carry out the responsibilities of parole supervision and to aid the courts in the supervision of those offenders placed on probation. The courts may, at their discretion, suspend the sentence of a convicted person and place him on probation. These probationers are usually under the strict supervision of the parole officer. The courts can, for due cause, revoke the probation of the offender and impose the original sentence. In some states, prisoners are eligible for parole consideration after they have served, for example, one-third of their sentence, or in the case of a 30-year or life sentence, after completion of 10 years. However, in the case of sex offenders, most statutes require an examination by a psychiatrist prior to granting of parole. In the late 1960's and early 1970's work-release programs were instituted in a number of states, and it seems that these are helping offenders to successfully return to society.

SUMMARY AND PRACTICAL SUGGESTIONS

In this chapter a general overview of the criminal justice system was presented. The officer should have a practical understanding of the system and of how it and the law affect his daily activities. He must recognize his role and its relation to those of others working in the system if the system is to operate at maximum efficiency. He should recognize from the outset his task in maintaining the routine functioning of our society. Only through continuing education and training will the police officer attain the highest professional status possible.

The officer should avail himself of every opportunity to learn more about statutes and ordinances, departmental rules and regulations, the courts and their procedure, and the disposition of convicted defendants. There is no substitute for experience and it cannot be learned from books or in a classroom; however, experience alone cannot fulfill even the basic needs of an officer and his work can only be enhanced by education and training. In addition, a good understanding and correct application of the law will gain more convictions for the officer.

REFERENCES

1. Commission Report on State-Local Relations in the Criminal Justice System, Advisory Commission on Intergovernmental Relations, U. S. Government Printing Office, 1971, p. 83.
2. 39 Am. Jur. 2d 188, Habeas Corpus, Sec. 14.
3. Commission Report on State-Local Relations in the Criminal Justice System, Advisory Commission on Intergovernmental Relations, U. S. Government Printing Office, 1971, pp. 112–113.
4. The Jail: Its Operation and Management, U. S. Bureau of Prisons, p. 9.
5. Task Force Report, Corrections, The President's Commission on Law Enforcement and Administration of Justice, U. S. Government Printing Office, 1967, p. 7.
6. Ibid., pp. 162–163.
7. The Jail: Its Operation and Management, U. S. Bureau of Prisons, pp. 9–10.
8. Ibid., pp. 17–18.
9. Commission Report on State-Local Relations in the Criminal Justice System, Advisory Commission on Intergovernmental Relations, U. S. Government Printing Office, 1971, p. 123.

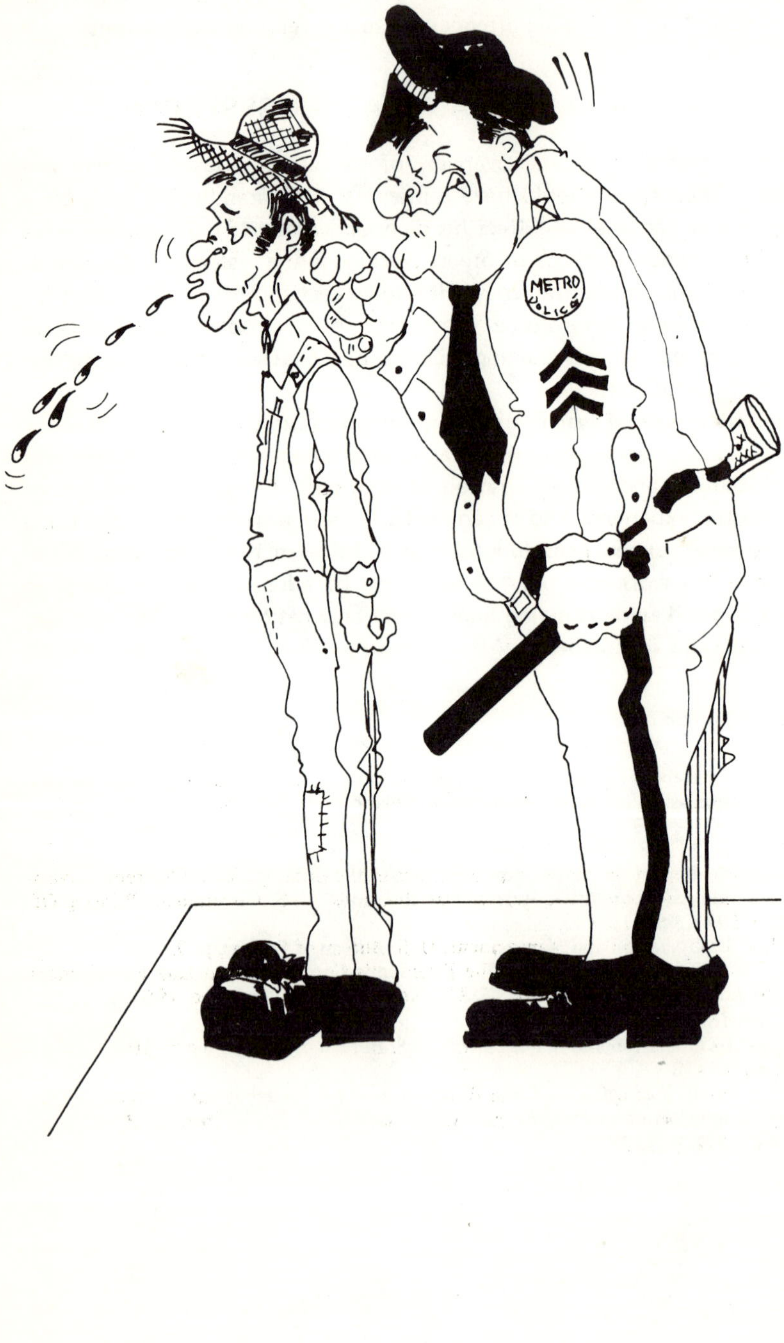
METRO
POLICE

CHAPTER II

LAWS OF ARREST

Our contemporary laws of arrest can be traced back directly to the early common law of England. References to the common law were made by the early Canonists and are also found in the *Dialogue of the Exchequer*, a treatise written in England about 1180. As Parliament made new written laws which modified these existing legal principles, the term "common law" was used to describe those laws in force prior to the passage of statutes.

When our forefathers came to America, they brought the English common law with them. These settlers made use of and governed themselves by it in the colonies until the American Revolution, but as legislatures were created and written laws were enacted, the common law became more restricted by the statutes. However, where it has not been superseded by statute, the common law remains in force in most states. Louisiana, however, is a unique exception. At the time the Louisiana Territory was ceded to this country, it was governed by French law, and even today parts of the Napoleonic Code are still in force in that state.

As with the common law, many of the arrest practices that had developed in England were brought to this country by the colonists and were used extensively prior to the adoption of our Constitution. For example, according to early English common law, sheriffs or constables appointed by the crown were the only "officers" possessing official arrest powers. However, the sheriff or constable had the power and authority to call upon the citizenry for aid in forming a *posse comitatus* to render assistance in making an arrest.

Early English common law forms a part of America's legal tradition, and history has played an enormous role in molding America's legal institutions. The decisions of America's courts today are directly influenced by the development and modernization of common law concepts and practices followed years ago.

ARREST DEFINED

Since this chapter is devoted to a specific area of the law, that of arrest, the officer should know and understand the meaning of the term. Often the lay person, who is only familiar with the "dictionary definition," does not understand the legal definition which the officer is legally bound to apply in his police activities. Therefore, the following definitions are offered for comparison:

> An arrest is the taking, seizing, or detaining of the person of another, by touching or putting hands on him; or by any act that indicates an intention to take him into custody and that subjects him to the actual control and will of the person making the arrest; or by the consent of the person to be arrested.[1]

> To stop the progress or movement of: to take or keep in custody by authority of law: the state of being stopped: the act of taking or holding in custody by authority of law.[2]

> To deprive a person of his libery by legal authority. Taking custody of another for the purpose of holding or detaining him to answer a criminal charge.[3]

> An arrest, as the term is used in criminal law, signifies the apprehension or detention of the person of another in order that he may be forthcoming to answer for an alleged or supposed crime.[4]

> In criminal procedure, an arrest consists in the taking into custody the person of another, under a real or assumed authority, for the purpose of holding or detaining him to answer a criminal charge, or of preventing the commission of a criminal offense.[5]

As one can readily see, a particular word or phrase may have many meanings. Often the officer has as much trouble as a lay person in determining which meaning should apply in a given circumstance. Actually, the different definitions cited here are not meant to create misunderstanding or confusion. They are intended to serve a two-fold purpose; first, the officer must certainly understand what the term "arrest" means, and second, since we are now entering a field of law which is based primarily on theory, the officer should begin to apply that theory at the earliest possible point.

Let us assume, for a moment, that you are a police officer in the city of Dallas, Texas, and you wish to apply at least one of the above definitions to an arrest you have made. Which would you apply—the first, second, third, fourth, or fifth? On the other hand, let us assume that you are employed by the Jackson, Mississippi, Police Department, have made an arrest, and wish to apply one of the definitions. Which one would you apply? Now you are a resident of New York City and have made a citizen's arrest. Which would you use?

For an officer to be able to answer these questions correctly, he must have some knowledge of how the law is applied. For example, we are here faced with the problem of applying different definitions to three separate and distinct jurisdictions. And, since we are primarily interested in presenting the best possible case, we want to apply the best possible definition. If we examine each definition closely, we see the first and the fourth are definitions taken from a legal encyclopedia, the second is taken from a regular dictionary, while the third is from a law dictionary. This leaves the fifth, which is from a Mississippi Supreme Court decision. If we had cited a definition from a United States Supreme Court decision, it probably would have been applicable in all three cases; however, none was cited. The officer in Dallas would probably use either the first or fourth definition, since those from legal encyclopedias usually are preferred over those from law dictionaries and would certainly be preferred over those from regular dictionaries. The officer in Jackson would probably use the definition of his own state's high court, as long as it did not conflict with a United States Supreme Court decision. A decision from a state high court would be preferred over more general definitions from legal encyclopedias or law dictionaries. In other words, an officer would and should apply decisions of his own state's supreme court in the absence of superseding United States Supreme Court decisions on the same issues. As far as the citizen's arrest in New York City is concerned, it might be unwise to apply any of the quoted definitions, since none of them really apply to a citizen's arrest.

At this point there might be a question as to why the officer must follow previous court decisions. The answer is relatively simple, since the officer and the courts are bound by the doctrine of stare decisis (sometimes referred to as state decisis in state courts). This means that once a court has applied a principle of law to a certain set of facts, it will adhere to the principle and apply it in future cases where the facts are substantially the same. As the court, in general, must abide by its past decisions, the officer must also abide by them or suffer the penalty of losing his case in court. The Supreme Court of the United States has, on many occasions, laid down certain guidelines which make it mandatory for the officer to do or not do certain things when acting officially. This was done in the case of *Ker* v. *California.*[6]

> Arrests by state and local police officers are to be judged by the same Constitutional standards as apply to the Federal government. In order for an arrest to be valid today, the officer must comply with the provisions of the Fourth Amendment as well as his own state constitution and statutes.

Here the Court was direct and to the point in its wording, leaving no doubt as to what the officer must do: he must follow the directives of the Fourth Amendment.

> The right of the people to be secure in their persons, . . . against unreasonable . . . seizures, shall not be violated, and no

> warrants shall issue, but upon probable cause, supported by oath or affirmation, and particularly describing the . . . persons . . . to be seized. (United States Constitution, Amendment IV.)

Notice that certain words have been deleted that are relevant to search and seizure but not to the arrest per se. This section of the Constitution, as quoted here, does protect the individual from illegal seizure of his person. (i.e., from illegal arrest).

> . . . the Fourth Amendment's guaranty of the right of privacy is enforceable against the states through the due process clause of the Fourteenth Amendment, and identical or similar provisions are found in the constitutions of the several states.[7]

The term "arrest" was derived from the French word "arreter" which means to stop or stay. It signifies the restraint of a person that deprives him of his liberty and freedom of movement, and it must bind him to the control and will of the person making the arrest.

ESSENTIAL ELEMENTS OF AN ARREST

INTENT

The actions relied upon as constituting an arrest must have been performed by the person wishing to make the arrest with the *intent* or purpose to take the alleged offender into the custody of the law. If there is no *intent* to deprive the other person of his liberty or to take him into custody, and stopping him is merely part of the proper exercise of some other official act or duty, *It Does Not Constitute an Arrest.*

For example, suppose an officer stops a motorist to check his driver's license. The actual stopping does not constitute an arrest because the intent to arrest is lacking. However, the intent could attach at the time of the stopping if a crime were being committed in the officer's presence and if the officer had authority to check the person's driver's license in the beginning. On the other hand, let us assume that the officer stops a car illegally—for instance, just to get a closer look at a pretty girl and maybe, if he is lucky, to get her phone number and address. Could intent to arrest attach at the time of this stopping if a crime were being committed in the officer's presence? It is very doubtful that the officer would have a valid arrest here, because he was standing where he didn't have a legal right to be. That is to say, the officer had no legal reason for stopping the car in the first place.

Even the forcible seizure of the person of another will not constitute an arrest when there is no intent to take him into the custody of the law. For example, an officer is assigned to a traffic detail at a ball game; the game starts and the officer now has time to watch it. Midway through the game, a "drunk" causes a disturbance and the traffic officer, who by now is really involved in the game, is called on to do something with the drunk. The officer approaches the drunk, takes him by the arm, and proceeds to take him out of the stands very hurriedly, because the officer doesn't want to miss a single play. Just as the two reach the gate and the officer tells the drunk to go on home and sleep it off, the drunk strikes the officer with his fist. Is the drunk now resisting arrest? Hardly, for the arrest had not been consummated—there was no intent to arrest.

> One who arrests without a warrant must manifest his intention to arrest and the offense or conduct for which the arrest is made, unless he is known to the arrested person as a peace officer and such information is not requested, or unless such action would be dangerous to himself or a third person, likely to imperil the making of the arrest, or useless, or unnecessary.[8]

AUTHORITY

The person making the arrest must act under a legal or real authority to take the arrested person into the custody of the law. Generally speaking, the extent of the authority vested in a person making the arrest distinguishes an arrest from other similar acts. If all the elements of an arrest are present and the person has actual or legal authority, the arrest is lawful; if he is acting under no authority, the arrest is unlawful or false. When all the essential elements are present the officer is protected from a suit for false arrest.

For example, in the case of the *District of Columbia* v. *Perry,*[9] a Maryland officer pursued a speeder across the state line into the District of Columbia where he halted the car and made an arrest for speeding. However, the Maryland officer had no authority to make the arrest in the District of Columbia. The same theory would apply to any officer who arrests for misdemeanors outside of his area of jurisdiction if he acts in his legal capacity as an officer. Generally, the laws of fresh or hot pursuit as they apply to misdemeanors do not extend across state lines. Could the Maryland officer call an officer of the District of Columbia and let the latter make the arrest? It is very doubtful that this would be a valid arrest, for the speeding violation was not committed in his presence and in addition was committed in Maryland. Hence, the District of Columbia officer would have no authority to arrest. In addition, the Maryland officer could not return the offender to Maryland by force, because one may not usually extradite for misdemeanors. How then could the Maryland officer bring the violator before the bar of justice? If a reciprocal agreement exists between Maryland and the District of Columbia, the Maryland officer should have gone before a magistrate and signed an affidavit asking for issuance of a warrant. Notice of the warrant would be sent and entered in the violator's driver's license files, and when the offender applied for renewal of his license he would be forced to make some disposition of the warrant before he could obtain a new license.

CONTROL (SEIZURE OR DETENTION)

The actions of the person making an arrest must result in *actual* or *constructive* control over the person arrested. There can be no arrest unless the officer takes possession of the person. The taking of possession of the person is normally accomplished by manual caption (a seizing with the hands). However, a seizing is not always necessary to consummate an arrest, because the person may submit himself to an arrest.

Actual seizure or detention is accomplished ordinarily by manual caption, as mentioned above. The actual seizure would often involve the use of physical force, and such force may consist not only of seizing with the hands but also of the use of firearms. However, actual physical force is not always necessary to constitute manual caption; the merest touching of the body may be sufficient. If an officer holds a suspect at gunpoint and tells him that he is under arrest, there would be manual caption in that the presence of the weapon directed toward the suspect would exert physical control over him. At the other extreme, an officer may confront a suspect, tell him that he is under arrest, and merely touch him on the arm. In either instance, the actions of the officer would probably constitute manual caption. One should not construe the foregoing statements to mean that an officer must touch everyone he arrests, for this is not so. Although manual caption is not the only valid method of seizure, it certainly would be preferable in many cases. In 1889 the Supreme Court of North Carolina stated:

> The certain and most unequivocal method of making an arrest is by the actual seizure of the person to be arrested, but this is not essential; it is sufficient if the person be within the control of the officer, with power of actual seizure if necessary. The officer need not touch the person of such party to make the arrest effectual, but he must have, and intend to have, control of the party's person. This seems to be necessary to constitute a valid arrest.[10]

Another example of an actual seizure is given in the following quotation from a 1963 decision of the Massachusetts Supreme Court:

> Though the police did not declare that the defendant was under arrest, the officer in charge of the police station testified that the defendant would not have been free to leave until the investigation had been completed and implied that the defendant would have been detained physically had he tried to leave . . . . We are of the opinion that it would be unrealistic to say that the defendant was not under arrest . . . .[11]

Now let us compare the circumstances in the following case, which happened in Baltimore, Maryland, with those of the two preceding cases. Officers of the Baltimore Police Department responded to a reported prowler call. Upon arriving at the address, they found the defendant inside a foyer obviously trying to break an inner door. The officers confronted the defendant and started to ask questions at which time he made a quick lunge to get away. The officers grabbed him but they were knocked down as he succeeded in breaking away. The officers then chased the defendant onto the sidewalk where he was finally subdued. The Maryland Court of Appeals affirmed the conviction in the lower court, saying:

> In determining the lawfulness of the arrest, we must do so with relation to the time when it occurred. It seems clear that there had been no arrest—merely an accosting—prior to [the suspect] Price's break . . . . We think . . . that the arrest, in a legal sense, occurred when the Officer first grabbed the appellant in the vestibule, even though he did not then succeed in holding him.[12]

In this case, the court applied the manual caption theory at the point when the defendant was first touched by the officer. In essence, the defendant was resisting a legal arrest when he tried to flee after the first physical contact was made.

As stated earlier, an officer may also make a valid arrest by constructive seizure. A constructive seizure or detention of the accused is accomplished by his submission to the officer's control and will suffice without manual caption (without touching or the use of any physical force). It consists in the suspect's submission to the control and authority of the officer in the belief and understanding that such submission is necessary. If the accused person signifies by word or act that he submits himself to the officer's control and authority, the arrest is consummated, provided the other necessary elements are present.

> The mere fact that an officer makes a statement to an accused that he is under arrest is not sufficient to complete the arrest. But if an officer having authority to make an arrest lays hands upon the person of the suspect, however slightly, with the intention of taking him into custody, it is an arrest, even though the officer may not succeed in stopping or holding the suspect even for an instant. If the person arrested understands that he is in the power of the one arresting and submits in consequence, it is not necessary that there be an application of actual force, a manual touching of the body, or a physical restraint that may be visible to the eye.[13]

In examining the sufficiency of a seizure or detention, we must consider the fact that mere words alone, however appropriate (such as "You are under arrest"), are insufficient to constitute an arrest unless they are accompanied by an actual or constructive seizure. For example, if an officer tells a person that he is under arrest but the person pays no attention, is not touched, and does not submit to the officer's control, the person is *not* under arrest. The officer *must* control the person's actions in order to make a valid arrest. Perhaps the following quotations will help to clarify this theory of constructive seizure:

> Neither a declaration of words indicating an intention to arrest nor the reading of a warrant is of itself sufficient to constitute an arrest.[14]

> If the party making the arrest professes to have authority to make the arrest and commands the person, by virtue of his pretended authority, to go with him, and the person obeys the order, the two going together in the direction pointed out by the person claiming the right to make the arrest, there is an arrest and imprisonment within the meaning of the law.[15]

In further discussing the sufficiency of words, we must relate the seizure to the officer's intent to arrest. The arresting officer must make known to the suspect his intention to arrest and should not utter unrelated or ambiguous statements, such as "Put your hands up," "Meet me at the rear of your car," or "Come sit in my car." From these statements a suspect may not understand an officer's intent to make an arrest, even though the suspect understands it is a police officer who has given a command to him. This need for the officer to clearly state his intent was apparent in the following situation:

> Where an individual was apprehended by two deputy sheriffs at a still in the middle of a swamp, and the evidence showed that he knew the deputies personally and knew that they were deputy sheriffs, it was the duty of the deputies to inform him to consider himself under arrest, or by some other language convey to him the idea that an attempt was being made to arrest him. Where a deputy sheriff, instead of doing that, said "Put up your hands," the attempted arrest was illegal, and the person had the right to resist the arrest and in doing so to use the necessary force to meet force.
>
> If it is known that the individual is a desperate and dangerous criminal, a well known killer or a would-be killer, the officer may be justified in drawing a gun and requiring the individual he is seeking to arrest to surrender before informing him that he is putting him under arrest.[16]

PROBABLE CAUSE FOR ARREST

What constitutes probable cause for arrest has been a point of debate in state and federal courts from the time the Fourth Amendment was adopted and added to the Constitution. Our courts have consistently declined to formulate a single, absolute definition of probable cause for arrest, because the facts and circumstances are unique in every case. The average officer is often confused by the many explanations he receives in answer to his questions about probable cause. For this reason, we will try to give a general idea of what might constitute probable cause.

Probable cause is an apparent state of facts, found to exist upon reasonable inquiry, which would induce a reasonably intelligent and prudent man to believe that, under the circumstances of the moment, a particular person committed a crime. It is more than mere belief or suspicion, but it is not necessarily proof beyond a reasonable doubt. On the evidentiary scale, probable cause lies somewhere between good faith suspicion and positive proof. The term is used by the courts to signify the "minimum knowledge" which an officer must possess in order to make a constitutionally valid arrest, with or without an arrest warrant. Therefore, probable cause is dependent on the facts and circumstances of each case, and these facts and circumstances are the very ones that confront the officer who is on the scene and has firsthand knowledge of *all* apparent facts. However, the officer must remember, when he goes into court, that a jury is composed of lay people who most often have no prior knowledge of the particular case and are not aware of exactly what circumstances confronted the officer at the scene of the crime. The officer should not assume that everyone knows exactly what circumstances he was faced with but instead should always strive to present a very clear picture of what *he* observed at the scene. He must not allow himself to overlook facts which seem insignificant or commonplace to him, because they may be of major importance in determining whether probable cause existed. Conversely, the officer must also be aware that circumstances that appear highly suspicious to him might seem unremarkable to others. For example, how many lay persons would think twice about seeing four or five people occupying the front seat of a vehicle while there is no one in the rear seat? Would a person with no knowledge of law enforcement notice that the occupants of a vehicle attempted to hide themselves or some object when passing a police vehicle? There are many, many, "seemingly insignificant" things which people do at different times that usually go unnoticed by the general populace. However, actions like these, which are often performed unconsciously by persons who have something to hide, should create some suspicion in the mind of the observant officer. Probably no single one of these acts alone would constitute probable cause for arrest, but as information is accumulated, the police officer does not make a single evaluation but rather a series of judgments. Some of the information and some of the factors which he observes will usually add up in support of probable cause, while others may undermine that support. Finally, at some point, the officer must balance the negatives and positives, make a decision, and then act on his decision.

For a better understanding of probable cause, one should study carefully the following excerpts from court decisions:

> We have indicated on many occasions that there are few absolutes in the area of the law dealing with what constitutes probable cause for arrest. We have also emphasized from time to time that probable cause is not to be evaluated from a remote vantage point of a library, but rather from the view point of a prudent and cautious police officer on the scene at the time of the arrest.[17]

> In dealing with probable cause, . . . as the very name implies, we deal with probabilities. These are not technical; they are the factual and practical considerations of everyday life on which reasonable and prudent men, not legal technicians, act . . . . Probable cause exists where "the facts and circumstances within the arresting officer's" knowledge are sufficient in themselves to warrant a man of reasonable caution in the belief that an offense has been or is being committed.[18]

> The issue of probable cause is controlled by the circumstances of the moment and the impression to be evaluated is the impression made upon the mind of reasonably prudent officers.[19]

> An arrest without a warrant by-passes the safeguards provided by an objective predetermination of probable cause, and substitutes instead the far less reliable procedure of an after-the-event justification for the arrest . . . too likely to be subtly influenced by the familiar shortcomings of hindsight judgment. Whether or not the requirements of reliability and particularity of the information on which an officer may act are more stringent where an arrest warrant is absent, they surely cannot be less stringent than where an arrest warrant is obtained. Otherwise, a principal incentive now existing for the procurement of arrest warrants would be destroyed.[20]

> . . . the pertinent circumstances are those of the moment, the actual ones, the ones that confronted the arresting officers. Officers patrolling the streets at night do not prearrange the setting and they cannot judge events in the calm of an office. Things just happen, and as they happen the officers must choose to act or not. Our inquiry is whether their action was that of reasonable and prudent police officers in view of the circumstances as they appeared at the time of arrest.[21]

> While the process of reaching a conclusion that probable cause for an arrest exists calls for exercise of judgment and is in that sense a judging process, it is, of course, not a judicial process. It is, rather, a very specialized form of judgment, an expertness in making evaluations under pressure in circumstances where an untrained person might well be at a loss. The police are entitled to rely upon hearsay which would be inadmissible in judicial pro-

> ceedings, and upon various other factors which would not be admissible in evidence against an accused on trial. Rumor, gossip, common conversation, general reputation, hearsay, all these may well go into the police evaluation of the total situation which confronts them. Inevitably this is something of a "balance sheet process." Some of the information, and some of the factors which they observe, will add up in support of probable cause; some, on the other hand, may undermine that support. Finally, at some point the officer must make a decision, culled from a balance of these negatives and positives, and then act on his decision.[22]
>
> Mere suspicion is not enough to constitute probable cause . . . especially if it is mere general suspicion. An arrest cannot be justified on the mere belief that a person has been guilty of an offense, if such belief has no foundation in fact or has insufficient circumstances on which to rest, or if the person arresting unreasonably acts at the request of a third person who himself has a mere suspicion of the guilt of the one arrested. Furthermore, to afford a justification, there must be not only a real belief and reasonable grounds for it, but also, where there is opportunity to make inquiry, proper investigation into the facts.[23]
>
> Mere suspicion, based on the arrested person's reputation and his presence in the vicinity where the crime occurred, does not constitute probable cause. Thus, the fact that the person arrested has a jail record and has admitted previous commissions of the same offense for which he is arrested does not enlarge the authority of an officer to arrest, and is no justification for an illegal arrest without warrant.[24]
>
> Flight of the suspect is an important circumstance in the knowledge of the officer, tending to justify arrest without a warrant. However, it has been said that every man has a right to oppose an illegal arrest by flight, and the fact that he does so will not authorize his arrest as a fugitive.[25]

One can readily see that probable cause is often hard to determine, partly because there is no clear line of distinction between probable cause and good faith suspicion. For example, a police officer is employed in an area where alcoholic beverages are illegal to possess and sell. It is a small town of 8000, and the officer knows everyone and most by their first name. He also knows that Mr. A has illegally transported and sold whisky in the past (A is a "known bootlegger"). The officer observes A leave town at midday, headed in the direction of several liquor stores which are located in another small town, just across the state line. Later the same day, about dusk, the officer observes Mr. A as he drives back into town. Mr. A's vehicle is sitting rather low in the rear; in fact, it is almost dragging on the ground. As Mr. A passes the police vehicle, he smiles and waves at the officer, just as if he is completely innocent of any wrongdoing. Now the officer is faced with a problem—to act or not to act. Does the officer have probable cause, at this point, to arrest Mr. A? Would the officer be acting in good faith if he used a driver's license check as a pretext to observe the suspect more closely? Perhaps if the officer did stop Mr. A to check his driver's license there might be contraband in plain view. If there was no contraband in plain view, would the officer have improved his situation? Could the officer use the *Carroll* doctrine[26] which makes probable cause a prerequisite for the search of a moving vehicle believed to be transporting contraband?

In order to reach an equitable solution to these questions, one must first understand the issue, which here is probable cause. Do the facts as they are presented constitute probable cause? What are the facts? First, the officer observed Mr. A leaving and returning to the town, but this, in and of itself, is certainly not unusual. Second, the officer knows Mr. A and is aware that he is a "known bootlegger." Frankly, it is doubtful that this knowledge would help the officer at all in support of probable cause. As Court pointed out in *Henry* v. *United States,*[27] "The fact that packages have been stolen does not make every man who carries a package subject to arrest," and analogously, the fact that a man is a known bootlegger does not mean that every automobile trip he makes is a bootlegging run. What facts are left then? There is only one and it is of no real significance; the vehicle was sitting rather low in the rear and this fact alone would surely *not* constitute probable cause.

Now, with the same officer, the same town, and the same Mr. A, let us rearrange the circumstances and add a fact to this hypothetical situation. The officer observes Mr. A leave town at midday. However, this time the officer receives a telephone call from Reverend B who had been in the small town just across the state line visiting the sick when he observed Mr. A loading whisky into the trunk compartment of his automobile in front of one of the liquor stores. The Reverend advised the officer that Mr. A would be heading his way shortly and stated that he felt an obligation to call him as he had done so many times in the past. A short time later, at about dusk, the officer observes Mr. A returning and the rear of his vehicle is again almost dragging the pavement. Has the officer's situation improved? What are his chances of establishing probable cause now?

One should be able to recognize immediately that the officer would have a better chance of establishing probable cause in the latter instance. The fact that a reliable informant had given him information and the information was firsthand knowledge would be of major significance. This information, coupled with the officer's observations, would add up in support of probable cause. However, if the officer was testifying in court, it might be unwise to mention that Mr. A is a "known bootlegger," because this would give the defense counsel an opportunity to challenge the arresting officer on the basis that the officer was prejudiced toward Mr. A because he had sold whisky illegally in the past. In this instance, it would probably be better to leave the defendant's previous behavior as an undisturbed issue.

The question of probable cause for the arrest of a suspected person has been called a mixed question of law and fact. The general rule is that, if the facts are conceded or uncontradicted, the question whether they show probable cause for arrest is one of law for the court. If the facts are disputed, it is the court's duty to instruct the jury as to what facts, if established, will constitute probable cause, and to submit to them only the question of the existence of those facts. And it seems that the trial court's conclusion is treated on appeal as a reviewable ruling on a question of law, rather than with the greater finality accorded a finding of fact. It has been suggested, however, that the question of what a reasonable or ordinarily prudent man would do under given circumstances is naturally and logically one for the jury, rather than the court.[28]

The view that probable cause for an arrest on a criminal charge is a question for the court where the facts are undisputed, but otherwise is for the jury under appropriate instructions, has been said to be a general rule in criminal as well as civil cases. In one jurisdiction, however, it has been held that the court in a criminal case can instruct that the defendant has established probable cause, although it cannot instruct that he failed to establish it. And in another it has been held that the court, in a criminal case, may not determine the question as a matter of law in the first instance, even though the facts are undisputed.[29]

ARRESTS UNDER A VALID WARRANT

As will be discussed later in this chapter, a valid arrest may be made without a warrant under certain conditions. However, the general rule is that, except when an offense is committed in the officer's presence or when a felony has been committed and the officer has reasonable grounds to believe that the person he is confronting committed the felony, no arrest can legally be made unless and until an arrest warrant is issued by the proper authority.

When the warrant is issued by a competent court having proper jurisdiction, appears valid on its face, and is delivered to the officer who has authority to execute it, the officer is obligated to carry out the commands of the warrant without unnecessary delay. The officer himself must be able to recognize whether a warrant is valid on its face, but in checking its validity, he is not obliged to go beyond the document itself. An officer who fails to execute a valid warrant and is obligated to do so could be held in contempt of court, and, in addition, could be prosecuted criminally in many states for failing to perform his statutory duties. Every officer should understand that if the warrant he serves contains all the necessary elements, he will be protected from civil suits for false arrest or false imprisonment; however, if he serves the warrant and the necessary elements are not present, he may be held liable for his actions if someone is injured by them.

In order to be able to recognize that a warrant is valid on its face and to avoid any liability for serving an invalid warrant, the officer should make himself thoroughly familiar with the requisites of an arrest warrant.

BASED ON PROBABLE CAUSE

The affidavit or complaint on which the warrant is based must show sufficient probable cause to allow the issuing official to make an independent assessment of whether or not the affiant or complainant has shown a strong probability that a crime was committed. In doing so, the affiant or complainant must affirmatively allege the commission of a crime, not merely state a suspicion that a crime was committed. For example an affidavit states, "From information received of a reliable informant who has been accurate and reliable in the past, we believe that Mr. X committed the crime of ______." This is an affirmative statement showing that the affiant himself believes a crime was committed. On the other hand, the statement "We have information from a reliable informant that Mr. X committed a crime," does not affirmatively allege anything other than that the affiants have certain information at their disposal. In order to make this distinction clearer, the officer should examine the following quotes:

> Under the view that a determination of probable cause for arrest, made by a neutral and detached magistrate, is constitutionally required, it has been held that a complaint which states as a mere conclusion that the accused has committed a specified crime, without alleging that the affiant speaks from personal knowledge, indicating any sources for his belief, or setting forth any other sufficient basis on which a finding of probable cause could be made, is an insufficient basis for the issuance of an arrest warrant, since it does not permit the magistrate to make independent assessment of the probability that the accused committed the crime charged. For the same reason, allegations that would suffice for an indictment are not necessarily sufficient for a complaint in a case in which probable cause for arrest must be determined by the magistrate, and the basis for a finding of probable cause must appear on the face of the complaint. Common rumor or report, suspicion, or even strong reason to suspect is not adequate to support a warrant for arrest.
>
> In an affidavit on which a criminal arrest warrant is based, the offense need only be stated with reasonable certainty, but the facts charged must constitute a criminal offense of some sort. However, where an affidavit filed with an information in two counts charges the commission of one of the two offenses, its failure to cover the other is an irregularity that may be waived, and the point cannot be raised for the first time after conviction.
>
> An information positively sworn to by the county, or prosecuting, attorney on the basis of an affidavit of someone else has been held to be a proper basis for an arrest warrant in *Ex parte*

> *Flowers,* 2 Okla. 430, 101 P. 860. But where the county attorney is the complainant, it is not sufficient for the complaint to be sworn to by his deputy as in *Marrow* v. *State,* 140 Neb. 592, 300 N.W. 843.[30]
>
> An affidavit that merely states belief in the guilt of the accused is insufficient to support a warrant of arrest, the reason being that it states no fact for which the affiant could be prosecuted for making a false statement under oath. The complaint or charge on which a warrant is issued must set forth the facts constituting the offense according to the knowledge of the person making the complaint, and if he does not know them, other witnesses must be examined who do know them. There is some authority to the effect that a statute purporting to authorize the issuance of a warrant on the basis of a complaint or information verified only on information and belief is unconstitutional. However, it has been held that a complaint on information and belief is sufficient basis for a warrant of arrest in the case of a misdemeanor triable before a police or justice court if the statute makes no provision for the taking of depositions to support the complaint.[31]

PARTICULARLY DESCRIBING THE PERSON TO BE ARRESTED

> An arrest under a warrant is not privileged unless the person arrested is sufficiently named or otherwise described therein or has caused the person making the arrest to believe him to be the person so described.[32]

In many instances, an arrest warrant will contain only the name of the suspect, and this creates many problems for the officer who must execute the warrant. Often the issuing official has access to much information about the suspect but neglects to enter the information in the warrant, and the officer will then have problems in identifying the proper person to be arrested. Too often the officer places too much reliance on a name, especially in those cases where the officer feels he knows the person well enough to avoid any mistakes in identifying him. Although the problem of arresting the wrong person is not of major importance, as this seldom happens, we nonetheless must remain aware that the Fourth Amendment specifically states that the person to be arrested must be particularly described. Many times the officer could assure a sufficient description in the warrant by including all the information he has access to in his affidavit. It has often been said that any description which will enable the officer to distinguish the one person from all others is sufficient. However, we might go a step further and say that a stranger, the proverbial "reasonable and prudent man," should be able to recognize the defendant from the description contained in the warrant.

We are well aware that if the name of a person is not known, the warrant must include a description which is sufficient to identify the person to be arrested with reasonable certainty. Therefore, a "John Doe" warrant without any further description or identification of the person to be arrested is a nullity. However, if the "John Doe" warrant includes an adequate description to identify the person to be arrested, the warrant is valid. A warrant left blank and later filled in by the arresting officer is a nullity and violates the Fourth Amendment. Consider the following quotations concerning the description of the suspect:

> There is no such process as a warrant to arrest all suspected persons, and an officer who makes an arrest under a warrant so reading stands on no better ground than if there had been no process.[33]

> . . . a warrant does not justify an arrest unless the person arrested is sufficiently named or otherwise described therein. Similarly, at common law, a warrant for the arrest of a person charged with a crime must truly name him, or describe him sufficiently to identify him. And it has been held that the name must appear in the mandatory part of the warrant, not merely in the reciting part.
>
> The common-law rule does not prevent the issuance and service of a warrant on a person whose name is unknown, since, in such case, the warrant may describe the person intended by stating his occupation, residence, appearance, peculiarities, and the like. But whenever the warrant contains no name, the description must be sufficient to identify clearly the person to be arrested. A slight variation between the name in the warrant and the true name of the accused is not fatal if the names are so nearly alike as to be idem sonans,* but a warrant for the arrest of a named person will not justify the arrest of another who merely has the same surname.[35]

STATING THE NATURE OF THE OFFENSE

It is not absolutely necessary that the offense be stated in the warrant with as much detail as is required for an indictment, affidavit, or information, but the warrant must include language which will specify the nature of the offense with sufficient clarity to advise the subject of the accusations against

---

*"Idem sonans: The doctrine that if two names may be sounded alike without doing violence to the power of the letters formed in the variant orthography, then the variance is immaterial, and the names are idem sonans. It has also been said that names are idem sonans if the attentive ear finds difficulty in distinguishing them when pronounced, or if common and long continued usage has by corruption or abbreviation made them identical in pronunciation. The doctrine is based on the idea that the variance is so slight that the person would be readily known by the variant name."[34]

him. Under the Constitution, an arrestee has a right to know what charges are made against him, and the warrant must be sufficiently specific to meet this constitutional requirement. As pointed out earlier, a warrant cannot merely state "Hold for investigation"; it must state a crime. Clearly, the officer must be familiar with the statutory provisions of his own area in order to comply with this requirement, as the following quotation points out:

> What a warrant of arrest should contain depends mainly on the applicable provisions of the constitution, statutes, or procedural rules in the particular jurisdiction, . . . apart from any special provision, it is generally held that a warrant is insufficient and void if, on its face, it fails to state facts sufficient to constitute an offense. A designation or description of the offense, in the warrant, is required under some statutes or procedural rules. However, the strictness required in an indictment is not essential. Inaccuracies and imperfections do not vitiate a warrant that does not wholly fail to charge an offense. There is some authority, however, to the effect that the warrant must clearly allege all constituent elements of the offense charged, although other cases take the view that the purpose of the requirement is merely to advise the accused that he is charged with some particular offense, and that the warrant need not give the elements of the offense or define it.
>
> Where an affidavit on which the warrant is based sets out the charge in full and the magistrate appends the warrant thereto, this incorporates the charge, and the warrant and affidavit must be construed together. But where a complaint, recited in substance in a warrant, is verified merely on information and belief and does not state facts sufficient to constitute an offense, the warrant must be held to have been improvidently issued and to be invalid on its face.
>
> A statute requiring a magistrate's warrant to recite the accusations does not apply to a warrant issued by order of court after indictment or information and describes the offense generally.[36]

WARRANT MUST BE ISSUED BY PROPER OFFICIAL

There has been much argument about who may issue a warrant for arrest. In many instances, warrants for arrest are issued by the desk clerk at the police station. In other cases, prosecutors, sheriffs, and others have believed that they had power to issue arrest warrants. Generally, the power to issue warrants is bestowed upon one particular class of persons—magistrates. The courts have reasoned that the magistrate would be more apt to be neutral and objective than the officer who is most often directly involved in the case. In 1971, the United States Supreme Court stated in *Coolidge* v. *New Hampshire,*[37] "That in order to satisfy the requirements of the Fourth Amendment as made applicable to the states by the Fourteenth Amendment, a warrant must be issued by a 'neutral and detached magistrate.' Where a law enforcement officer assumes both roles he will, at best, be unconsciously biased in his finding." The *Coolidge* case cited *Johnson* v. *United States,*[38] in which the court said, "The point of the Fourth Amendment, which often is not grasped by zealous officers, is not that it denies law enforcement the support of the usual inferences which reasonable men draw from evidence. Its protection consists in requiring that those inferences be drawn by a neutral and detached magistrate instead of being judged by the officer engaged in the often competitive enterprise of ferreting out crime." And in the case of *United States* v. *Ventresca,*[39] the court stated, "The informed and deliberate determination of magistrates, empowered to issue warrants, are to be preferred over hurried actions of officers."

Since we have mentioned magistrates several times, it would be appropriate to give a brief description of their function. In one state, they are referred to by statute as a "person clothed with power as a public civil officer." The Constitution of that state provides that "all civil officers shall be conservators of the peace, and shall be by law, vested with ample power as such." In both cases, no mention is made of power to issue warrants.

In some states, the power to issue warrants is bestowed by statute. The Mississippi statute[40] provides that:

> The clerk of the municipality shall be the clerk of the police court, . . . and he shall be under the direction of the police justice . . . . The clerk shall issue all process from the court . . . . The clerk shall have power to take acknowledgements, administer any oaths required by law to be taken by any person, take affidavits charging any crime against the municipality or state . . . .

This statute makes no mention of a clerk's having power to issue warrants on his own; he must rely on the direction of the police justice. However, the clerk would have the power to take the affidavit charging the crime, and could also do the actual paper work for the warrant. However, he could not, without the direction of the police justice, sign the warrant for arrest.

In *State* ex rel. *White* v. *Simpson,*[41] the court held that a state statute empowering the district attorney to authorize issuance of a warrant violated the Fourth Amendment to the United States Constitution. In *Martin* v. *State,*[42] the court held that a clerk of a circuit court is without power to issue a warrant for the arrest of a person by an affidavit lodged with him. In *Smith* v. *Grady,*[43] the court held that the desk sergeant of a municipal police force who was also the deputy clerk of the police court had no authority to take the affidavits of private persons which charged the commission of misdemeanors, and without the direction of the police justice, he had no authority to issue warrants of arrest for the persons charged in the affidavits.

> While the power to issue warrants is most frequently executed by justices of the peace and police magistrates, it can be conferred by statute on other officials. Although this power implies

the power and duty to hear and determine probable cause, it is not such a judicial power that it cannot, for example, be conferred by statute on clerks of court.[44]

NECESSITY OF OATH OR AFFIRMATION BEFORE ISSUANCE

There is a presumption in law that the warrant was issued upon an affidavit supported by an oath or affirmation. However, if the defense can prove there was no affidavit or no oath, the warrant is a nullity under the Fourth Amendment. Careful study of the following quotations will make the reason for this requirement apparent:

> With certain exceptions based on the gravity of the offense, or on commission of the offense in the presence of the arresting person, the common law requires that an arrest be made on a warrant issued only after a formal charge made under oath. Thus, no arrest for a misdemeanor committed outside the presence of the one complaining should be made without a warrant based on proper affidavit. This procedure, the purpose of which is to secure freedom from illegal restraint for trivial causes, is now frequently a constitutional requirement. For instance, a federal rule which, apart from a warrant of arrest upon an indictment or information, requires a sworn complaint as the basis for issuance of an arrest warrant, implements the Fourth Amendment provision that no warrant shall issue, but upon probable cause, supported by oath or affirmation. Similar language in state constitutions has been held to make an affidavit, or a complaint or information positively verified by oath or affirmation, an essential basis for the issuing of a warrant. Under such a provision, a statute purporting to authorize the issuance of a warrant on the basis of a complaint or information verified only on information and belief has been held to be unconstitutional. But where the facts leading to a warrant are reported by a public official body, the members of which acted on their own knowledge, it has been held that no oath to the specific report was necessary, since the constitutional requirement of an oath was met by the fact that the members acted under their oaths of office.
>
> Generally speaking, where a sworn statement of probable cause is a constitutional requirement, a warrant issued upon an unsworn statement is void, and any arrest thereunder is illegal. It has been held, however, that where a complaint was on information and belief, failure to support it by examination of witnesses, although fatal to the jurisdiction of the magistrate to issue the warrant, did not keep the warrant from being fair on its face so as to protect the arresting officer, since the officer, in serving process, has a right to rely on the warrant and is not compelled to examine the complaint or other preliminary proceedings. On the other hand, where the complaint and warrant together constitute the precept, if the complaint shows on its face that the magistrate had no authority to issue the warrant, the warrant is void.[45]

OTHER GENERAL REQUIREMENTS

A warrant must bear the date of issuance, and if the date is not affixed thereto the warrant is invalid. The warrant must also bear the name of the issuing authority (i.e., city, county, judge), and this is true even though the warrant may be issued in the name of the state or federal government. Of course, the officer is duty-bound, after execution, to make a proper return on the warrant as to what he has done. The following quotation presents some general points about the return made by the officer:

> In order to justify an arrest under a warrant, the officer must act in strict compliance with the law, and failure to do so makes him a trespasser ab initio [from the beginning]. He must show that he has done all that was commanded by the warrant or some legal reason for not having done so. Thus, where it is part of his duty to make return of all that he has done, the writ will not protect him unless he makes such return.
>
> The return must contain substantially all that the officer did within the scope of proper execution. But if the officer has done other things that were not commanded by the warrant, and which were done by virtue of his general legal authority rather than by virtue of the warrant, he need not include them in his return.
>
> Even where the officer becomes a trespasser ab initio because of failure to return the process, persons who were legally obliged to assist him are protected if the arrest was lawful at the time; they cannot be held responsible for the officer's later omission over which they had no control.[46]

EXECUTION OF THE WARRANT

Even though the arrest warrant has been properly issued on an adequate showing of probable cause and particularly describes the person to be arrested, the arrest will not be legal unless the warrant is properly executed. Certain requirements must be met in order to have proper execution of the arrest warrant.

The officer who is to execute the arrest warrant must fall within the class of officer designated on the warrant. That is to say, if a warrant for arrest is directed to and commands a specific class of officer to serve it, then an officer not within the specified class could not legally serve or execute it. For example, most warrants are directed to "any lawful officer of ______ county." In this case, then, any officer having full police power within that county could properly serve or execute the warrant. However, if the warrant was directed to the sheriff of county X, for example, then only he or his deputy may execute the warrant. Usually an application for a warrant of arrest does not specify a specific officer to serve it; most are directed to "any lawful officer." There are exceptions to this general rule, but they usually occur in cases involving search and seizure, narcotics, federal jurisdiction, and other matters not normally associated with an ordinary arrest.

The arrest warrant must be executed within the officer's jurisdiction and within the jurisdictional limits of the warrant. Generally speaking, the warrant would have no legal effect outside of its original jurisdiction of issuance. This rule is certainly true in misdemeanor cases; however, in felony cases, greater latitude is allowed, simply because an accused felon may be extradicted from one state to another and returned to the original jurisdiction in which the crime was committed. Although the power of extradition can, in effect, extend the jurisdictional limits of the warrant, the officer is definitely restricted to acting within his area of primary jurisdiction except in cases of fresh pursuit, but even this power of fresh pursuit does not extend beyond the borders of his own state.

If the arrest is for a felony and the officer who makes the arrest does not have the warrant in his possession at the time of arrest, the officer must show the warrant to the arrested person as soon as possible if the accused requests to see it. However, this rule does not apply in cases of misdemeanors, because the misdemeanor must be committed in the officer's presence or he must have a warrant in his possession in order to make a valid arrest.

ARRESTS WITHOUT WARRANT

In general, warrantless arrests create the most problems for law enforcement officers, especially those who have no formal training. Almost daily, the officer will be called on to make an immediate decision as to whether, under the circumstances of the moment, he has a right to make the arrest on the spot or should first apply for an arrest warrant. If the officer makes the arrest without a warrant and his decision was wrong, he will have problems; but if he doesn't make the arrest, he may still have problems. To make the proper decision, the officer must be knowledgeable about the laws of arrest and understand how they are applied. The officer must understand the difference between a felony and a misdemeanor, because the arrest procedure and the rules governing it are not the same for each.

An officer may make an arrest without a warrant for a felony when he has reasonable grounds to believe, and does believe, that the person he is confronting has committed a felony. He should be reasonably sure that a felony has been committed, but it is not necessary that the felony be committed in his presence. Several general rules for the felony arrest are discussed in the following quotation:

> A peace officer may arrest without warrant for a felony committed or attempted in his presence. It is sufficient, as the rule is sometimes stated, if the officer has probable cause to believe that a felony is being committed in his presence. There is authority

> that an officer may also make an arrest without warrant when he reasonably believes the person arrested is about to commit a felony, although such a belief will not justify him unless it is based on reasonable grounds. A peace officer is usually authorized to arrest without warrant where he has reasonable cause to believe a felony has been committed and that the person to be arrested is the one who committed it. The rule often stated is that the officer may make an arrest when he believes, on reasonable grounds, that the person to be arrested has committed or is committing a felony. Under this rule, an officer who arrests on reasonable cause in a felony case is not required to show the actual guilt of the person arrested. Such an arrest is not invalidated by the fact that the person taken into custody proves to be innocent, or that, as it turns out, no felony was actually committed.
>
> In the case of a felony, there is some authority that the actual guilt of the party arrested justified the arrest whether or not the officer had reasonable grounds to believe that a felony had been committed when he acted, and that the officer is required to show reasonable grounds only when no felony has in fact been committed. And the power to arrest without warrant one who has committed a felony, though not in the officer's presence, is sometimes stated independently of the power to arrest on probable cause. But there is authority that a subsequent confession after the arrested person is in custody cannot legalize an arrest that was illegal in its inception.[47]

As these rules may vary by statute in different jurisdictions, the officer should be familiar with his own state's statutory provisions relating to felony arrests.

An officer may make an arrest without warrant for a misdemeanor only when the misdemeanor is committed in his presence. If time permits, however, and the arrest is not made immediately after the misdemeanor is committed in the officer's presence, an arrest warrant is required.

OFFICER'S PRESENCE DEFINED

A crime is committed in the officer's presence when the officer is made aware of the commission of the crime by any one or a combination of his five senses—sight, hearing, touch, smell, and taste. Too many officers rely on sight alone in many instances, and thereby weaken the case against the accused. For instance, an officer may be able to smell marijuana burning even though he can't see it. He may hear a car crash or he may hear noises immediately prior to a collision which would allow him to determine that a crime was committed without seeing the actual crash. In the application of the "stop and frisk" rules, an officer may feel a weapon while patting down a suspect, thus allowing an arrest. However, every officer should remember that mere suspicion, luck, or good guessing will not justify an arrest even though the officer turns up evidence of the crime as a result of the arrest.

The officer also needs to be aware that he is not required to witness the entire crime, but is only required to witness enough of the action to make him aware that the crime is being committed. For example, in *People* v. *Foster,*[48] when the officers arrived at a place of business and found the defendant kicking at the door and yelling, and the bleeding shop operator told the police that she had been attacked by the defendant, the affray was still sufficiently in progress to allow the officers to make an arrest even though they were not present when the actual attack took place. Many times at the scene of an automobile accident, the officer is permitted to charge for traffic violations even when he arrives on the scene 15 or 20 minutes after the initial impact of the vehicles. In this situation, the officer relies on any relevant evidence which is part of the *res gestae.* *

Another frequently disputed issue is whether the officer in whose presence the crime was committed had a legal right to be where he was when the crime was observed. For instance if the officer is sent to investigate a domestic complaint, knocks on the door of an apartment, and is invited inside by a person who has a right to possess or control the premises (such as a husband or wife), he may make an arrest for any crime occurring in his presence because he is on the premises lawfully. It has been said that if an officer is standing where he has a right to be, he is not required to turn away and allow a crime to go unnoticed.

The rules governing the misdemeanor arrest are very strict, and an arrest without warrant for a misdemeanor must be made immediately, or else an arrest warrant must be obtained. Many times the officer, upon losing a traffic violator in a high-speed chase, will call officers in surrounding areas and ask them to stop and hold the violator for him. Under these circumstances fresh pursuit is lost, and in order to make a valid arrest the officer must obtain a warrant. In this situation, the officer who actually apprehends the violator is sticking his neck out, so to speak, for his fellow officer, for if something unforeseen happens whereby someone is injured, the apprehending officer could be held liable for his wrongful actions.

THE CITATION

Issuing a citation (arrest ticket, uniform arrest ticket, or whatever it may be called in a particular area) does not constitute an arrest and can never be construed as such. Of course, a person can be issued a citation and arrested as

*"Matter incidental to the main fact and explanatory to it, including acts and words which are so closely connected therewith as to constitute a part of the transaction, and without a knowledge of which the main fact might not be properly understood. They are events themselves speaking through the instinctive words and acts of the participants; the circumstances, facts and declarations which grow out of the main fact are contemporaneous with it and serve to illustrate its character."[49]

well, since anyone may be arrested for committing a crime. The citation is actually a notification to the violator that he must appear in court at a stated time and place to answer charges made on the citation. It is a very useful device in traffic enforcement and is preferred over physical arrest whenever feasible.

Some of the advantages of a citation as opposed to a physical arrest are: 1) it saves the officer considerable time and effort, because he does not have to take the violator to jail for an offense which is relatively minor; 2) it provides a less drastic method of bringing a violator who is not truly a criminal before the bar of justice; and 3) the proper use of the citation will help to elevate the public image of all law enforcement officers by lessening the antagonism between the public and the police.

We must keep in mind that the citation is only a notification to appear in court, and in no way is it, in and of itself, sufficient to institute a criminal case. The affidavit is the legal document that must be lodged with the judge in order for a case to go to trial. However, if a person is issued a citation and he desires to appear immediately, plead guilty to the charge, and pay a fine (if any fine be assessed), he may do so without an affidavit being on file with the court, because in this case no trial is required.

Although in some instances, the inferior courts have been known to hold a person in contempt for not appearing on the date stated on the citation, this procedure is both improper and illegal, since the citation was not issued by the court. The proper procedure to follow would be to make an affidavit on the basis of the citation; a warrant could then be issued and presented to the proper person for service. If the violator is located out of state, notice of the warrant could be sent to his own state's driver's licensing bureau, and if a reciprocal agreement exists between the two states, the violator would be estopped from renewing his operator's license until there is some disposition of the outstanding warrant.

FRESH PURSUIT

Under the proper circumstances, the area in which an officer can make an arrest may extend beyond the borders of the area in which he has actual jurisdiction. This occurs when the officer is attempting to make an arrest, and the criminal, in order to escape, flees from the area. Keeping in mind that most states have statutory provisions governing fresh pursuit, the officer should compare the following general rules with the applicable statute in his state.

1. The officer must have had valid authority to make an arrest in the beginning. For example, an officer is on vacation outside his own state and his own area of jurisdiction; he sees a violation of law occur and immediately begins to chase the fleeing criminal. Although he may have authority to arrest as a private citizen, he certainly would not have authority based on fresh pursuit.

2. The pursuit must be of a fleeing criminal who is attempting to avoid immediate capture. Many times an officer will chase a person just because the person runs from the immediate area where he is confronted by the officer. Although the officer may often be correct in assuming that a person who is in flight has done something illegal, the officer has no right to pursue unless the person he is chasing has committed a crime. The first rule (valid authority initially to arrest) would likewise apply.

3. The pursuit must have been started promptly and maintained continuously. In order for the rule to apply the pursuit must be *fresh.* In other words, it should flow from the act of attempting to make an arrest and be part of the continuous process of apprehension. For example, the officer is chasing a speeder on a limited-access highway; it is night and the road has many curves and small hills. Although the officer momentarily loses sight of the vehicle he is chasing as they speed over hills and around curves, he has not lost fresh pursuit because of the fact that there is no other place for the violator to go except on that particular highway. However, let us assume that the officer is chasing a speeder on city streets; it is night and there is a distance of approximately three-fourths of a block between the two vehicles. The speeder turns into a particular street and the officer also turns into this same street but no longer can see the violator. The officer accelerates in order to shorten the distance between him and the speeder, and as he passes an alleyway he glances down it and sees the vehicle at the other end of the alley. It would take too much time for the officer to turn his vehicle around, so he decides to circle the block and "head him off at the pass." When the officer reaches the other end of the alley, the violator's vehicle is not in sight, so the officer drives around for a few minutes and finally spots the unoccupied vehicle parked in front of a house. At this time fresh pursuit has been lost, and the officer may not forcibly enter any house looking for the driver of the vehicle. He must retreat, make an affidavit, and acquire an arrest warrant in order to make a valid arrest for the speeding violation.

The problem now narrows to deciding whom to issue the warrant for. The officer has only one alternative. He should run a check on the license plate and acquire the name and address of the registered owner of the vehicle, then obtain a warrant for his arrest. This would create a rebuttable presumption that the owner was driving, and he would be obliged to prove that he was not driving if in fact he was not. In this way, the officer would eventually find the driver, unless the vehicle turned out to be stolen. (In many cases, the stolen-vehicle argument is used as a defense to a traffic charge.)

Let us look at another situation often encountered in fresh pursuit. The officer chases the criminal to his home, and both the violator and the officer jump out of their vehicles and run toward the building. The officer is within 10 feet of the person, but when the officer arrives at the door someone else appears in the doorway and tells the officer that he cannot come into the building. Must the officer stop and explain the situation or may he continue his pursuit? If the officer stops to explain he will certainly lose fresh pursuit and would have to retreat and acquire an arrest warrant. However, he could pass over, under, or around the person, and fresh pursuit would still be in effect. In this case, the officer's actions would largely depend on the gravity of the offense, and it is in situations of this sort that the officer needs to make a sound judgment based on experience and common sense.

4. If fresh pursuit is lost, the officer must retreat and obtain an arrest warrant in order to make a lawful arrest for that particular violation.

The foregoing general rules should be most strictly applied in misdemeanor cases. The officer would not, however, be so restricted in apprehending a fleeing felon. Under most statutes, an officer may freshly pursue the fleeing criminal wherever he may go as long as he remains in the state. The officer may not cross the state line unless his state has a statutory agreement with the other state allowing him to do so. However, even if such an agreement exists, the officer might be wise to retreat and obtain a warrant.

AUTHORITY TO DETAIN WITHOUT PHYSICAL ARREST

Generally, an officer has no authority to detain a person for an unreasonable length of time without making a physical arrest. Some officers believe that they have the authority to hold persons for investigation or other purposes for as long as 24 or 36 hours, but this cannot legally be done. However, Section 2 of the Uniform Arrest Act states:

> 1. A peace officer may stop any person abroad who he has reasonable ground to suspect is committing, has committed or is about to commit a crime, and may demand of him his name, address, business abroad and whither he is going.
>
> 2. Any person so questioned who fails to identify himself or explain his actions to the satisfaction of the officer may be detained and further questioned and investigated.
>
> 3. The total period of detention provided for by this section shall not exceed two hours. The detention is not an arrest and shall not be recorded as an arrest in any official record. At the end of the detention the person so detained shall be released or be arrested and charged with a crime.

Although the supreme courts of Rhode Island, New Hampshire, and Delaware have upheld this section of the act, the United States Supreme Court has not reviewed an entire case on this specific point. However in *Kavanaugh* v. *Stenbouse,*[50] the United States Supreme Court declined to review the case and remanded it, thus upholding the lower court's decision that to detain a person for a period of two hours is not unreasonable.

What do these court decisions mean to the officer on the street? They mean that if his particular governmental jurisdiction has adopted the Uniform

Arrest Act or enacted laws or ordinances having the same effect, he may legally question and detain persons without violating their constitutional rights. For example, the officer notices two men acting suspiciously, going from one house to another at 3:00 A.M. in a residential district. In any jurisdiction, the officer would have authority to stop the two, inquire of their business at that particular location, and find out who they are. If the two refuse to give this information, the officer could hold them for further investigation if there is a statute allowing such detentions. However a few states do not have such a statute, nor have they adopted the Uniform Arrest Act, and in these jurisdictions, the officer could not hold the two for an "unreasonable" amount of time in order to check further nor could he arrest them for failing to give the requested information. At present, there are several cases pending in both state courts and federal district courts in which acts of this nature are being challenged by persons who were detained without a physical arrest. Until a firm answer is given by the United States Supreme Court, the officer should follow the existing statutes covering this area. Those officers whose jurisdictions have no such statutes should follow existing state court decisions.

Another area of concern is the extent of the officer's authority to detain motorists in order to check such things as operator's license, vehicle registration, and faulty equipment. The state supreme court held in *Miami* v. *Aronowitz*[51] and *Morgan* v. *Heidelburg*[52] that "it is universally held that a car may be stopped to check the driver's operators license. However, this act of stopping does not constitute an arrest and therefore any privileges that usually accompany a lawful arrest may not be employed at this time." Other cases have upheld the officer's authority to open doors in order to check the vehicle identification number; to detain a motorist long enough to run a check on the license plate and state inspection sticker number; and to check any faulty equipment which might create a safety hazard. However, to detain a motorist for a period of five or six hours as a pretext for some other action would be unreasonable, and a court would subsequently find that the officer was not acting in good faith. Every officer should be aware of the fact that he must go into court with "clean hands."

USE OF FORCE IN MAKING AN ARREST

Almost every arrest by an officer technically involves a show of force or the actual use of force. Generally speaking, the officer is the judge in each case of the amount of force necessary to accomplish the arrest. However, he must keep in mind that at trial he may have to justify the amount of force he has used. In making a lawful arrest, the officer is only entitled to use that amount of force which is necessary to secure the prisoner, overcome resistance, prevent escape, effect recapture, or protect himself from impending bodily harm. He is never permitted to use unnecessary force or to employ dangerous methods when less violent ones would suffice.

Some of the factors to be considered in regulating the amount of force used in making an arrest are:

1. Is the offense a felony or misdemeanor, and if it is a felony, is it a crime against the person or property. Even in making a felony arrest, the officer may be restricted if it was not one of the more serious felonies.

2. The reputation of the suspect must be considered. Perhaps he has made a statement such as "I will not be taken alive," or he may have a history of violent behavior.

3. At the time of the arrest, the officer must observe the suspect's actions very closely, since the amount of force used to consummate the arrest will largely depend on the suspect's actions. Whether the officer calmly makes his authority evident or is compelled to meet *force* with *force,* the officer must control the situation.

4. Until recently, the officer did not have to concern himself with the actions of members of the public who are present when the arrest is attempted. However, he must now utilize his knowledge and skills to control any potential dangers or problems brought about by the presence of others at the arrest scene.

5. Before getting himself into a dangerous situation in making an arrest, the officer should consider whether there are other units nearby to back him up, and if not, how long it would take for help to arrive. If the situation appears to be actually or potentially dangerous, the officer should *always* call for support—it is better to be safe than sorry.

6. The officer must consider the possibility that the defendant or others present at the scene may be carrying weapons. The officer, if acting lawfully, is justified in taking another's life if the other is attempting to take his. The laws which empower the officer to act do not demand that he sacrifice his life in order to enforce them.

FELONY VS. MISDEMEANOR ARREST

More force may be used in making felony arrests than in arrests for misdemeanors. If the prevailing circumstances require it, the officer may even fire his weapon in order to effect the felony arrest. However, it would be very difficult to justify shooting a fleeing felon, except in cases where the officer and the public may be endangered by the felon's continued freedom or in cases of violent crimes against the person, such as murder, rape, or armed robbery. If the officer does fire his weapon to effect the felony arrest, he must have actual knowledge that a felony has been committed, not merely a suspicion. If the officer is in doubt, he should treat the offense as a misdemeanor, since the rules governing arrest are more restrictive for misdemeanors than for felonies. The officer will be protected if he mistakenly employs the misdemeanor procedure for what later turns out to be a felony.

In making a misdemeanor arrest, the officer may use whatever physical force is necessary to consummate the arrest, short of deadly force. He may not ever fire his weapon except to save his own life, and this danger of loss of life must be immediate and present in order to justify such extreme force. For example, the officer cannot resort to firing his gun just to stop a traffic violator who is fleeing from arrest. It is obviously better that the misdemeanor suspect escape than be shot. A person's life is certainly worth more than a $20 fine.

In attempting a felony or a misdemeanor arrest, the officer must keep the safety of the public in mind at all times—they are the ones whom the officer is duty bound to protect. The officer should never shoot into a crowded street, even if the accused did commit a felony. He should never be so concerned with making an arrest that he forgets about the public and endangers their lives just to write a ticket or to stop a motorist to check his driver's license. Common sense is always of great importance in making an arrest.

ENTRAPMENT

Since the defense of entrapment has been increasingly claimed by defendants in the last few years, the officer should be aware of its meaning so that he may avoid damaging his case because of it. The term in its literal sense means merely the act of trapping, but it has a broader legal meaning. Entrapment is the act of inducing or leading a person to commit a crime which was not originally contemplated by him for the sole purpose of apprehending him in its commission and prosecuting him for the offense.

> When used in its original sense of merely trapping the criminal, the fact of entrapment is obviously not a defense. Thus, a defendant cannot raise a defense that money was marked by means of which he was detected; that marked goods were exposed to a suspected thief; that a door was purposely left open for him; or that an opportunity was intentionally given him to commit the crime. Similarly, it is no defense that the victim, on learning of the proposed crime, does nothing to stop its commission but allows the defendant to begin the commission of the crime so that he may be apprehended in the act.
>
> When the doing of a particular act is a crime regardless of the consent of anyone, and the criminal intent originates in the mind of the accused, the fact that an opportunity is furnished, or that the accused is aided in the commission of the crime in order to secure the necessary evidence to prosecute him therefore, constitutes no defense.
>
> The purpose of a law enforcement officer is not to solicit the commission of, nor to create, an offense, but to ascertain if the accused is engaged in an unlawful business, or to entrap the defendant in the act of committing an offense which he has reasonable grounds to believe the accused has commenced, or is about to commence.
>
> In the case of those crimes into which enters as an essential element the violation of individual rights of persons, such as the

offenses of Larceny, Burglary, and Robbery, the situation is somewhat different. Here, it will be seen, the entrapment must not be under such circumstances as would amount to the consent of the person affected, or a necessary ingredient of guilt, the want of such consent, will be lacking, and the crime will not have been committed. The line of distinction seems to be whether there has been an active, as distinguished from passive, inducement to the taking on the part of the person affected or his duly authorized agents; and where such active inducement can be shown, no conviction can be had.

Where the owner, in person or by his duly authorized agent, suggests to the accused the criminal design, and actively urges, cooperates with, and assists the accused in the taking of the goods, such conduct amounts to a consent to the taking, and the criminal quality of the act is wanting. Consent to the crime is not shown, however, by proof that the owner or victim remained passive and made no effort to prevent the commission of the crime, such as Larceny, Burglary, or Robbery. It is likewise no defense that the agent of the owner or victim or law enforcement officer pretended to cooperate with the defendant. The fact that the defendant was led to commit the crime by his friends or confederates does not, under any circumstances, constitute entrapment.[53]

SUMMARY AND APPLICATION

In order to test his understanding of and ability to apply the theory presented in this chapter, the officer should try to arrive at an equitable solution to the following hypothetical problems. The important issues are hidden in the problems. Read very carefully and place as much emphasis on the circumstances as you would if you were confronted by them on the street.

PROBLEM I

The officer has chased a vehicle for several miles at speeds over 100 miles per hour. He is unable to overtake the speeding vehicle but does make note of the make, model, color, and license number and, in addition, is able to gain a good physical description of the driver. Although the violator completely eluded the officer, he would still like to see him brought to trial for the violation. What legal steps must the officer take in order to bring the violator into court? If an arrest is later made, how strong would the officer's case be?

PROBLEM II

An officer is chasing a drunk driver when they turn into a driveway leading to a house; the drunk jumps out of his car and runs into the house.

The officer is very close behind him and as he enters the front door he finds he is face to face with a nude woman whom the officer suspects is the drunk's wife. She screams and tries to find something to cover her voluptuous, nude body. The officer is inanimate for a few seconds, but recovers his presence of mind when he hears a noise that seems to emanate from an adjacent bedroom. At this time, the officer can see into all the other rooms except the one bedroom, but he cannot see the drunk. It is the officer's desire to arrest the drunk. What legal actions should the officer take?

PROBLEM III

While trying to turn his police cruiser around at a muddy construction site, the officer gets his car stuck in the mud. He cannot get his car out without assistance and is forced to call a wrecker. The wrecker arrives and hooks onto the cruiser as a carload of teenagers passes by, then stops several yards from the officer's position. His situation seems to be very funny to them, because they laugh and heckle the officer. This perturbs the officer, but he is powerless to act at the moment since his car is hooked onto the wrecker and he cannot get to them. Later the same night, after washing the mud from his car and changing into a clean uniform, the officer observes the same car full of teenagers, whereupon he stops the car and asks the occupants why they thought the earlier situation was so funny. At this time, the officer notices that all four occupants of the back seat are drunk. There is a crime now occurring in the officer's presence. What legal actions may the officer take?

PROBLEM IV

While driving along, Sam Smutt is stopped at a "driver's license check." The officer who approaches the car sees several pornographic pictures on the back seat in plain view. It is a crime to possess such pictures. At this time Sam, realizing that the officer has seen the pictures, places the vehicle in forward gear and "burns rubber" as he quickly speeds away. The officer immediately gives chase and after several miles succeeds in apprehending Sam. In addition to several traffic charges, the officer also charges Sam with resisting arrest. Would the officer be likely to have a good resisting-arrest case against Sam?

PROBLEM V

At 3:00 A.M., an officer sees a known burglar driving a car in an area which he does not usually frequent and also notices other passengers trying to hide inside the car after seeing the police car. The officer stops the car and questions the occupants as to their presence at the particular location but does not make an arrest. He contacts his supervisor and gives the information to him, and he directs the officer and other units to set up surveillance in the area of the stop. A trailer truck is seen parked in an enclosed yard and this appears very suspicious to the officer. At about 9.00 P.M., the known burglar and his group are seen entering the yard where the truck is parked. At this time, all the officers on the detail enter the yard and announce their presence. The subjects in the yard open fire on the officers; a gun battle ensues and four of the men are captured. The next day, the known burglar surrenders. Did the officer act correctly in each instance? Should he have acted any differently?

PROBLEM VI

An officer follows a wanted felon for several miles, and the subject finally pulls to the shoulder of the road and stops. It is the officer's intent to arrest the subject under the provisions of an outstanding felony warrant. As the officer approaches the vehicle, he notices that the felon is the only occupant of the vehicle. He has both hands on the steering wheel, his eyes are focused straight ahead, and all windows are closed and the doors locked. The officer, with weapon in hand, knocks on the windows and makes several statements to the person in a loud voice, but the driver does not move or acknowledge the officer's presence in any way. At this point, what actions may the officer legally take and what reasoning should be applied to determine what actions are appropriate?

PROBLEM VII

Following the sale of narcotics to three undercover agents, two suspects leave the scene and are trailed by two of the agents in an unmarked car. The agents notice an officer in uniform who is parked on the side of the street in a marked police cruiser. The agents pull alongside the police car, identify themselves, explain the situation, and ask the uniformed officer to stop the suspect car and arrest the occupants for them. The uniformed officer does as requested. Would the arrest be likely to be valid or not? What reasoning should be applied in this case?

PROBLEM VIII

A young undercover narcotics agent who is very interested in making his first arrest, approaches L. S. Dee, a known dealer in marijuana, and tries unsuccessfully to make a buy. L. S. explains that he has quit dealing in drugs and is going straight. However, the young agent is persistent and tries again and again to get L. S. to sell him marijuana. After growing tired of being pestered by this young man, whom he does not know to be a narcotics agent, L. S. acquires the desired amount of marijuana and sells it to the agent. The agent immediately arrests L. S. Would the agent have a good case and what defenses are available to L. S. Dee?

REFERENCES

1. 5 Am. Jur. 2d 695, Arrest, Sec. 1.
2. Webster's New Students Dictionary, Springfield, Mass., G. & C. Merriam Co., 1974, p 46.
3. Black's Law Dictionary, rev. 4th ed., St. Paul, West Publishing Co., 1968, p. 140.
4. 5 Am. Jur. 2d 698, Arrest, Sec. 3.
5. *State* v. *Lightcap,* 179 So. 881 (1938).
6. *Ker* v. *California,* 374 U. S. 23 (1963).
7. 5 Am. Jur. 2d 697, Arrest, Sec. 2.
8. Restatement of Torts, Sec. 128.
9. *District of Columbia* v. *Perry,* 215 A.2d 845 (1966).
10. *Lawrence* v. *Buxton,* 102 N.C. 129 (1889).
11. *Commonwealth* v. *Wallace,* 346 Mass. 9 (1963).
12. *Price* v. *State,* 227 Md. 28 (1961).
13. 5 Am. Jur. 2d 696, Arrest, Sec. 1.
14. *Wyatt* v. *State,* 120 Tex. 3 (1932).
15. *Christ* v. *McDonald,* 152 Ore. 494 (1936).
16. *Hinton* v. *Sims,* 171 Miss. 741 (1935).
17. *Ellis* v. *United States,* 264 F.2d 372 (1959).
18. *Draper* v. *United States,* 358 U. S. 307 (1959).
19. *Dixon* v. *United States,* 296 F.2d 427 (1961).
20. *Beck* v. *Ohio,* 379 U. S. 89 (1964) (quoting *Wong Sun* v. *United States,* 371 U. S. 471 [1963]).
21. *Ralph* v. *Pepersack,* 335 F.2d 128 (1964).
22. *Jackson* v. *United States,* 302 F.2d 194 (1962) (citing *Brinegar* v. *United States,* 338 U. S. 160 [1949]).
23. 5 Am. Jur. 2d 736, Arrest, Sec. 45.
24. 5 Am. Jur. 2d 737, Arrest, Sec. 45.
25. 5 Am. Jur. 2d 738, Arrest, Sec. 45 (quoting *Porter* v. *State,* 124 Ga. 297 (1905).
26. *Carroll* v. *United States,* 267 U. S. 132 (1925).
27. *Henry* v. *United States,* 361 U. S. 98 (1959).
28. 5 Am. Jur. 2d 741, Arrest, Sec. 49.
29. 5 Am. Jur. 2d 742, Arrest, Sec. 49.
30. 5 Am. Jur. 2d 706, Arrest, Sec. 13.
31. 5 Am. Jur. 2d 707, Arrest, Sec. 14.
32. Restatement (Second) of Torts, Sec. 25.
33. *Blocker* v. *Clark,* 126 Ga. 484 (1906) (quoting *Grumon* v. *Raymond,* 1 Conn. 40 [1814]).
34. College Law Dictionary, 2d Student's ed., Rochester, N.Y., The Lawyers Co-operative Publishing Co., 1948.
35. 5 Am. Jur. 2d 702, Arrest, Sec. 9.
36. 5 Am. Jur. 2d 701, Arrest, Sec. 8.
37. *Coolidge* v. *New Hampshire,* 403 U. S. 443 (1971).
38. *Johnson* v. *United States,* 333 U. S. 10 (1948).
39. *United States* v. *Ventresca,* 380 U. S. 102 (1965).
40. Mississippi Code of 1972, Revised and Annotated, Chap. 21, Title 23, Sec. 11.
41. *State* ex rel. *White* v. *Simpson,* 137 N.W. 2d 391 (1965).
42. *Martin* v. *State,* 190 Miss. 32 (1940).
43. *Smith* v. *Grady,* 411 F.2d 181 (1969).
44. 5 Am. Jur. 2d 703, Arrest, Sec. 10.
45. 5 Am. Jur. 2d 705, Arrest, Sec. 12.
46. 5 Am. Jur. 2d 709, Arrest, Sec. 17.
47. 5 Am. Jur. 2d 715, Arrest, Sec. 25.
48. *People* v. *Foster,* 176 N.E.2d 397 (1961).
49. 20 Am. Jur. 2d 553, Courts, Sec. 220.
50. *Kavanaugh* v. *Stenbouse,* 174 A.2d 560 (1961).
51. *Miami* v. *Aronowitz,* 114 So.2d 784 (1959).
52. *Morgan* v. *Heidelburg,* 246 Miss. 481 (1963).
53. Guy N. Rogers, Esq. Lecture given at the Mississippi Law Enforcement Officers' Training Academy, Jackson, Miss., 1972.

CHAPTER III

EVIDENCE

IN GENERAL

Evidence, defined legally, includes all the means by which an alleged matter of fact is established or disproved. Most courts recognize three major classes of evidence: (1) direct evidence, (2) circumstantial evidence, and (3) real evidence. The testimony of an officer who is describing what he actually saw as he witnessed a crime being committed would be direct evidence. A motion picture of the crime being committed would likewise fall into the category of direct evidence. From circumstantial evidence, an alleged fact might be inferred from one or more circumstances which have been directly established. For example, if the officer investigating a burglary finds a prybar with Joe's fingerprints on it and an address book belonging to him at the crime scene, there is circumstantial evidence that Joe committed the burglary. Circumstantial evidence may, of course, also be used to establish innocence. For example, if the victim claims that Joe shot him, but examination of the wound by a physician reveals that a knife caused the puncture, this fact would create circumstantial evidence tending to clear Joe of the alleged shooting. Here the circumstantial evidence resulting from examination of the victim would be beneficial to Joe in his defense and would probably carry more weight than the direct testimony of the victim. Real evidence is simply physical evidence; those things which speak for themselves and require no explanation, but which must be identified. Real evidence includes physical objects, such as weapons, photographs, and drugs. Although it is obvious that one would recognize a gun as being a gun and a photograph as being a photograph, each piece of evidence must be identified and its significance explained by the person introducing it.

It should be noted from the foregoing examples that real evidence can be either direct or circumstantial. The testimony of an officer who saw the crime being committed would be direct evidence. A motion picture of the crime could be both real and direct evidence. Testimony from the officer about the significance of prybar and address book would be circumstantial evidence; however, if the prybar and address book themselves were admitted in evidence, they would then constitute both real and circumstantial evidence.

The officer should realize that, in the majority of cases, direct evidence is normally given more weight by the jury than circumstantial evidence and that real evidence is usually more persuasive than a witness' testimony. For these reasons, the officer should always endeavor to acquire the evidence which would be of greatest value in the presentation of his case. For example, a motion picture of the crime in progress would certainly be of more value than the testimony of a witness about the crime.

It is important to recognize that the rules governing evidence are concerned with its admissibility and have no bearing on the weight the jury might place on it. Once the evidence is admitted, the weight to be given it is a matter for the jury to decide.

In considering the admissibility of evidence, we must look to its relevancy. When evidence is relevant it has a tendency to prove or disprove a material fact, has probative value, and is related to the issue. In other words, there must be a logical connection between the fact offered as proof and the fact to be proved. Although only relevant evidence is admissible, all relevant evidence may not be admitted, since certain evidence might take up an undue amount of time, cause undue prejudice, confuse the issue, or mislead the jury in some way. Judges are given broad discretion to decide whether to admit or exclude evidence, but many cases are reversed on appeal because the judge in a lower court abused this discretion. Unless excluded on some other ground, any fact which has a direct bearing on or tends to aid in the determination of the issue will usually be admitted as relevant evidence.

In this general discussion of evidence, we must mention the competency of a witness. Generally speaking, competency means that a person is legally qualified to give testimony. It is not so much a matter of age or mental capacity, but a question of whether the witness is capable of giving testimony having probative value. Competency further denotes that the witness is not disqualified by some other rule of evidence, such as that which excludes privileged communications. The three general rules which govern the determination of competency are: (1) the witness must be capable of expressing himself so that he can be readily understood either directly or through someone who interprets for him; (2) he must be capable of understanding his duty as a witness to tell the truth; and (3) he must have personal knowledge of the issues in question. For example, if a 17-year-old mentally retarded female is raped, she could, even though mentally retarded, still be a competent witness in the trial of the person accused of the crime, provided she could meet the three general requirements for competency.

At this point, we should examine another matter relevant to the field of evidence: the impeachment of a witness. The officer should be familiar with impeachment and should suggest its use to the prosecutor whenever feasible. In simple terms, to impeach a witness is to discredit his testimony. This does not mean that the technique is designed to establish perjury by the witness; it is used to make the witness appear less reliable in the eyes of a jury. Impeachment is usually attempted on cross-examination. The prosecutor may attack the witness on the grounds that he is biased, that he has given a prior inconsistent statement, or that he lacks veracity. Thus, the officer can aid the prosecutor by inquiring fully into the statements and character of both the accused and the defense witnesses. Of course impeachment is also available to the defense counsel and is used quite often to challenge the arresting officer's testimony. This often happens when the officer has presented a very strong case, and the defense counsel has no apparent legal basis on which to defend his client. In this situation, for the defense counsel to try to impeach the officer's testimony might be his *only* means of defense. The officer should realize that any animosity directed toward the officer on cross-examination by defense counsel is not personal but is a "professional discourtesy" designed to shake the officer up, confuse him, or discredit him to the jury to impeach his testimony. Although the officer may often feel that he, rather than the accused, is on trial, he must force himself to smile, to give direct and concise answers to questions by the defense, and in general, to be as courteous to the defense attorney as he is to the prosecutor! He should remember that the defense attorney is obligated to *defend* his client, and he may do so in any way that is legal and ethical. If there is any indication that the officer acted out of prejudice or spite toward the accused, the defense attorney has a duty to his client to challenge the officer's actions. In this way, our adversary system helps to protect the accused person's constitutional rights.

There are other tests of admissibility which, for the most part, provide alternative means of obtaining the fullest yet fairest presentation of the facts. One objection quite often made in a criminal trial is that certain evidence is unduly prejudicial. As mentioned earlier, this theory is usually applied to any evidence which might unduly bias or prejudice the jury in its search for the truth. A good example would be a *color* photograph of a deceased person. Unless it is essential, it would not be admitted for the sole purpose of proving that the person was dead. This issue often arises in cases of brutal murders where the deceased was beaten or cut to death. However, if the photograph is offered to show other relevant facts, such as the proximity of the murder weapon to the dead body, it may be admitted even though the scene itself is gory.

Many times a court will take "judicial notice" of certain facts, accepting them as true facts without requiring any proof. It is said that "the judge and jury are presumed to know what every well-informed person knows." In other words, a judge will not close his mind to what others know. This dispenses with the necessity of proof on certain subjects and will usually apply to facts which cannot be contradicted. Some facts of which judicial notice is taken are: (1) matters of general knowledge, (2) qualities of matter, (3) the courses of law and nature, (4) scientific facts and principles, (5) geographical facts, (6) historical facts, (7) words, phrases, and abbreviations, and (8) weights and measures.

The officer should not forget that the burden of proof in a criminal case lies with the prosecution. It is necessary that the defendant be found guilty beyond a reasonable doubt, except in cases founded solely on circumstantial evidence when the proof must exclude every other reasonable hypothesis except that of guilt. The burden of proof rests on the prosecution from the beginning of the trial to its conclusion and never shifts. However, a defendant may be required to prove his own allegations if he offers a defense such as insanity, intoxication, or self-defense. If there is any doubt in the mind of a single juror as to the defendant's guilt, he is entitled to a judgment of acquittal under our present system.

In many cases, a *presumption* is created during the trial. Every officer should know the meaning of this term, because the proper use of a presumption may create a prima facie case against the defendant. A presumption is a conclusion which is arrived at by an assumption of fact or by inference from other facts. There is a presumption when there are strong grounds for believing something to be so in spite of lack of proof or when something is believed to be so but is not proved. A presumption would include prima facie evidence which is good and sufficient on its face to establish a given fact. For example, by the doctrine of *res ipsa loquitur,* a presumption of negligence will arise if the defendant had exclusive control of the instrument of injury and if the accident was one that would not ordinarily occur in the absence of negligence. The presumption would arise, for example, against a driver who hit a pedestrian who was crossing on a green light. Another example of a presumption is expressed in the old adage, "ignorance of the law is no excuse," which means that everyone is presumed to know the law.

Rebuttable presumptions are those which may be overcome by showing evidence to the contrary. The burden of producing evidence to rebut the presumption rests upon the opposing party, once the basic fact giving rise to the presumption is presented. The following are examples of rebuttable presumptions:

1. A court order is presumed to be correct.
2. A person is presumed to be sane.
3. A person's character is presumed to be good.
4. An accused person is presumed to be innocent.
5. One who commits an act is presumed to realize the natural consequences of that act.
6. In many states, a child under 10 years of age is presumed incapable of committing a crime.
7. A child born in wedlock is presumed to be legitimate.

EXCLUSIONARY RULES OF EVIDENCE

THE BEST EVIDENCE RULE

Disputed questions of fact must be established by the best evidence available. The "best" or "primary" evidence is that which affords the greatest certainty regarding the fact in question. Secondary evidence is that which is inferior to primary evidence and which proves on its face that better evidence exists. As a general rule, the best evidence rule applies only to writings, the contents of which are essential and related to the issues at hand. However, a copy of the original document will usually be accepted if the original has been lost or destroyed; if the original is in the possession of a third party who will not surrender it; if it is an official document; or if it would take too much time or would be impracticable to produce the original in court. Although the best evidence rule applies primarily to written documents, it may also apply to other evidence. For example, a weapon used in the commission of a crime is primary evidence as opposed to testimony concerning the weapon. Simply speaking, this rule requires that the best evidence available be produced.

THE HEARSAY EVIDENCE RULE

It is a general rule, subject to many exceptions, that hearsay evidence is incompetent and inadmissible to establish a fact. Hearsay evidence is defined as "statements coming from one not a party in interest and not a party to the proceeding, and not made under oath. Such evidence is inadmissible because the statements thus made are not subject to the ordinary tests required by law for ascertaining their truth, the author not being exposed to cross-examination in the presence of a court of justice and not speaking under the sanction of an oath, no opportunity being afforded to investigate his character and motives, and his deportment not being subject to observation."[1] The rule simply requires a witness to have firsthand knowledge of the facts he wishes to relate to the court. For example, if a witness says, "I saw Joe break into the building," this is not hearsay since he is merely telling what he actually observed. However, if the witness says, "Sam told me he saw Joe break into the building," he is not telling what he himself observed but merely what another said he saw, and the statement would therefore be inadmissible as hearsay evidence. The following are some of the general rules applied by our courts in the regulation of hearsay evidence:

1. The person alleged to have made a statement or to have executed a written instrument must be present and available for cross-examination.

2. The court and jury must have an opportunity to observe the demeanor of the person being quoted.

3. Statements sought to be quoted must be made under oath.

4. There is a high probability of inaccuracy in reporting "passed on" or "secondhand" information.

5. The defendant has a constitutional right to be confronted by the witnesses against him.

Exceptions to the Hearsay Rule

Although there are at least 30 exceptions to the hearsay rule, only a few will be mentioned here. Since we are primarily interested in criminal law, we will discuss those exceptions that are most relevant to criminal cases.

Former Testimony. Testimony from a former hearing or trial is admissible if the witness who testified on the prior occasion is unavailable and the defendant had the opportunity to cross-examine him on the prior occasion. The reasoning here is that the prior testimony was given under oath and so is presumed to be true. If the defendant did not have an interest in or was not a party to the former proceeding, testimony from that proceeding is not usually admissible.

Declarations. A *declaration against interest* is generally admissible when a person is unavailable to testify and it is presumed that such person would not make a statement against himself if it were not true.

Spontaneous declarations are generally admissible as part of the res gestae. These are statements about an event made under the stress of excitement immediately before or after the event and before the speaker has had time to reflect or contrive. Words which are spoken contemporaneously with a relevant act are admissible under this rule. For example, the officer arrives at the scene of an automobile accident only five minutes after it happened. One driver is dead and the other, who is standing beside his car and appears excited and remorseful, says to the officer, "I was in a hurry and was driving too fast. I ran the stop sign and killed him." The officer may testify about this statement under the spontaneous declaration exception to the hearsay rule.

Dying declarations are admitted if it can be shown that the person making the statement was in a condition that would lead to death, knew that he was facing death with no hope of recovery, and actually died from the existing condition. For example, John is rushed to a hospital emergency room for treatment of a gunshot wound of the chest. After working frantically for several hours, the doctor tells John that there is very little hope for recovery. John says, "Old Joe shot me, Doctor, and when I get out of here I'm going to get him!" and dies ten minutes later. This statement would not be admissible as a dying declaration because John did not believe he was going to die. On the other hand, if John knew he was going to die and had told the doctor that Joe shot him, the statement would be admissible as a dying declaration.

Records of Past Recollections. Records of past recollections may be used to refresh the memory of a witness and to prove facts contained in those records. Such records must have been made while the event sought to be testified about was still fresh in the witness' memory and must be a product of firsthand knowledge. To be admissible, these records must have been made by the witness himself or under his direction, or made by another person for the purpose of recording the witness' statements at the time they were made.

This exception to the hearsay rule allows the officer to use his accident reports, investigative reports, or other records to refresh his memory while giving testimony in a court of law. However, the officer should use caution when taking such reports into the courtroom and using them on the witness stand. He should take only those reports or records which relate to the issue at hand, because the defense counsel has a right to examine every entry in them, and they may contain other information which might be detrimental to the prosecution's case.

Tacit Admissions. As a general rule, when a statement is made in a person's presence that tends to incriminate him, and he does not deny, contradict or object to the statement, the statement and the fact that he failed to deny it may be admitted against him as a *tacit admission.* This rule is based on the assumption that the natural reaction of an innocent person is to deny accusations of wrongdoing made against him. However, the officer should not put too much emphasis on this particular exception, since it does not apply if the person is in police custody.

Other Exceptions. There are other exceptions to the hearsay rule, but for the most part, they are of less importance to the officer than those just discussed. However, the officer should be aware of them, because he may need to use one or more of them on occasion. Entries in regularly kept account books, made by the party himself or someone in the normal course of his employment at or reasonably near the time of a particular transaction, are admissible. Statements made in public records and in documents which are intended to be made public are admissible. Statements of a deceased person which relate to his reputation, pedigree, or family history are admissible if they were made before any prospective litigation involving those issues. Statements made in ancient documents are admissible. In some states, a document is considered ancient after it is 30 years old, but this is usually controlled by statute in each state. Market quotations and market reports which are published in trade bulletins or reliable writings upon which particular dealers depend are admissible.

OTHER INADMISSIBLE EVIDENCE

Certain evidence may not be used in a case because of the manner in which it was obtained or the effect it will have on the jury. When evidence is obtained by an illegal search and seizure or statements are obtained illegally, a motion to suppress will usually be sustained. Conversely, evidence not obtained by force, trespass, or fraud is usually admissible, and will not be excluded on constitutional grounds. Because of its importance in the field of evidence, a separate chapter (Chapter IV) is devoted to the issues involved in search and seizure. Confessions will be discussed later in this chapter.

Admission of testimony for which a necessary predicate was not established or of unnecessarily prejudicial evidence is usually cause for reversal if the guilty verdict is appealed. However, the United States Supreme Court has said that errors made in the lower courts which are not prejudicial to the constitutional rights of a defendant are not grounds for reversal.

In many states, the *contemporaneous objection* rule is applied whereby the failure of an attorney to make timely objection to the introduction of evidence acts as a waiver of the defendant's right to have such evidence ruled inadmissible. The general rule is that objection to evidence may be made before the trial, at the beginning of the trial, or at the time such evidence is sought to be introduced, but if the attorney objects at a later point, his objection will not be allowed. The United States Supreme Court has consistently held the contemporaneous objection rule to be valid where the state has made it a part of its rules of trial procedure.

PRIVILEGED COMMUNICATIONS

Our laws recognize and sanction certain privileged relationships in order to encourage freedom of communication between the persons involved. By sanctioning such relationships, the law provides that those parties to the privilege cannot be forced to divulge the protected confidential communication. This protection is personal in the sense that it can only be claimed by a party to the privileged relationship.

Husband and Wife. The privilege generally extends between husband and wife and protects both of them. Either may claim the privilege as to any communication or acts done by either while they were married. However, the privilege does not apply to matters occurring prior to marriage or after divorce, to child abuse cases, or to relevant facts in a divorce case. Because of the privilege, a married person cannot be required to testify against the spouse in a criminal case, unless one spouse is charged with a crime against the other. Even if one spouse does take the stand to testify in a criminal case in which the other is the defendant, the former may claim the privilege for any confidential communication or the latter may prevent the former from disclosing such information.

Attorney and Client. Under most statutes, the privilege accorded to attorney-client communications extends only in favor of the client and may not be claimed by the lawyer. The following guidelines are applicable to attorney-client communications.

> The privilege applies only if:
>
> 1. the asserted holder of the privilege is or sought to become a client;
>
> 2. the person to whom the communication was made is a member of the bar, or his subordinate and in connection with this communication is acting as a lawyer;
>
> 3. the communication relates to a fact of which the attorney

was informed by his client, without the presence of strangers, for the purpose of securing either an opinion of law, legal services or assistance in some legal proceeding, and not for the purpose of committing a crime or tort;

4. and the privilege has been claimed and not waived by the client.[2]

Physician and Patient. This privilege prohibits a physician from disclosing confidential information given to or acquired by him in the course of his professional attendance upon the patient. However, as in the attorney-client relationship, this privilege extends only to the patient and cannot be claimed by the doctor. This privilege is not applicable to criminal proceedings. However, a client may prevent a psychotherapist from giving testimony against him in a criminal case if the psychotherapist was not court appointed. A physician's records may be subpoenaed by a *subpoena duces tecum,* whereby he would be required to present himself in court, along with those records enumerated in the subpoena.

Communications to Clergy. Most states (about 44) have statutes making confidential communications to clergymen privileged. In those states, and in some that have no such statute, clergymen are not required to testify as to penitential communications entrusted to their confidence.

The Confidential Informant. In several recent decisions, the United States Supreme Court has made it quite clear that, in most instances, the prosecution does not have to disclose the identity of a confidential informant as long as his reliability is established. In some cases, the presiding judge has required the informer to be brought before him, in private, so that he himself could determine the informer's reliability. In these cases, the informer's identity was not disclosed to the defense.

Governmental Privilege. Until the Watergate affair, when the federal government claimed that disclosure of certain information would be against public policy, the courts usually complied. However, in *Nixon* v. *United States,*[3] the Supreme Court found that the privilege that applied to confidential communications between the President and his advisors was a presumptive rather than an absolute privilege. The effect of this decision would seem to be that, in cases where the federal government claims that certain communications are privileged, the court will balance the need for confidentiality against the need for the evidence sought, rather than accept the government's claim on its face.

Although some states have statutes granting governmental privilege to state officials, the courts have not generally recognized the privilege. In many states, a person who voluntarily gives information to a legislative investigative body would be privileged to object to the use of that information in a prosecution against him.

OPINION EVIDENCE

It is a general rule that a lay or nonexpert witness may not give his opinion or draw a conclusion except in instances where the opinion or conclusion is one which normal persons form constantly and correctly. This rule is based on the theory that the witness' duty is to furnish the facts and that the jury's duty is to form opinions and reach a conclusion based on those facts.

An expert witness is not limited to furnishing facts; he may, after being qualified as an expert, give opinions and conclusions. In order for an expert witness to give opinion testimony, it must be shown that he has sufficient knowledge, skill, training, education, or experience in the specific field so that his opinion will be an aid to the jury in its search for the truth. His expertise must, of course, go beyond that of the average layman.

Often after a particular expert witness has established his reputation as an expert in a given field, the opposing party will stipulate that he does qualify as such, thus eliminating the need for cross-examination on this point. However, until such reputation is established, the expert witness must be prepared to demonstrate his qualifications, give sufficient reasons for his opinions, and specifically relate his knowledge to the issues of the trial. Expert witnesses may also be cross-examined on the sources of information on which their opinions are based and on how they arrived at the opinion given.

Generally speaking, the average officer would not qualify as an expert witness. However, since many police officers are now acquiring college degrees in their specialized field, and indeed are becoming more educated in general, many of them do qualify as experts in such areas as ballistics, accident investigation, narcotics, and fingerprint identification. The officer should understand that to qualify as an expert is not an easy task. He will be subjected to often grueling cross-examination, since he must show that his knowledge relates to the issue and is greater than that of the average layman. Further training, education, and experience acquired by an officer will better qualify him as an expert witness.

CONFESSIONS AND ADMISSIONS

The courts of our land have applied the "free and voluntary" rule to the taking and use of a confession made by one accused of committing a crime. To state the rule simply, one could say, "A confession is admissible in evidence, against an accused, only if freely and voluntarily made, without duress, fear, or compulsion in its inducement and with knowledge of the nature and consequences of the confession." There are several reasons for the rule, but the two most important are that (1) the confession cannot be relied on as being true unless it is freely and voluntarily given, and (2) if the confession is obtained by force, duress, or fraud, it violates the rights guaranteed by the Fifth Amendment to the United States Constitution.

In determining the voluntariness of a confession, most courts will consider three basic factors: (1) the use of force, (2) threats of bodily harm, and (3) psychological coercion. Everyone knows what "use of force" means, and most would understand that saying to a suspect, "If you don't tell us what we want to know, you are going to get hurt!" would constitute threats of bodily harm. All officers know that brute force may not be used in order to gain a confession. However, courts today are changing their attitude toward the taking of a confession, and they are beginning to place much more emphasis on the use of psychological force or coercion to obtain a confession. This is not to say that all officers are intentionally using psychological coercion, but many of them use it unconsciously and realize too late that they have done so. For example, to show how easily this happens, let us assume that George is in custody and is charged with murder. George has not waived any of his rights, and one of the officers says to him, "Look George, we are trying to be as nice as we can and we are not going to hurt you. All we want you to do is to tell us the truth about this matter, and you don't need a lawyer for that." Although this statement may have been innocently made with no ulterior motive, it none the less violates the defendant's right to counsel and could be construed as psychological coercion. Quite often the arrested person will place a great deal of confidence in the officer who has arrested him by asking the officer for advice as to whether he should seek the services of an attorney or would do better to confess and seek the mercy of the court. If the officer is confronted with a question such as this, he can give only one answer and still have a good case. The officer may only advise the suspect of his rights; he cannot give any other advice and expect to have a good case. If he tells the suspect that an attorney is not needed, the officer will have violated the defendant's rights, and if he tells the defendant that he should not waive his rights and should have counsel, the officer will be unlikely to obtain a confession.

Since we will be discussing Fifth and Sixth Amendment rights, the following pertinent excerpts are included here (with emphasis added) to help the officer to understand his obligations to a defendant in a criminal case.

> No person shall be held to answer for a capital, or otherwise infamous crime, unless on a presentment or indictment of a Grand Jury, . . . nor shall any person be subject for the same offense to be twice put in jeopardy of life or limb; *nor shall be compelled in any criminal case to be a witness against himself,* nor be deprived of life, liberty, or property, without due process of law . . . . (United States Constitution, Amendment V.)
>
> In all criminal prosecutions, the accused shall enjoy the right to a speedy and public trial, . . . and to be informed of the nature and cause of the accusation; *to be confronted with the witnesses against him; . . . and to have the assistance of counsel for his defense.* (United States Constitution, Amendment VI.)

Both these and other amendments contained in the Bill of Rights are made applicable to the states by and through the Fourteenth Amendment; thus, they are applicable to the actions of every police officer in this nation. One of the first Fourteenth Amendment due process confession cases originated in the state of Mississippi. In this case, state officers obtained a confession by force and torture, and the confession was allowed into evidence in state court. The resulting conviction was appealed to the United States Supreme Court and was reversed under the Due Process Clause of the Fourteenth Amendment.[4]

Since this decision, many other cases have been decided that held that every law enforcement officer must afford the accused his Fifth and Sixth Amendment rights and that these constitutional requirements are binding on the states through the Fourteenth Amendment. Since we know that these rights are guaranteed to every accused, we must determine at what point in a criminal proceeding these rights attach.

Basically we are dealing with two main constitutional guarantees: the privilege against self-incrimination and the right to counsel. We will first consider the self-incrimination protection. In the case of *Malloy* v. *Hogan,*[5] the Court stated that "the right of a person to remain silent unless he chooses to speak in the unfettered exercise of his own will, and to suffer no penalty for such silence" is a right secured against the state by the Fourteenth Amendment. In *Griffin* v. *California,*[6] the Supreme Court reinforced the *Malloy* ruling by saying:

> In accord with our decision today, it is impermissible to penalize an individual for exercising his Fifth Amendment privilege when he is under police custodial interrogation. The prosecution may not, therefore, use at trial the fact that he stood mute or claimed his privilege in the face of accusation.

The decision in *Miranda* v. *Arizona,*[7] left no doubt that the Fifth Amendment privileges are not confined to the actual criminal court proceedings. The Court said:

> The prosecution may not use statements, whether exculpatory or inculpatory, stemming from custodial interrogation of the defendant unless it demonstrates the use of procedural safeguards effective to secure the privilege against self-incrimination. By custodial interrogation, we mean questioning initiated by law enforcement officers after a person has been taken into custody or otherwise deprived of his freedom of action in any significant way.

Although the Court here mentions *custodial interrogation* and depriving a person of his freedom in *any significant way,* one must be aware that these are guidelines and that the particular circumstances of each case will determine when these rights attach and what procedural safeguards are required.

At this point, we should also examine the Sixth Amendment right to counsel, which is closely related to the privilege against self-incrimination. In 1963, in *Gideon* v. *Wainwright,*[8] the Court held that the Sixth Amendment right to counsel was applicable to the states, thus overruling the prior controlling decision, *Betts* v. *Brady.*[9] The effect of the decision in *Gideon* was that all indigent defendants charged with felonies must be provided with counsel at the trial stage of the proceedings. After *Gideon,* the Court began to develop the concept of "critical stage" as a guideline for determining when counsel must be provided. The rule that evolved was that counsel must be provided at every critical stage of the proceedings, which was defined as any stage where substantial rights of an accused could be affected. The Court has applied this standard on a case-by-case basis to decide which stages of the proceedings are critical stages.

Hamilton v. *Alabama*[10] was one of the first cases in which the court used the term "critical stage." In this case, the Court decided that the *arraignment* was a critical stage of the criminal procedure and that "denial of counsel at that stage in a capital case violates due process . . . ." In *Hamilton,* the Court gave definite guidelines for police actions. We must now look at the subsequent decisions to understand the concept of "critical stage" and how it is applied today.

In the case of *White* v. *Maryland,*[11] the Court applied the critical stage reasoning to the preliminary hearing and held that when the defendant was required to plead to the charge without the assistance of counsel, his Sixth Amendment right to counsel was violated. In *Massiah* v. *United States,*[12] the Court moved the critical stage back to an earlier point. In this case, federal agents overheard, by surreptitious means, certain incriminating statements made by the defendant after he was indicted and was out on bail and awaiting trial. The Supreme Court reversed his conviction and said, "The petitioner was denied the basic protection of the right to counsel when there was used against him at his trial evidence of his own incriminating words, . . . after he had been indicted and in the absence of counsel."

In *Escobedo* v. *Illinois,*[13] the United States Supreme Court, in a 5 to 4 decision, applied the "critical stage" reasoning to custodial interrogation. Mr. Justice Goldberg, delivering the opinion of the Court, stated:

> We hold, therefore, that where, as here, the investigation is no longer a general inquiry into an unsolved crime but has begun to focus on a particular suspect, the suspect has been taken into police custody, the police carry out a process of interrogation that lends itself to eliciting incriminating statements, the suspect has requested and been denied an opportunity to consult with his lawyer, and the police have not effectively warned him of his absolute constitutional right to remain silent, the accused has been denied 'the Assistance of Counsel' in violation of the Sixth Amendment to the Constitution, . . . and that no statement elicited by the police during the interrogation may be used against him at a criminal trial.

With this decision, the court extended the right to counsel to the earliest possible point in the criminal process, to that point when "the process shifts from investigatory to accusatory—when its focus is on the accused and its purpose is to elicit a confession." This decision created a great deal of confusion for law enforcement officers, since it gave no definite guidelines for them to follow. It was not until two years later that many of the questions raised by *Escobedo* were answered in the *Miranda* decision.

The decision in *Miranda* was not primarily concerned with the Sixth Amendment right to counsel; the focus was on the Fifth Amendment privilege against self-incrimination. The presence of counsel was held necessary as a means of enforcing the immunity against self-incrimination, except in cases where the accused effectively waives that right. Under this decision, the accused need not request counsel during custodial interrogation. The burden is on the officer to inform the suspect of his Fifth and Sixth Amendment rights and to refrain from asking *any* further questions unless and until the accused knowingly and intelligently waives those rights.

When *Miranda* and *Escobedo* are applied together, we arrive at the following definition of a "critical stage": "when the individual is first subjected to police interrogation while in custody at the station or otherwise deprived of his freedom of action in any way" *(Miranda)* or "when the process shifts from investigatory to accusatory—when its focus is on the accused and its purpose is to elicit a confession" *(Escobedo)*. For example, assume that an officer is called to investigate a shooting at the country club. When he arrives at the scene, the officer observes a group of people standing around a body. The officer approaches the group and says, "What is going on here?" Mr. Y steps from the group and says, "I shot him, he's dead, and I'm glad!" The statement made by Mr. Y would probably be admissible at his trial for murder because of the fact that the officer did not ask him a direct question. His question was a general on-the-scene inquiry into an unsolved crime which was still in the investigation stage. Mr. Y was not a suspect at the time, nor was he deprived of his freedom in any significant way. As the Court said in *Miranda*, "Our decision is not intended to hamper the traditional function of police officers in investigating crime . . . . Such investigation may include inquiry of persons not under restraint."

Now let us change some of the facts. Again, the officer is called to the scene of the shooting. Upon arrival he observes Mr. Y with a gun in his hand, standing apart from the group which is gathered around the dead body. The officer approaches Mr. Y, and standing face to face, says directly to him, "What is going on here?" Mr. Y answers the officer with exactly the same words used in the preceding example. Would Mr. Y's statement be admissible? It is likely that it would not, because although Mr. Y had not been formally charged, he certainly had become the accused in the officer's mind. Also, in this example, the officer did ask a direct question of Mr. Y, which he answered with the incriminating statement. However, the officer might possibly present the incriminating statement as a spontaneous declaration, and if it was accepted as such, it would probably be admissible.

As another example of the critical stage, let us assume that the officer arrives at the scene of a shooting and observes Mr. Y standing alone next to the dead body, holding a gun in his hand. The officer says to Mr. Y, "Do you know what happened here?" Mr. Y answers, "I don't know what happened. I just walked here, found this body, and picked up this gun." The officer calls the information to his investigative bureau via radio and is asked by a detective, who knows Mr. Y, to bring Y in to the office for questioning. The officer then turns to Mr. Y and says, "Get in my police car and go to the office with me. Detective Smith would like to talk to you." Mr. Y answers, "O.K.," and gets into the police vehicle. While on the way to the office, Mr. Y says to the officer, who has not been talking to Mr. Y, "I just gotta tell somebody. I shot that man and I'm glad he is dead. Somebody should have killed him ten years ago." These statements made by Mr. Y would probably be inadmissible. Although he may or may not have been a suspect, he was deprived of his freedom in a significant way, even though he was not under arrest or in formal custody. This situation seems to meet the description in *Miranda* of a "police-dominated atmosphere, resulting in self-incriminating statements without full warnings of constitutional rights."

Since warnings of constitutional rights are required by the Court's decision in *Miranda,* it would be appropriate to discuss them at this point. Before any warnings are given to the suspect, the officer should make the suspect aware of his identity and authority as a police officer, whether in or out of uniform. If the suspect is not aware that the person to whom he is speaking is an officer, then the fact that he did not know could be a ready-made defense when the officer seeks to admit the confession as evidence. When the officer advises a suspect of his Fifth and Sixth Amendment rights, the Supreme Court, in *Miranda,* said that the suspect must be told: (1) that he does not have to say anything and that he has an absolute right to remain silent; (2) that anything he might say can and will be used against him in a court of law; (3) that he has a right to consult with an attorney before speaking to police and that he has the right to have the attorney present during any questioning; (4) that he will be provided with an attorney if he wants one and that even though he is without funds to retain one, the attorney will be provided without charge to him; and (5) that if he does not desire to answer any questions, or if he desires to discontinue the interview at any time, he will not be compelled to continue. It is not necessary that these exact words be used in giving the warnings; however, these five points *must* be covered.

For an example of how the *Miranda* ruling affects interrogations, let us assume that the officer is questioning a suspect who is in custody. The suspect has been given the Miranda warnings and has effectively waived his rights. He is alone with the officer in an office which is used for the purpose of interrogation. During the process of questioning, the suspect notices that the time is 11:45 A.M. and calls this to the attention of the officer. The suspect tells the officer that he is hungry and that since it is nearly noon, he would like to stop the interrogation and eat lunch. The officer immediately stops the questioning; they leave, eat lunch, and return one hour and ten minutes later. The officer must now decide whether to continue the interrogation without acquiring another waiver. In analyzing this problem, the officer should review the five warnings and decide which would apply in this situation. Before giving a solution, however, let us change some of the facts. This time, instead of the suspect being the one who suggests stopping the interview for lunch, suppose the officer makes the suggestion and asks the suspect to stop. Would an additional waiver be required upon their return in this instance? In the first example, the warnings would probably have to be given again and a new waiver obtained, since the suspect discontinued the interview, as the fifth warning provides. However, in the second example, a new waiver should not be required, since the officer discontinued the interview. In applying these and other legal theories, the officer should remember that the situations presented here and throughout this book are purely hypothetical and may or may not occur in real life. They are designed to be thought-provoking and to give the officer an opportunity to consider the issues in a factual setting.

Since the *Miranda* decision, a confession is admissible at trial only when the accused intelligently waived his rights to remain silent and to have an attorney. In any case when a confession is made without the presence of an attorney, a very heavy burden is placed on the state to show that the accused person knowingly and intelligently waived his rights. Because of this, the United States Supreme Court takes pains to scrutinize waivers made by uncounseled defendants.

To insure that confessions obtained will be admissible, the officer should follow these guidelines. A *verbal* waiver to a single police officer, if contradicted by the defense at trial, will usually result in an inadmissible confession. A waiver of rights should be in *written* form, recorded as *precisely* as possible, and whenever practicable, the warning *procedure* should be taken verbatim by a stenographer. If a stenographer is not available, the officer who is interrogating the suspect should incorporate the exact warnings given and the suspect's exact answers directly into the statement. The person who is taking the statements should use great care to avoid changing any words used by the suspect, for even if this is done in good faith to make the statement sound better or more understandable, it would not then be the suspect's statement.

The officer should be aware that since the decision of *Jackson* v. *Denno,*[14] the trial judge decides whether the confession was voluntary, not the jury. This means that a voluntariness hearing will be held out of the presence of the jury, before the confession in question is admitted into evidence. The officer must have clear and positive proof that the confession was voluntary. He cannot infer, simply from the fact that after being given the warnings the accused answered questions, that a waiver of rights was made. The most effective way to prove that a suspect waived his rights is by a completed *written* waiver, supported by a proper number of witnesses. The number of attesting witnesses desired by the different courts varies, but as a general rule, two are sufficient. In any case, each witness attesting to the waiver *must* appear in court to give testimony as to what happened in regard to the waiver.

The officer must be sure that the suspect understands what his rights are and that he understands the warnings given. If the suspect is not sufficiently familiar with English or lacks the mental capacity to understand, the officer could not gain an admissible confession. (It has been argued that anyone who waives his rights against self-incrimination shows a lack of intelligence, but the majority of state courts have rejected this theory.) The Mississippi Supreme Court held that:

> Where defendant, who had an intelligence quotient of 60, and who was diagnosed by competent physicians to be moderately mentally retarded or a moderate mental defective, which retardation or deficiency increased under stress, [he] could not knowingly, voluntarily and effectively waive his Constitutional right against self-incrimination.[15]

It is very possible that other state supreme courts have decided cases similar to this. The officer should know the rule in his state and should govern his actions accordingly.

In questioning the accused, the officer must take great care to avoid using any language which might be construed as an attempt at psychological coercion. He should not say anything which indicates what he thinks the suspect ought to do; the suspect must make his own decision. The old "good guy-bad guy" routine, leaving the suspect in an empty room for long periods, using four or five different interrogators in succession, and the various other means by which the police break down the suspect's resistance are usually very effective in gaining a confession. State courts tend to resolve the inevitable "swearing contest" between the police and the defendant over what happened behind the closed doors in favor of the police. Although the officer may have to resort to the practices just mentioned, he should, at the least, be aware that they usually constitute psychological coercion. Every officer should also be aware that all courts look with disfavor upon lengthy interrogation and incommunicado detention. For example, if a person is questioned for an unreasonable length of time or has been in custody for a long period without being allowed to talk to his family, friends, or attorney, a court may find that a subsequent statement was not freely and voluntarily given, even though the suspect may have effectively waived his rights prior to making the statement. The courts usually view these practices as psychological coercion.

SCOPE OF THE CONSTITUTIONAL PROTECTIONS

In order to understand the extent of the Fifth and Sixth Amendment protections, we should examine the various categories of evidence separately. The Supreme Court has repeatedly held that the privilege against self-incrimination applies only to testimonial or communicative acts.

PRIVATE BOOKS AND PAPERS

Unfortunately, there have been few cases of major importance on the precise issue of the admissibility of incriminating statements found in private books or papers. However, most authorities agree that the Fifth Amendment privilege against self-incrimination extends to papers, books, and other documents of a testimonial nature. For example, if a woman writes in her diary, "Dear Diary, I killed my husband today because he was unfaithful to me," this statement would be a private writing and is certainly testimonial in nature. Therefore, unless the woman waives her rights against self-incrimination and the diary is properly obtained by the police, the statement would be inadmissible. On the other hand, let us assume that the woman wrote, "Dear Diary, I certainly hope my financial situation improves soon, because I don't like the idea of stealing all those pension checks, forging the names, and cashing them. I'm afraid of getting caught." Without a waiver, the statement itself would not be admissible as a confession in a prosecution for larceny. However, the diary would be admissible for the purpose of handwriting comparison in a prosecution for forgery if it was properly obtained. This is because it would be offered as real, physical evidence, not as testimony.

FINGERPRINTING AND PHOTOGRAPHING THE ACCUSED

Most states have statutory provisions authorizing the taking of fingerprints and photographs of suspects who have been taken into police custody. Many of these are worded like the Mississippi statute:[16]

> . . . there is hereby conferred and imposed upon [names the various agencies with police power] the powers of taking or causing to be taken, *upon arrest,* fingerprints and thumbprints, and, if necessary, photographs of every person *arrested* and *charged* with a crime under the laws of the state . . . . *(Emphasis added.)*

Until recently many of the statutes applied only to felony crimes. However, today most statutes use the phrase, "charged with *a crime,*" making the statute applicable to both felony and misdemeanor arrests.

The United States Supreme Court has decided several cases on this issue and in one case the court stated that "it is elementary that a person *in lawful custody* may be required to submit to photographing and fingerprinting as part of the routine identification process."[17] *(Emphasis added.)*

Another Supreme Court case, *Davis* v. *Mississippi,*[18] involved a conviction for the rape of an 87-year-old woman. Twenty-four young boys were picked up and taken to the police station or other places for interviews. Fingerprints and palmprints were taken from 12 of the boys, including John Davis. An F.B.I. expert testified at the trial in the circuit court that Davis' prints matched those taken from the victim's window. The state supreme court affirmed the conviction on appeal, but the United States Supreme Court reversed and remanded the case for a new trial on the theory that even though Davis had been immediately released after the taking of his prints, he was technically under arrest at the time the prints were taken, and the prints were therefore the fruit of an unlawful arrest. The Court based its decision on the Fourth Amendment provisions concerning arrest:

> Detentions for the sole purpose of obtaining fingerprints are no less subject to the constraints of the Fourth Amendment. It is arguable, however, that, because of the unique nature of the fingerprinting process, such detentions might, under narrowly defined circumstances, be found to comply with the Fourth Amendment even though there is no probable cause in the traditional sense. Detention for fingerprinting may constitute a much less serious intrusion upon personal security than other types of police searches and detentions. Fingerprinting involves none of the probing into an individual's private life and thoughts that marks an interrogation or search. Nor can fingerprint detention be employed repeatedly to harass any individual, since the police need only one set of each person's prints. Furthermore, fingerprinting is an inherently more reliable and effective crime-solving tool than eyewitness identifications or confessions and is not subject to such abuses as the improper line-up and the "third degree." Finally, because there is no danger of destruction of fingerprints, the limited detention need not come unexpectedly or at an inconvenient time. For this same reason, the general requirement that the authorization of a judicial officer be obtained in advance of detention would seem not to admit of any exception in the fingerprinting context.

THE POLICE LINEUP

Normally a police lineup, if properly conducted, does not violate the accused's constitutional rights. However, the courts have imposed certain guidelines that the police must follow. In *Kirby* v. *Illinois,*[19] the Supreme Court cited its prior decisions in *United States* v. *Wade*[20] and *Gilbert* v. *California:*[21]

> . . . a post-indictment pretrial lineup at which the accused is exhibited to identifying witnesses is a critical stage of the criminal

> prosecution; that police conduct such a lineup without notice to and in absence of his counsel denies the accused his Sixth (and Fourteenth) Amendment right to counsel and calls in question the admissibility at trial of the in-court identifications of the accused by witnesses who attend the lineup. Those cases further held that no "in-court identifications" are admissible in evidence if their "source" is a lineup conducted in violation of this constitutional standard.

In essence, the Court said that a lineup, per se, does not violate the defendant's right against self-incrimination. It is, however, a critical stage and the accused is allowed counsel at the lineup in order to insure that the procedure is conducted properly. In the *Kirby* case, the Court was asked to "extend the *Wade-Gilbert* rule to identification testimony based upon a police station showup that took place before the defendant had been indicted or otherwise formally charged with any criminal offense." The Court responded by saying:

> In this case we are asked to import into a routine police investigation an absolute constitutional guarantee historically and rationally applicable only after the onset of formal prosecutorial proceedings. We decline to do so . . . . We decline to depart from that rationale today by imposing a *per se* exclusionary rule upon testimony concerning an identification that took place long before the commencement of any prosecution whatever.[22]

PHOTOGRAPHIC AND EYEWITNESS IDENTIFICATION

Closely related to the lineup are identifications made through the use of photographs or on-the-scene eyewitness confrontations. If photographs are used in such a way as to suggest to the witness the identification of a particular suspect, there is a good possibility that the in-court identification will be contaminated. This type of pre-trial identification was challenged in *Simmons* v. *United States*[23] as being suggestive and conducive to misidentification and violative of the Due Process Clause of the Fourteenth Amendment. The court responded:

> It must be recognized that improper employment of photographs by police may sometimes cause witnesses to err in identifying criminals. A witness may have obtained only a brief glimpse of a criminal, or may have seen him under poor conditions. Even if the police subsequently follow the most correct photographic identification without indicating whom they suspect, there is some danger that the witness may make an incorrect identification. This danger will be increased if the police display to the witness only the picture of a single individual who generally resembles the person he saw, or if they show him the pictures of several persons among which the photograph of a single such

> individual recurs or is in some way emphasized. The chance of misidentification is also heightened if the police indicate to the witness that they have other evidence that one of the persons pictured committed the crime. Regardless of how the initial misidentification comes about, the witness thereafter is apt to retain in his memory the image of the photograph rather than of the person actually seen, reducing the trustworthiness of subsequent lineup or courtroom identification.
>
> Despite the hazards of initial identification by photograph, this procedure has been used widely and effectively in criminal law enforcement, from the standpoint both of apprehending offenders and of sparing innocent suspects the ignominy of arrest by allowing eyewitnesses to exonerate them through scrutiny of photographs. The danger that use of the technique may result in convictions based on misidentification may be substantially lessened by a course of cross-examination at trial which exposes to the jury the method's potential for error. We are unwilling to prohibit its employment, either in the exercise of our supervisory power or, still less, as a matter of constitutional requirement. Instead, we hold that each case must be considered on its own facts, and that convictions based on eyewitness identification at trial following a pretrial identification by photograph will be set aside on that ground only if the photographic identification procedure was so impermissibly suggestive as to give rise to a very substantial likelihood of irreparable misidentification.

In another case, which involved an immediate on-the-scene confrontation at 5 o'clock in the morning, when there would by necessity be a long delay in summoning the suspect's counsel to observe a formal lineup, the court stated:

> Such delay may not only cause the detention of an innocent suspect; it may also diminish the reliability of any identification obtained, thus defeating a principal purpose of counsel requirement. We wish to make clear that the holding of this case approves only those on-the-scene identifications which occur within minutes of the witnessed crime.
>
> . . . recognition of a person or face would seem to be as much the product of a subjective mental image as of articulable, consciously remembered characteristics. A man may see clearly in his "mind's eye" a face or a figure which he is hard put to describe adequately in words. Though the image of an "unforgettable face" may occasionally linger without any translation into words, photographic recall is most often ephemeral. Vivid in the flash of direct observation, it fades rapidly with time. And the conscious attempt to separate the ensemble impression into particular verbalized features, in order to preserve some recollection, may well distort the original accurate image so that it is the verbalized characteristics which are remembered and not the face of the man.
>
> Balancing all the doubts left by the mysteries of human perception and recognition, it appears that prompt confrontation in

circumstances like those of this case will "if anything promote fairness, by assuring reliability."[24]

The case of *Stovall* v. *Denno*[25] was another instance in which the decision was based on "the circumstances of the moment." This case presented the following facts: Dr. Behrendt was stabbed to death in his kitchen. His wife leaped at the assailant, and he knocked her to the floor and stabbed her 11 times. The police found a shirt on the floor of the kitchen; in the pocket were keys which were traced to the defendant. Mrs. Behrendt was hospitalized immediately because her life was in danger. The police, without affording the accused time to retain counsel, took him to her hospital room so that she could identify him. She identified him both there and in the courtroom. The court of appeals, sitting en banc, stated:

> Here was the only person in the world who could possibly exonerate Stovall. Her words, and only her words, "He is not the man," could have resulted in freedom for Stovall. The hospital was not far distant from the courthouse and jail. No one knew how long Mrs. Behrendt might live. Faced with the responsibility of identifying the attacker, with the need for immediate action and with the knowledge that Mrs. Behrendt could not visit the jail, the police followed the only feasible procedure and took Stovall to the hospital room. Under these circumstances, the usual police station line-up which Stovall now argues he should have had, was out of the question.

BLOOD SAMPLES AND OTHER TESTS

In *Breithaupt* v. *Abram,*[26] the Supreme Court summarily rejected the argument that the withdrawal of blood and the admission of the analysis into evidence violated the Fifth Amendment privilege against self-incrimination. In *Schmerber* v. *California,*[27] the Court again dealt with this issue:

> It could not be denied that in requiring petitioner to submit to the withdrawal and chemical analysis of his blood the State compelled him to submit to an attempt to discover evidence that might be used to prosecute him for a criminal offense. He submitted only after the police officer rejected his objection and directed the physician to proceed. The officer's direction to the physician to administer the test over petitioner's objection constituted compulsion for the purpose of the privilege. The critical question, then, is whether petitioner was thus compelled "to be a witness against himself."
>
> * * *
>
> It is clear that the protection of the privilege reaches an accused's communications, whatever form they might take, and the compulsion of responses which are also communications, for example, compliance with a subpoena to produce one's papers. . . .

> On the other hand, both federal and state courts have usually held that it offers no protection against compulsion to submit to fingerprinting, photographing, or measurements, to write or speak for identification, to appear in court, to stand, to assume a stance, to walk, or to make a particular gesture. The distinction which has emerged, often expressed in different ways, is that the privilege is a bar against compelling "communications" or "testimony," but that compulsion which makes a suspect or accused the source of "real or physical evidence" does not violate it.
> * * *
>
> In the present case, however, no such problem of application is presented. Not even a shadow of testimonial compulsion upon or enforced communication by the accused was involved either in the extraction or in the chemical analysis. Petitioner's testimonial capacities were in no way implicated; indeed, his participation, except as donor, was irrelevant to the results of the test, which depend on chemical analysis and on that alone. Since the blood test evidence, although an incriminating product of compulsion, was neither petitioner's testimony nor evidence relating to some communicative act or writing by the petitioner, it was not inadmissible on privileged grounds.

Before the *Schmerber* decision, the Court had dealt with the problem of bodily extractions in another case. In *Rochin* v. *California,*[28] officers confronted Rochin in his bedroom, and when he tried to swallow two capsules the officers "jumped upon him" and attempted to extract the capsules. Their efforts were to no avail, so they handcuffed Rochin and took him to the hospital where, at the direction of one of the officers, a doctor pumped his stomach. The pumping produced vomiting and in the vomited matter were two capsules which contained morphine. Rochin was convicted for possession of morphine. In the Court's decision to reverse the conviction, Mr. Justice Frankfurter said:

> ... we are compelled to conclude that the proceedings by which this conviction was obtained do more than offend some private sentimentalism about combatting crime too energetically. This is conduct that shocks the conscience .... They are methods too close to the rack and screw to permit of constitutional differentiation.

In this case, the reversal did not hinge on the claim of compulsory self-incrimination or violation of the Sixth Amendment right to counsel but was based on the theory that the officers' actions constituted cruel and unusual conduct which violated fundamental rights. Mr. Justice Black said in his concurring opinion, "What the majority hold is that the Due Process clause impowers this Court to nullify any state law if its application 'shocks the conscience,' 'offends a sense of justice' or runs counter to the 'decencies of civilized conduct.' " Although *Schmerber* and other cases decided since *Rochin* have allowed bodily extractions, the officer should take care to avoid any acts which might "shock the conscience" or "offend a sense of justice."

Implied Consent Statutes. Most states now have implied consent statutes which primarily deal with the "drunk" driver or persons "driving while under the influence of alcohol." The reasoning behind such statutes is that driving a motor vehicle is a privilege and is therefore subject to certain rules and regulations. When a person purchases his license to operate a motor vehicle he impliedly gives his consent to have certain tests administered to him if he is arrested and accused of operating the vehicle while under the influence of alcohol. There have been many cases challenging the constitutionality of such statutes, especially in Kansas, which was one of the first states to adopt an implied consent statute.

In the cases of *Newhouse* v. *Misterly*[29] and *State* v. *Pugas,*[30] the courts stated the general rule that "since evidence acquired from the body, as in *Schmerber,* violates no privilege against self-incrimination, neither does testimony concerning the refusal to give bodily evidence." It would seem from these and other decisions that an officer may testify to the fact that a person, when confronted with the tests, refused to allow them to be administered. In some states, there are provisions for on-the-spot revocation of the operator's license of any driver who refuses to submit to the tests provided for in the pertinent statute.

RIGHT TO COUNSEL IN MISDEMEANOR CASES

The question of whether counsel is required in a given misdemeanor case has proved to be a confusing one for both the police and the courts. To answer this question, the officer not only must know what elements make up a particular crime, but also must be aware of what sentence can be imposed on conviction. In 1965, the circuit court upheld the right to counsel in a misdemeanor case in *Harvey* v. *Mississippi.*[31] Then in 1969, the same court, in *James* v. *Headley,*[32] stated that "all charges against an accused must be cumulated in measuring the possible sentence which could be imposed for the purpose of calculating whether the offense is 'petty' or 'serious.' " The court then quoted *Duncan* v. *Louisiana,*[33] "In the federal system, petty offenses are defined as those punishable by no more than six months in prison and a $500 fine." In the 1970 Fifth Circuit decision of *Shepherd* v. *Jordan,*[34] the Sixth Amendment right to counsel was held to apply to all criminal prosecutions except those for "petty" offenses. In the 1971 decision of *Wall* v. *Purdy,*[35] the court explained that "to require counsel in all misdemeanor cases would be impossibly costly." So, as a result of these decisions, the officer is provided with the general rule that counsel is required in "serious" misdemeanor cases but not in "petty" cases. In determining whether the offense is serious or petty, the officer should follow the "six months–$500" guideline stated in *Duncan* v. *Louisiana.*

CONSTITUTIONAL RIGHTS OF JUVENILES

Until 1967, there was little uniformity among the states in the constitutional protections afforded to juvenile offenders. However, in *In re Gault,* [36] the Supreme Court enunciated the constitutional requirements for juvenile proceedings:

> Fourteenth Amendment Due Process requires that in juvenile court proceedings which may result in the juvenile's commitment to an institution, the child and his parents or guardian must be: (1) given notice sufficient to permit preparation of defense to charges, (2) notified of the child's right to be represented by counsel (including assigned counsel), and (3) the child must be afforded the privilege against self-incrimination and the rights of confrontation and cross-examination.

In his dissent, Mr. Justice Stewart questioned the wisdom of applying uniform standards:

> The Court today used an obscure Arizona case as a vehicle to impose upon thousands of juvenile courts throughout the Nation restrictions that the Constitution made applicable to adversary criminal trials. I believe the Court's decision is wholly unsound as a matter of constitutional law, and sadly unwise as a matter of judicial policy.

In the aftermath of the *Gault* decision, courts were faced with the issue of waivers of constitutional rights by juveniles. This issue was addressed in the case *In re R. M.*[37]:

> . . . although it has been frequently argued that a juvenile is not competent to waive his right to counsel because of his young age, this proposition has been generally rejected by the weight of authority. It cannot be said that a juvenile cannot waive constitutional rights as a matter of law. It may be difficult to prove because of his young age but it is a factual matter to be decided by the trial judge in each case.

In order to avoid any possibility of tainting his case, especially when the juvenile is not being tried as an adult, the officer should follow the requirements of *Gault* and should advise the juvenile of his rights in the presence of his parents, guardian, or attorney.

RIGHT TO FREELY COMMUNICATE WITH COUNSEL

As the Supreme Court made clear by its denunciation of incommunicado detention in *Miranda,* an accused has the right to freely communicate with his counsel. However, there has frequently been some conflict between this right and jail rules governing visits with prisoners. In some instances, an attorney has been allowed to speak with his client for only a few minutes, and in other cases, conversation between the accused and his counsel was either video-taped or recorded. Decisions like *State* v. *Cory*[38] have provided guidelines for regulating communications between the accused and his counsel. In the *Cory* case, the court said "A defendant and his lawyer have a right to talk together by telephone or personal interview without being monitored by the police or prosecution in any way." One must assume, from this decision at least, that counsel should be allowed to talk with the accused during normal business hours. However, if a particularly timed visit or telephone call would jeopardize the security of the jail, neither should be allowed, because the primary obligation of the police is to protect the public safety.

WHEN WARNINGS OF RIGHTS ARE NOT REQUIRED

Warnings of Fifth and Sixth Amendment rights are not required in any case in which a person volunteers a statement. It is important to note the difference between a volunteered statement and a voluntary answer to an incriminating question, because the latter must be preceded by the *Miranda* warnings, while the former need not be. For example, a person runs into the police station and says to the officer on duty, "I just shot my wife, her body is outside in my car and the gun is in my pocket." Under these circumstances, there would be no need for the officer to stop him midway through the statement and give the warnings because this is a volunteered statement, given without any inquiry from police, and the investigation has yet to reach the "critical stage."

The *Miranda* warnings need not be given when the officer does not ask a suspect for incriminating testimony. Although there is some difference of opinion on this issue, the majority rule is that if the question would require an "inculpatory" answer, it should be preceded by the Miranda warnings. For example, as mentioned in Chapter II, under the provisions of the Uniform Arrest Act a suspicious person may be stopped on the street and inquiry made as to his name, address, and business at that particular location. However, once the person becomes a suspect in the officer's mind, the warnings should be given before any further questions are asked.

In the language of *Miranda,* the warnings need not be given as long as the suspect is not in custody or has not been deprived of his freedom of action in a significant way. Here we must note that an officer cannot hold a suspect without the benefit of a valid arrest in order to question him and gain the desired information before formally placing him under arrest. The officer must remember that the Fifth and Sixth Amendment guarantees attach at the critical stage, as defined earlier in this chapter.

No warnings are required in cases where motorists or other persons are stopped simply for the purpose of inquiry, provided that they are not suspects of crime and the questioning is in furtherance of some other valid police function. For example, a police officer could stop and detain a motorist for a reasonable time without advising him of his rights in order to check his operator's license, vehicle registration, vehicle identification number, or the vehicle's safety equipment, such as brakes, lights, and steering.

Generally, no warnings would be required in investigating a traffic accident, since most traffic offenses are only petty misdemeanors. However, the officer's intent must be to charge the person with only the petty violation. In more serious cases, such as those where the person could be charged with manslaughter, the officer would be required to give the warnings at the critical stage. For example, if at a point midway through the investigation the officer decides to charge for a felony, the warnings must be given before any further questioning.

STATEMENTS OF ACCUSED USED FOR IMPEACHMENT

In the 1971 decision, *Harris* v. *New York,*[39] the Supreme Court stated the following general rule:

> *Miranda* barred the prosecution from making its case with statements of an accused, made while in custody, prior to having or effectively waiving counsel. It does not follow from *Miranda* that evidence inadmissible against the accused in the prosecution's case in chief is barred for all purposes, provided of course the trustworthiness of the evidence satisfies legal standards.

In simple language, this means that if the defendant takes the stand in order to testify in his own behalf, the prosecution may use statements made by him while in custody for impeachment purposes. To be admissible for impeachment, the statements must be inconsistent with those made by the accused during the trial and must satisfy other legal standards. Normally only those statements or parts of a statement which are contradictory to the answers given by the defendant at trial are admissible. For example, a person is arrested and gives the officers a full and factual confession. The trial judge rules the confession to be inadmissible for the purpose of establishing the prosecution's case in chief. However, later in the trial, the defendant takes the stand and, when answering questions on cross-examination, contradicts certain statements made in his confession. The prosecution may now use the statements to impeach the defendant.

OTHER TYPES OF EVIDENCE

Many of the court decisions previously discussed have had the effect of limiting the use of confessions in establishing guilt. The officer should realize this and should understand that other cases have encouraged the use of real or physical evidence. Therefore, to build a strong case, the officer should devote his energy to making a thorough investigation so he can obtain the best tangible evidence and will not be forced to base his case on a confession.

INSTRUMENTS USED IN A CRIME

Generally, a device, article, or instrument which was used or was intended to be used in the commission of a crime may be admissible evidence if it is known that there is a connection between the article, the accused, and the crime. Murder weapons and weapons used for assault may be admitted, and even simulated weapons are admissible. For example, X used a toy pistol in the robbery of a bar. Technically, X committed the crime of armed robbery, and the toy pistol would be admissible because the gist of the offense is the fear created in the mind of the victim who believed that the gun was real. On occasion other items, such as saws, pliers, hammers, and other common tools, may become instruments of crime, depending on their use or attempted use by the accused. Burglary tools are admissible, and in some states, the possession of them by one who does not customarily use such tools in the normal course of his occupation is prima facie evidence of an intention to use them for illegal purposes. The list of instruments that might be used or intended to be used in the commission of a crime could go on and on, but the important thing for the officer to remember is that a connection must be shown between the person, the instrument, and the offense.

CLOTHING AND OTHER MATERIALS

Clothing worn to commit a crime, bloodstained clothing of a victim, and clothing containing hair or fiber may be examined and tested in a laboratory. The accused may be required to put on particular clothing for viewing by an eye-witness. Fiber imprints from clothing on the metal of automobile bodies are often used in the prosecution of hit-and-run accident cases. In a rape case, examination of the bedclothes and the victim's nightclothes will usually produce pubic hair and semen stains of the attacker; likewise, the clothes of the accused will usually show pubic hair and stains from the victim. A traffic accident scene would generally contain such evidence as debris, paint chips, dust and dirt, broken chrome or glass, skidmarks, and other items which will enhance the officer's case if obtained properly, examined expertly, and preserved correctly throughout the criminal proceedings.

EXHIBITING THE PERSON IN COURT

Since the duty of a jury is to determine the truth, people may be exhibited in the courtroom in order to aid the jury in its determination. For example, witness may be exhibited so that the jury might see at first hand the nature and extent of an injury in a criminal case. In a suit for damages, the plaintiff may exhibit himself to the jury to show the seriousness of an injury sustained in a traffic accident. A man and child may be directed to stand or sit close together so that the jury can observe any physical or facial similarity between the alleged father and illegitimate child in a paternity suit.

VIEWING OF THE CRIME SCENE

There are two general rationales for allowing the jury to view the crime scene. One is that it will supply them with firsthand knowledge of the locality where the crime occurred pictured in their minds. The other is that the viewing will allow them to more effectively evaluate and understand the evidence presented during the trial. In any case, viewing of the crime scene is permitted by statute in some states and by court decision in others, with the exception of Texas, where it is not allowed by either. As with most types of evidence, the trial judge can allow or not allow the viewing at his discretion.

PHOTOGRAPHS

As a general rule, photographs are admissible if they are original, if the correct foundation is laid, if they are a part of the testimony of a qualified witness, and if it is shown that they are an accurate representation of the scene depicted. Usually the person who took the photographs would be required to come into court to identify each and establish its accuracy. Posed photographs are admitted in some states if the proper foundation is established, and the hypothetical scene depicted by them shows conditions that actually existed. Color photographs are generally admissible, subject to the limitations just mentioned. However, gruesome photographs are usually inadmissible unless they have probative value and will not prejudice the jury. The time when the photographs are taken is important, and it is recommended that they be taken either at the time or immediately after a crime is committed. For example, if an officer wanted to show the weather and road conditions that existed when a crime was committed on a particular rainy day, it would be pointless to take a photograph of the scene on another day when there was no rain.

SOUND RECORDINGS

As long ago as 1936, the courts were admitting sound recordings in evidence. In *State* v. *Perkins,*[40] the court stated:

> The phonograph, the dictaphone, . . . and similar recording devices . . . are now in such common use that the verity of their recording and reproducing sounds . . . is well established; and as advances in such matters of scientific research and discovery are made and generally adopted, the courts will be permitted to make use of them by way of presenting evidentiary facts to the jury.

In later cases, the courts gave the officer guidelines which he must abide by if the recording is to be ruled admissible. The following quotation presents the guidelines which are used today:

> The party offering the recording in evidence must make a showing with reference to its preparation, that is, whether the mechanical device was sufficiently capable of taking the testimony; and also there should be a proper showing as to the manner of the preservation of the recording, that is, as to whether any changes have been made, deletions, or additions to the recording, and of the correctness. The genuineness or the authenticity of the recording must be established.[41]

Two years later, three more provisions were added to the guidelines: the operator of the recording device must be competent to operate it; the speakers who are recorded must be identified; and the conversation which was elicited must have been made voluntarily, in good faith, and without duress of any kind.[42]

For a recording to be admissible, the prosecution must establish a foundation by showing that the prescribed guidelines were followed. If the recording is of a confession made by an accused, the *Miranda* warnings must have been given. The trial judge will usually hold a preliminary hearing to determine the admissibility of all or part of the recording. Since *wiretapping* and *eavesdropping* using a recording device fall under the search and seizure provisions of the Fourth Amendment, the methods by which such recordings can be obtained legally will be discussed in detail in Chapter IV.

Closely related to the sound recording is the *voice spectrograph* which is being studied and experimented with in several universities in the United States. Because the voiceprint has not yet been scientifically perfected, its reliability has not been established. For this reason, the courts will probably hold voiceprints to be inadmissible until their accuracy and reliability can be demonstrated.

THE POLYGRAPH (LIE DETECTOR)

The officer should understand that the results of a polygraph examination have been consistently held to be inadmissible in evidence to establish either the guilt or innocence of the defendant. However, in one case the court said, "In a criminal case the prosecution and defense may stipulate to the taking of the test and the admission in evidence of the results." The court added, "The defendant may not invalidate the stipulation merely because the results are unfavorable to him."[43]

In another case, the court discussed the admissibility of the test results:

> In the absence of stipulation, our courts, without exception, reject the results of lie-detector tests when the same are offered in evidence for the purpose of establishing the guilt or innocence of one accused of a crime. . . . There are no cases on record in which a lie-detector test has been admitted by stipulation without the presence and qualification of the operator and interpreter of such tests as an expert witness during the trial.[44]

In at least one case, even in the absence of the stipulation, testimony about the test was admitted for a limited purpose. In this case, the officer was allowed to testify to what the test indicated in order to prove that the accused's subsequent confession was voluntarily made.[45] In another case, the court left open the issue of admissibility because the defendant had stipulated merely to the taking of the test, not to admitting the results in evidence.[46] In still another case, the court held it improper for the prosecutor to comment on an accused's willingness or unwillingness to submit to or volunteer for polygraph test. The reasoning of the court was that the issue is not relevant to consciousness of guilt and that such comments are self-serving and may improperly influence the jury.[47]

A defendant is not deprived of his right to counsel if he voluntarily and with full knowledge of all rights, submits to a polygraph test without the presence of his attorney.[48] It has been held that an officer can be dismissed from his department for refusal to take the test when ordered to do so by his superior in a disciplinary hearing, even though, as an individual, he has a right to refuse.[49]

CHARTS, DIAGRAMS, MAPS, AND MODELS

As a general rule, the use of visual aids to supplement a witness' testimony has been firmly established since the 1950's. As stated in the legal encyclopedia, *Corpus Juris Secundum,* the usual test of the admissibility of such visual aids is their capacity to inform a jury. If they are accurate and fully explained, they are generally admissible even though they may be abstract in nature.[50] Even writings on chalkboards have been allowed in the courtroom in order to prevent jury confusion. The theory is that such writings are not evidence in and of themselves but are only extensions of counsel's arguments or witnesses' testimony.[51] Models, drawings, charts, and sketches are commonly used. Whenever practicable, they should be presented to the trial judge for examination before trial, because it is within his discretion to allow or disallow them.

EXPERIMENTS

Since the purpose of a trial is to ascertain the truth, most courts strive to furnish the jury with the best possible evidence. For this reason, experiments made in the courtroom or outside the court are usually admitted along with the results thereof.

As an example of the value of experiments, consider the following story. Even though the story is "hearsay" at this point, having been told to this writer by one of his law professors, it was presented as a true story. It seems that the plaintiff in this case (before becoming the plaintiff, of course) approached a soft drink dispensing machine and placed 25¢ in the coin slot, but the soft drink did not emerge. To add insult to injury, the machine would not return his money. After saying a few choice words, he beat, shook, and kicked the machine in an attempt to recover his money. During these "violent acts" directed toward the machine, it fell upon him and broke his leg. Needless to say, the plaintiff sued the vending company for damages. The defendant vending company, wishing to avoid liability, hired a prominent attorney to defend it. The attorney, wise in the rules of trial procedure and evidence, wasted no time in setting the case for trial. His main defense strategy was to install a vending machine, exactly like the machine which fell on the plaintiff, in the courtroom in order to show the jury that, even under extreme experimental conditions, the machine could not topple over. As the court and jury sat spellbound, the defense counsel shook, beat, and pounded on the machine. Finally, he turned his back to the machine in order to kick it as a mule would, caught his foot in the opening where the canned drink emerges, and lost his balance. As the attorney fell to the floor of the courtroom, the machine toppled onto his leg, and the result of this experiment was another broken leg. To say the least, the results were more than expected, and the findings of the jury need not be mentioned. Although this was not a criminal case, the officer can learn a worthwhile lesson from it.

SPEED DETECTION DEVICES

The courts have now recognized, in some states by "judicial notice," that devices such as radar and vascar do accurately measure the speed of moving vehicles. The results of these speed detecting devices are usually admissible without the requirement of expert testimony to establish accuracy. Both these devices are widely used, and although they are not fully understood by the motoring public, the results are seldom challenged in court.

FORENSIC BALLISTICS

Today, forensic ballistics has become a recognized science. In most cases, the person wishing to testify to the results of ballistics tests would have to be a qualified expert. The expert ballistics witness may testify to a number of facts which relate to the identification of firearms and bullets, provided his qualifications are properly demonstrated.

OTHER EVIDENCE

Other evidence, such as fingerprint identification, blood grouping tests, urine tests, blood tests, and x-rays, is admissible if it is shown to be relevant, material, properly obtained, and correctly preserved. These requirements would likewise apply to all evidence previously discussed. The officer should use caution when gathering evidence and should make certain that he marks and identifies it properly. The officer should retain personal custody of the evidence until it is delivered for examination by laboratory personnel, and he should then acquire the proper receipt for it. In other words, the "chain" of evidence must be kept unbroken if the evidence is to be admissible. Partly as a result of federal funding, many crime laboratories, staffed by qualified experts and furnished with ample, up-to-date equipment, have been established in most states and in many cities. The officer should avail himself of every opportunity to utilize the services offered by these laboratories so that he can improve his case.

SUMMARY AND APPLICATION

Since thought-provoking problems are beneficial to the learning process, the same method of applying theory through hypothetical situations used in Chapter II is used here. The officer should begin to recognize the important issues with more ease as he becomes more familiar with the problem method.

PROBLEM I

An officer was suspended and his superior instituted disciplinary proceedings before a review board. The superior demanded that the officer submit to a polygraph test, which he took without argument. The officer requested that his attorney be allowed to attend the hearing and his request was denied. The officer now claims that his constitutional rights were violated. Do you think the officer's right to counsel was violated? What theory should be used to arrive at the answer?

PROBLEM II

S. A. M. Bogus was arrested, charged with committing a felony, and advised of his Fifth and Sixth Amendment rights. He knowingly and intelligently waived his right to remain silent and stated that he did not want or need an attorney to be present at the time. The arresting officer asked S. A. M., "Would you like to tell the truth about the crime?" Immediately, the suspect gave the officer a full and factual confession. Would a court be likely to construe the officer's question to be psychological coercion? Do you think a court would allow the confession?

PROBLEM III

Joseph Truthful was arrested and charged with a felony. Without being advised of his rights as provided for in *Miranda,* Joe gave the officers a confession. During the voluntariness hearing, the trial judge ruled the confession to be inadmissible. The prosecutor established his case on evidence other than the confession, withholding it by necessity for the time being. During the trial Joe took the stand in his own behalf and contradicted certain statements made in his confession. At this time the prosecutor asked that the statements be admitted for impeachment purposes. Defense counsel objected and was overruled by the judge. Would the judge likely be correct in his ruling? Would the results be the same if the confession had been legally gained?

PROBLEM IV

Donnie C. Dream was shot and severely wounded. D. C. was immediately taken to a hospital and rushed into the emergency room where two doctors hurriedly administered medical treatment. After about an hour, the doctors had exhausted all means of saving D. C.'s life and told him that there was no hope of recovery from the injury. After being told that his death was imminent, D. C. told the doctors that A. C. Trueheart was the one who shot him but he didn't think A. C. really meant to hurt him as severely as he did and that it was probably an act committed in the heat of passion. Fifteen minutes later, D. C. died from the gunshot wounds. A. C. was later arrested and charged with murder. The only evidence that A. C. committed the crime was the statement made by D. C. to the doctors before he died. Would the doctors' testimony relating D. C.'s statements be likely to be admissible? What theory would the court apply in arriving at this decision?

PROBLEM V

Clancy D. Clue was arrested on a felony charge. He was advised of his Fifth and Sixth Amendment rights but did not immediately waive them. However, the next day, Clancy did agree to sign a written waiver and answer questions, and he stated that he did not want or need a lawyer, since he knew enough about the law to protect his own rights. The arresting officer, after acquiring the written waiver, started to interrogate Clancy. After about an hour the officer had not gained any helpful information, so he called in five detectives and allowed each of them to ask questions in the hope of gaining the desired information. After several hours of interrogation, Clancy finally broke down and confessed. Would the trial judge likely rule Clancy's confession inadmissible? What factors would he consider in arriving at his decision?

PROBLEM VI

An officer is called to investigate an auto accident which involved two vehicles. Upon arriving at the accident scene, the officer finds that both drivers have already been taken to a hospital with unknown injuries. After finishing the on-the-scene investigation, the officer proceeds to the hospital to talk with those involved. When he finishes the interview with one driver, the officer is told that the other was D. O. A. As a result of certain statements made by the living driver and certain evidence found at the scene, the officer decides to charge him with manslaughter, which is a felony. Would the statements of the suspect be admissible at his trial on the felony charge? Which rule of evidence could be applied in order to have the statements admitted? Could an officer apply more than one rule in this situation?

PROBLEM VII

Mr. X, who was a suspect in a felony case, requested an interview with the prosecutor. The prosecutor fully warned X of his rights and asked if he wanted his attorney present during the interview. X stated that the attorney's presence was not necessary. X made a statement which was later introduced in evidence against him at his trial. Defense counsel strongly objected to its introduction, claiming it was inadmissible. What do you think? Which rule of evidence would be applicable in this case?

PROBLEM VIII

Nine armed officers entered the defendant's drug store at night with a search warrant that authorized a search for illegal narcotics and named the defendant as possessor of suspected contraband. The defendant was summoned from a back room, where he was lying down, in order that he might witness the search. A brown paper bag containing a white powdery substance was found hidden under a display case. Without giving any warnings, one officer showed the sack to the defendant and asked, "What is this?" The defendant replied, "It's heroin. You've got me this time!" The validity of the search was not challenged at trial. However, the judge ruled that the statement made by the defendant was inadmissible. What theory did the judge use in arriving at his decision?

PROBLEM IX

The defendant was arrested on multiple traffic violations. Before being put in jail, he demanded that the officer allow him to telephone an attorney. The officer did allow him a phone call which lasted for approximately 15 minutes. Before being put into a cell, the defendant requested another phone call to his attorney and stated that the first call he made was to a friend and they had talked about the golf game they had planned for the following week. The officer refused the second request. Would the officer be correct or incorrect in his decision to not allow the second call? Would the defendant be likely to have counsel appointed to defend his case if he is indigent?

REFERENCES

1. 29 Am. Jur. 2d 493, Hearsay Evidence, Sec. 497.
2. *United States* v. *United States Shoe Corp.,* 89 F. Supp. 357 (1950).
3. *United States* v. *Nixon,* 417 U. S. 683 (1974).
4. *Brown* v. *Mississippi,* 297 U. S. 278 (1936).
5. *Malloy* v. *Hogan,* 378 U. S. 1 (1964).
6. *Griffin* v. *California,* 380 U. S. 609 (1965).
7. *Miranda* v. *Arizona,* 384 U. S. 436 (1966).
8. *Gideon* v. *Wainwright,* 372 U. S. 335 (1963).
9. *Betts* v. *Brady,* 316 U. S. 455 (1942).
10. *Hamilton* v. *Alabama,* 368 U. S. 52 (1961).
11. *White* v. *Maryland,* 373 U. S. 59 (1963).
12. *Massiah* v. *United States,* 377 U. S. 201 (1964).
13. *Escobedo* v. *Illinois,* 378 U. S. 478 (1964).
14. *Jackson* v. *Denno,* 378 U. S. 368 (1964).
15. *Dover* v. *Mississippi,* 227 So.2d 296 (1969).
16. Mississippi Code of 1972, Revised and Annotated, Chap. 99, Title 15, Sec. 13.
17. *Smith* v. *United States,* 324 F.2d 879 (1963).
18. *Davis* v. *Mississippi,* 394 U. S. 721 (1969).
19. *Kirby* v. *Illinois,* 32 L. Ed. 2d 411 (1972).
20. *United States* v. *Wade,* 388 U. S. 218 (1967).
21. *Gilbert* v. *California,* 388 U. S. 263 (1967).
22. *Kirby* v. *Illinois,* 32 L. Ed. 2d 411 (1972).
23. *Simmons* v. *United States,* 390 U. S. 377 (1968).
24. *Russell* v. *United States,* 408 F.2d 1280 (1969).
25. *Stovall* v. *Denno,* 388 U. S. 293 (1967).

26. *Breithaupt* v. *Abram,* 352 U. S. 432 (1957).
27. *Schmerber* v. *California,* 384 U. S. 757 (1966).
28. *Rochin* v. *California,* 342 U. S. 165 (1952).
29. *Newhouse* v. *Misterly,* 415 F.2d 514 (1969).
30. *State* v. *Pugas,* 252 La. 345 (1968).
31. *Harvey* v. *Mississippi,* 340 F.2d 263 (1965).
32. *James* v. *Headley,* 410 F.2d 325 (1969).
33. *Duncan* v. *Louisiana,* 391 U. S. 145 (1968).
34. *Shepherd* v. *Jordan,* 425 F.2d 1174 (1970).
35. *Wall* v. *Purdy,* 8 Cr. L. 2334 (1971).
36. *In re Gault,* 387 U. S. 1, (1967).
37. *In re R. M.,* 106 N.J. Super. 372 (1969).
38. *State* v. *Cory,* 382 P.2d 1019 (1963).
39. *Harris* v. *New York,* 401 U. S. 222 (1971).
40. *State* v. *Perkins,* 355 Mo. 851 (1946) (quoting *Commonwealth* v. *Clark,* 187 A. 237 [1936]).
41. *State* v. *Williams,* 49 Wash.2d 354 (1956).
42. *United States* v. *McKeever,* 169 F. Supp. 426 (1958).
43. *State* v. *Valdez,* 91 Ariz. 274 (1962).
44. *People* v. *Qozzetta,* 27 Ill.2d 302 (1963).
45. *Tyler* v. *United States,* 343 U. S. 908 (1951).
46. *People* v. *La Forest,* 106 N.H. 159 (1965).
47. *State* v. *Mottram,* 158 Me. 327 (1962).
48. *Harris* v. *State,* 208 So.2d 108 (1968).
49. *Coursey* v. *Board of Fire & Police Commissioners,* 234 N.E.2d 339 (1967).
50. 32 C.J.S. 1044, Evidence, Sec. 730.
51. *Fischer* v. *Fischer,* 31 Wisc.2d 293 (1966).

CHAPTER IV

SEARCH AND SEIZURE

INTRODUCTION

Many years ago, when the Colonies were under the control of Great Britain, the individual and his property were subject to almost unlimited searches and seizures. Unrest was rampant throughout the Colonies, and abusive invasions of privacy were regularly practiced by representatives of the Crown. During this period, many men became prominent in the fight for individual freedoms, and one man was especially eloquent in his denunciation of unlawful invasions of privacy. This was James Otis, an American patriot and statesman who entered the legal profession in 1750. He was appointed King's Advocate General but resigned in 1760 so that he could appear as counsel for the merchants of Boston. In 1761, he argued their cause against the "writ of assistance" (known today as the search warrant), which allowed customs collectors to search the establishments of those suspected of violating the Sugar Act of 1733.

Otis referred to the writ as "the worst instrument of arbitrary power, the most destructive of English liberty and the fundamental principles of law, that was ever found in an English law book." Although he failed in his attempt to prevent issuance of the writs, he was recognized as a most able pleader for the cause of freedom for the colonists.

From even this brief look at history, it is apparent that the laws which today govern the officer's actions in regard to search and seizure are not new; they have been with us as long as we have been a nation. The United States Constitution was ratified in 1789, and the Fourth Amendment adopted in 1791. This amendment protects the individual from unlawful invasions of privacy by the government. As early as 1886, the Supreme Court stated that the doctrines of the Fourth Amendment "apply to all invasions on the part of the government and its employees of the sanctity of a man's home and the privacies of life. It is not the breaking of his doors, and the rummaging of his drawers, that constitute the essence; but it is the invasion of his indefeasible right of personal security, personal liberty and private property . . . ."[1]

In order to understand our present rules of law governing search and seizure, we must examine Supreme Court and other court decisions which interpret the Fourth Amendment. These decisions give the law enforcement officer guidelines which he must follow if he wishes to legally obtain evidence to present in a court of law. If these guidelines are not followed, the evidence the officer wishes to present will be ruled inadmissible because it was illegally obtained.

In this chapter, we will be dealing with the *exclusionary rule.* Simply stated, the rule is this: evidence *will not* be admitted if it is illegally obtained. The cases discussed in this chapter will help the officer to understand how this rule is applied and how the Fourth Amendment is interpreted by the courts.

> The right of the people to be secure in their persons, houses, papers, and effects, against unreasonable searches and seizures, shall not be violated, and no warrants shall issue, but upon probable cause, supported by oath or affirmation, and particularly describing the place to be searched, and the persons or things to be seized. (United States Constitution, Amendment IV.)

The constitution of almost every state contains a similarly worded provision, and our courts usually interpret the state's provision as they do the Fourth Amendment. The general rule of interpretation applied by the courts is that statutes authorizing searches and seizures are to be strictly construed against the state. In addition, the officer must only look within the particular article or statute for its meaning; he cannot rely on any other *statute* for help in interpretation. This leaves the officer only one alternative in applying the Fourth Amendment and other state constitutional provisions relating to search and seizure: he must look to case decisions and court interpretations to learn how these provisions are to be applied.

The Fourth Amendment does not specifically provide for the exclusion of illegally gained evidence. However, as a result of various court decisions over the last 60 years, the exclusionary rule has developed, which prevents evidence gained by unreasonable search and seizure from being admitted into evidence at trial. The rule was first enunciated in 1914 when the United States Supreme Court stated that:

> . . . in a federal prosecution the Fourth Amendment barred the use of evidence secured through an illegal search and seizure. This ruling . . . was not derived from the explicit requirements of the Fourth Amendment; it was not based on legislation expressing Congressional policy in the enforcement of the Constitution. The decision was a matter of judicial implication.[2]

Here we see that the rule was first applied only to evidence in federal court cases, and it was not until 35 years later that the question arose as to whether the rule applied to state courts. By 1949, over 30 states had rejected the *Weeks* doctrine, and only 16 had adopted it. At the same time, in other countries, including the United Kingdom, evidence gained by illegal search and seizure was held to be admissible. In *Wolf* v. *Colorado,*[3] the Supreme Court held that "in a prosecution in a State court for a State crime the Fourteenth Amendment does not forbid the admission of evidence obtained by an unreasonable search and seizure."

Two years later, in 1951, the Supreme Court again refused to apply the *Weeks* doctrine to state courts through the Fourteenth Amendment.[4] However, Mr. Justice Douglas in his dissenting opinion said, "To hold first that the evidence . . . may be admitted and second that its use may not be enjoined is to make the Fourth Amendment an empty and hollow guarantee so far as state prosecutors are concerned." In this dissent we can see the rule followed today taking shape.

Seven years after the *Wolf* decision, the Supreme Court extended the *Weeks* rule by enjoining federal officers from turning over evidence they had gained illegally to state authorities for use in a state prosecution and from giving testimony concerning the evidence.[5] However, state officers were not precluded from gaining evidence illegally and turning it over to federal officers, and this rule, which became known as the "silver platter" doctrine, was not overturned until 1960.[6] State courts still operated under a less strict rule until the following year when Mr. Justice Clark, delivering the opinion of the Court in the landmark decision of *Mapp* v. *Ohio,*[7] stated:

> Today we once again examine *Wolf's* constitutional documentation of the right to privacy free from unreasonable state intrusion, and, after its dozen years on our books, are led by it to close the only courtroom door remaining open to evidence secured by official lawlessness in flagrant abuse of that basic right, reserved to all persons as a specific guarantee against that very same unlawful conduct. *We hold that all evidence obtained by searches and seizures in violation of the Constitution is, by that same authority, inadmissible in a state court.* (emphasis added)
>
> The ignoble shortcut to conviction left open to the State tends to destroy the entire system of constitutional restraints on which the liberties of the people rest. Having once recognized that the right to privacy embodied in the Fourth Amendment is enforceable against the States, and that the right to be secure against rude invasions of privacy by state officers is, therefore, constitutional in origin, we can no longer permit that right to remain an empty promise. Because it is enforceable in the same manner and to like effect as other basic rights secured by the Due Process Clause, we can no longer permit it to be revocable at the whim of any police officer who, in the name of law enforcement itself, chooses to suspend its enjoyment.

Although in this decision, the Court left no doubt as to what the officer must do, in many states it was four or five years before the *Mapp* ruling was applied. Today, every state must "follow decisions of the United States Supreme Court in regard to standards that must be applied by state courts."[8]

Every officer should understand from the outset that there are basically eight different ways to search for or seize evidence legally. In the following sections, each of these methods will be discussed. Since the courts have consistently indicated their preference that a search be made under the provisions of a valid search warrant, and since the officer is on the safest legal ground when he uses a warrant, we shall begin by discussing that method.

THE SEARCH WARRANT

A search warrant has been defined as "an order, in writing, in the name of the state, signed by a judicial officer, directing a law enforcement officer to search for personal property and bring it before the court."[9] Many officers would read this definition and feel that they fully understand it; however, when they apply it to an everyday situation it would seem much less clear. For example, let us take the average officer who executes a valid search warrant describing six F.M. radios which have been stolen in a burglary of an appliance store. The officer searches the premises described in the warrant and finds the stolen radios in the possession of Mr. X. The issue is whether the officer should or should not arrest Mr. X for the crime of possessing stolen property? At first glance, the answer would seem to be yes, because Mr. X has apparently committed a crime. But upon closer observation, the correct answer becomes less obvious.

In order to arrive at a correct answer, we must consider the essential elements of the crime. In order to arrest a person for the crime of possessing or receiving stolen property, the officer must have probable cause to believe that the property was stolen by a person other than the one possessing it. Otherwise, the person might be guilty of robbery, burglary, or larceny. The officer must also have reason to believe that the accused actually received the stolen property and concealed it, that he actually knew the property was stolen at the time he received it, and that he received the property for his own gain.

At this point, the reader should look again at the definition of a search warrant. He should notice that the search warrant commands the officer to search for the property described, and if he finds it, to seize it and bring it before the court. It does not direct the officer to make an arrest. Although an officer may make an arrest for any crime committed in his presence, the possession of radios is not a crime per se. On the other hand, let us substitute illegal narcotics for the stolen radios. The officer searches under the provisions of a valid warrant and finds the illegal narcotics in Mr. X's possession. Should he arrest Mr. X at this time? The answer is yes, because the possession of illegal narcotics is a crime in and of itself. For greater understanding, we must now examine the specific requirements of the search warrant.

PROPERTY SUBJECT TO A SEARCH WARRANT

Since most states have statutory provisions covering those items for which a search warrant may be issued, we will discuss this requirement in general. In the past, it was a general rule that a search warrant could be issued for stolen or embezzled property, property or objects used or intended to be used in committing a criminal offense, and other objects or items if authorized by statute. This rule was designed to prevent an officer from searching for items which he had no legal right to seek out. However, through usage, the general rule has been broadened to include even "mere evidence," as the following excerpt from a Supreme Court decision points out:

> Nothing in the language of the Fourth Amendment supports the distinction between "mere evidence" and instrumentalities, fruits of crime, or contraband. On its face, the provision assures the "right of the people to be secure in their persons, houses, papers, and effects . . . " without regard to the use to which any of these things are applied. This "right of the people" is certainly unrelated to the "mere evidence" limitation. Privacy is disturbed no more by a search directed to an instrumentality, fruit, or contraband . . . . Moreover, nothing in the nature of the property seized as evidence renders it more private than property seized, for example, as an instrumentality; quite the opposite may be true. Indeed, the distinction is wholly irrational, since, depending on the circumstances, the same "papers and effects" may be "mere evidence" in one case and "instrumentalities" in another. . . . there is no viable reason to distinguish intrusions to secure "mere evidence" from intrusions to secure fruits, instrumentalities, or contraband.[10]

In another case, federal agents legitimately discovered unregistered firearms as a result of a lawful search of a gun shop's records. They were free to seize the weapons without warrant as evidence of illegal activity.[11] The agents were not required to overlook the "mere evidence."

PROBABLE CAUSE REQUIREMENT

An officer who requests a search warrant must show probable cause in his affidavit. In a 1925 decision, the Court said, "If the facts set out in the affidavit are such that a reasonable, discreet and prudent man would be led to believe that there was a commission of the offense charged, there is probable cause justifying the issuance of a warrant."[12]

Many cases have been decided in which there was a determination that certain facts did or did not constitute probable cause. The officer should not look for a clearly defined rule, because no such rule exists. He must understand that the same facts might constitute probable cause in one case and might not in another. The following case excerpts are offered to give some insight into what circumstances might constitute probable cause.

In one case, two police officers applied to a justice of the peace for a warrant to search for narcotics in the defendant's home. To support their application, the officers submitted an affidavit, which stated in part:

> Affiants have received reliable information from a credible person and do believe that heroin, marijuana, barbiturates and other narcotics and narcotics paraphernalia are being kept at the described premises for the purpose of sale and use contrary to the provisions of law.

The search warrant was issued, and officers executed it and seized narcotics. The defendant was convicted and he appealed on the issue of the validity of the affidavit and search warrant. On this issue the Court stated:

> An evaluation of the constitutionality of a search warrant should begin with the rule that "the informed and deliberate determinations of magistrates empowered to issue warrants . . . are to be preferred over the hurried actions of officers . . . who may happen to make arrest." The reasons for this rule go to the foundations of the Fourth Amendment. A contrary rule "that evidence sufficient to support a magistrate's disinterested determination to issue a search warrant will justify the officers in making a search without a warrant would reduce the Amendment to a nullity and leave the people's homes secure only in the discretion of police officers." Under such a rule resort to warrants would ultimately be discouraged. Thus, when a search is based upon a magistrate's, rather than a police officer's, determination of probable cause, the reviewing courts will accept evidence of a less "judicially competent or persuasive character than would have justified an officer in acting on his own without a warrant" and will sustain the judicial determination so long as "there was substantial basis for the magistrate to conclude that the evidence was properly presented . . . ."
>
> Although an affidavit may be based on hearsay information and need not reflect the direct personal observations of the affiant, the magistrate must be informed of some of the underlying circumstances from which the informant concluded that the narcotics were where he claimed they were, and some of the underlying circumstances from which the officer concluded that the informant, whose identity need not be disclosed, was "credible" or his information "reliable." Otherwise, "the inferences from the facts which lead to the complaint" will be drawn not "by a neutral and detached magistrate," as the Constitution requires, but instead, by a police officer "engaged in the often competitive enterprise of ferreting out crime," or, as in this case, by an unidentified informant.

> We conclude, therefore, that the search warrant should not have been issued because the affidavit did not provide a sufficient basis for a finding of probable cause and that the evidence obtained as a result of the search warrant was inadmissible in defendant's trial.[13]

In *Nathanson* v. *United States,*[14] a warrant was issued upon the sworn allegation that the affiant "has cause to suspect and does believe" that certain merchandise was in a specified location. The court, noting that the affidavit "went upon a mere affirmation of suspicion and belief without any statements of adequate supporting facts," stated the following rule:

> Under the Fourth Amendment, an officer may not properly issue a warrant to search a private dwelling unless he can find probable cause therefore from facts or circumstances presented to him under oath or affirmation. Mere affirmance of belief or suspicion is not enough.

In another case, the affidavit stated: "Affiant is advised by reliable informer who was familiar with drug trafficking that marijuana would be removed from a stated address within twenty-four hours." In deciding this case, the court said that the affidavit failed to set forth facts or underlying circumstances necessary to enable the magistrate independently to judge the informant's conclusion and that the warrant was invalid.[15]

In another case, in an affidavit in support of the application for a search warrant, it was stated that an informant who had been reliable in the past had stated that he had purchased marijuana on several occasions from the defendant at a named address. The warrant was issued and executed and marijuana was found. Later it was found that the informer had not given reliable information in the past. The court stated:

> In spite of the incorrect statement, there was a basis for crediting the statements made by the informant. The informant admitted committing a crime for which there was a substantial penalty. He also described the place of the sale and the marijuana. An admission against penal interest is a significant and sometimes conclusive reason for crediting an informer.[16]

Many times an officer will get too involved in what he is doing, and won't give enough thought to the details of a particular case he may be involved with. For example, examine the following facts and try to determine the factors overlooked by the officers. Defendant Barker went to the home of an informer. The informer was not at home, but his wife was. While there, Barker gave three marijuana cigarettes to the informer's wife and then left the house, presumably returning to his own home. When the informer returned home, his wife gave him the cigarettes and he took them to police and related his wife's story. The police went before a municipal judge and made an affidavit based on the foregoing facts for a search warrant to search Barker's home. The search warrant was executed and marijuana was found. Barker was convicted of possession of marijuana in the lower court. However, on appeal, the state supreme court reversed the conviction, saying:

> Affidavit stating that defendant had three marijuana cigarettes in his possession at informer's home . . . was not sufficient for a detached and neutral magistrate to find that probable cause existed to search defendant's residence.[17]

In this case, the officers should have realized that the possession of contraband at one location does not necessarily prove possession of contraband at another location. In the *Barker* case, the police could not *conclude* that there was marijuana in defendant's home, because no one observed him with it there. However, this was not the only mistake made in the *Barker* case. It seems that the officers were so excited at the prospect of seizing a relatively small amount of contraband that they overlooked the fact that Barker could and should have been charged with a more serious crime—delivering or dispensing marijuana. If they had handled the situation properly, the officers might have legally seized the marijuana incident to the arrest.

Some years ago, before our later court decisions, the defendant, in challenging a search, was not allowed to go beyond the warrant to show error. However, today he may question the affidavit on which the search warrant was based. The officer must show probable cause in his affidavit or, in some states, he may give oral testimony in support of the affidavit. In either instance, the officer must provide the magistrate with more than mere belief or suspicion. He must have knowledge before the search, not after it.

WHO MAY ISSUE SEARCH WARRANTS

Often a question arises as to who may issue a search warrant. There have been instances when a deputy clerk of a police court, a district attorney, and even a sheriff of a county thought they had authority to issue a warrant. The general rule is that only a *judicial* officer may issue a search warrant, and only after he has made an independent assessment of the probable cause shown in the officer's affidavit. Otherwise, the warrant would be invalid, and any evidence seized under the invalid warrant would surely be ruled inadmissible. This rule is not stated explicitly in the Fourth Amendment but is a result of the courts' interpretation of it. In a 1971 decision in a case in which the state attorney general had issued the warrant, the United States Supreme Court found that "the warrant was not issued by a neutral and detached magistrate as required by the Constitution." The Court further stated:

> . . . in order to satisfy the requirements of the Fourth Amendment, as made applicable to the states by the Fourteenth Amend-

ment, a warrant must be issued by a "neutral and detached magistrate." Where a law enforcement officer assumes both roles he will, at best, be unconsciously biased in his finding.[18]

"OATH OR AFFIRMATION" REQUIREMENT

There exists a presumption in law that the affidavit on which a search warrant is based was made after oath or affirmation. If the defense can prove otherwise, the warrant would be held invalid, and therefore any search or seizure made under it would be a violation of the defendant's rights under the Fourth Amendment. A minority of our lower courts feel that the oath taken by an officer when he is sworn in as an officer is sufficient to fulfill the oath or affirmation requirement. In many instances, however, the judicial officer may overlook this requirement entirely. For instance, in one particular case, several officers appeared before a circuit judge to make affidavit requesting a search warrant for narcotics. The officers had put much time and effort into their investigation for several months in order that the case would be a strong one. The judge started to ask the officers questions, but before they answered, one officer asked the judge if he would administer an oath to them. The judge replied, "Oh, I know you are telling the truth, we shouldn't worry about taking an oath." However, one officer did persuade the judge to administer an oath. It was fortunate that the officers took time to do this, because the first question asked of them by the defense on cross-examination was, "Were you under oath when the affidavit was made?"

REQUIREMENT TO "PARTICULARLY DESCRIBE"

The "places" to be searched and the "things" to be seized must be "particularly described" in a search warrant. Since the courts have not placed an ironclad definition on the word "particularly," the officer often becomes confused when trying to fulfill this requirement in his search warrant. The general rule is that if the description is sufficiently definite to clearly distinguish the one premises or things from all others so that the ordinary, reasonable, and prudent man could recognize them with reasonable certainty, then the requirement is satisfied. In one case, the court stated, "Any description of places and things in the affidavit and search warrant which will enable the officer making the search to locate them with reasonable certainty is sufficient."[19]

In a few jurisdictions, legal descriptions of the premises, such as those that appear in land conveyances, are used, while in others, a house number and street name may be used. We cannot say that either of these methods is right or wrong; we can say, however, that "the first house on North Street" is not specific enough. The officer might be wise to include in his description a step-by-step account of the route he intends to take, from his starting point to the exact place described in the search warrant.

Like the premises, the items sought in a search warrant must also be particularly described. In one case, officers had a valid search warrant for suits and shoes which had been stolen. On the way to serve the warrant, they met two vice squad officers and asked them to come along. The suits and shoes were found, but the labels were missing. As the search continued, the vice squad officers started to search for narcotics. A pistol and a bottle of unidentified pills were seized. The court said that this was a general exploratory search and was illegal.[20]

In another case, a warrant described the article to be seized as a "Bendix-Westinghouse Compressor" and listed a serial number; however, the number was incorrect. There was only one air conditioner and one Bendix Compressor on the premises. The evidence was seized and the court admitted it, saying that descriptive error is not necessarily fatal to a warrant. Under the facts of this case, the warrant did not authorize a general search; since the incorrect serial number did not give the executing officers discretion to seize anything else, the requirement of particularity was met.[21]

In another case, the defendant and his wife were attempting to induce a young lady to become a prostitute. A search warrant was issued for various specified items sought as evidence of this crime. In executing the warrant, police found written instructions describing how to turn the lady into a prostitute. These were seized even though they were not listed in the warrant. The court in affirming the conviction said that the seizure was proper because the instructions reasonably related to the crime on which the warrant was based.[22]

OTHER REQUIREMENTS

Most states have statutory provisions regulating the amount of time in which the search warrant may be returnable. Generally speaking, once the warrant is properly issued it becomes *functus officio,* which means that the warrant begins to operate officially. The officer should make every effort to execute the warrant as soon as possible after its issuance unless there are exigent circumstances which would justify a reasonable delay. A warrant left blank and filled in by the police officer after his search is a nullity. Likewise, a warrant written by the officer and signed by the judge after the search is also invalid. In either case, the purpose of the Fourth Amendment would be defeated. The officer should make himself aware of his own state statutes regarding such matters as time, date, and return requirements.

EXECUTING THE WARRANT

The officer or officers to whom the search warrant is directed must be the ones who execute it, unless it is directed to "any lawful officer" of a particular jurisdiction. If it is directed to any lawful officer, it may be executed by any officer possessing full police power within his and the warrant's jurisdiction. Usually an application for a search warrant is not an application for appointment of a special officer to serve it, since most statutes dealing with search warrants make no provisions for appointment of a special officer to serve them.[23] The officer who makes application for the warrant is usually the one who executes it. In one case, the court said that a city policeman could serve, within the city, a warrant issued by a justice of the peace, because it was directed "to any lawful officer of the county," and evidence secured under the provisions of such a warrant would be admissible.[24]

In considering the time limitations for execution of the search warrant, the officer should keep in mind that this is generally controlled by state statute. In many cases, this issue will be controlled by the probable cause the officer has shown in his affidavit. For example, the officer has shown probable cause that a suspect will be arriving at a described place with narcotics at 5:00 A.M. on the 15th. The warrant would probably be invalid if it was served at 2:00 P.M. on the 18th, because, in the first place, the officer would have implied by his actions that his probable cause was somewhat lacking. In addition, if the probable cause was supported by information from an informant, his reliability might be challenged because his information was incorrect. Normally, the search warrant will be returnable "instanter" (immediately; without delay), but some courts have held that the fact that the warrant was not executed until the next day did not render the process void.[25] However, a search warrant on which a search of the premises has already been made is functus officio; that is, it has fulfilled the purpose of its creation and is of no further effect.[26]

The duration of the search based on a warrant often creates problems for the officer. The general rule is that the duration of the search must be determined by the size of the objects one is looking for. Obviously, it would take more time to search for small objects than large objects. It must also be kept in mind that once the objects enumerated in the warrant are found, the search must stop. A 1947 case gives a good example of how the circumstances might control the duration of the search with a warrant. In this case, the court upheld a search which extended over a five-hour period, because the officers were looking for small objects. The nature and size of the objects were considered in determining the reasonable duration of the search.[27]

While by virtue of a search warrant, law enforcement officers do have a legal right to break into a house and make a search even though the house may be locked with no one at home and are entitled to take a reasonable time to make the search, they do not have a right to remain in a house in darkness from, for example, 10:00 o'clock until midnight.[28] Here again, the officer would defeat his purpose, because he would prove by his actions that he was not searching. More than likely he found no one home, entered, and searched, but did not find what he was looking for and so decided to wait until the subject came home in the hopes that he would have the illegally possessed articles with him. While waiting, he was not searching and to search was his only purpose under the warrant. The seized articles would therefore be ruled inadmissible.

It is also a general rule that an officer may use whatever force is necessary to carry out his *legal* actions, without being liable for any damages caused by such *lawful* actions. Generally speaking, an officer in possession of a valid warrant *may not* break into a private dwelling without first stating his identity and purpose. A knock on the door is not usually sufficient. However, if the officer identifies himself as a law enforcement officer, knocks, and receives no response, he may then break in without invalidating the warrant or the search.

There are at least two exceptions to this general rule. One is found in the provisions of the Drug Abuse Prevention and Control Act of 1970. Under this act, an officer may acquire a "no-knock" search warrant for offenses involving controlled dangerous substances if he shows that "the property sought may and, if such notice is given, will be easily and quickly destroyed or disposed of" or that "the giving of such notice will immediately endanger the life or safety of the executing officer or other person." The second exception is also applied when exigent circumstances are found to exist. The courts accept this exception in those few cases in which it is shown that the officer's life may have been put in extreme danger had he been forced to announce his presence. However, if the officer is aware of this danger at the time the search warrant is requested, he should ask for a "no-knock" warrant, stating his reasons for doing so at that time.

The officer should be very careful to use the least force necessary to carry out his *legal* actions. If the officer's actions are not legal, the person against whom they are directed may use force to repell the unlawful attack. For example, in one case, an officer armed with a *void* search warrant (the search had already been made) returned to and forcibly entered the defendant's house without permission and without stating his purpose. The officer was killed in the attempt.[29] Often the officer is reluctant to attempt a forcible entry because he fears that he may have to pay for the damages to the person's premises. He should not let this concern him, because as long as his actions are lawful, he will not be liable for the damages.[30] However, as mentioned previously, the officer may be held liable if he executes the search warrant knowing it to be invalid or knowing that it was issued by someone not having the authority to do so.

AREA WHICH MAY BE SEARCHED

As a general rule, only the place specified in the search warrant may be searched, and in doing so an officer may only look in places where the articles described might be found, according to their size, shape, and so forth. For example, an officer could not search a small drawer while looking for stolen television sets, nor could he search a yard if the warrant called for a search of the building only. Likewise, if the warrant described only a room, the officer would not be allowed to search the whole house. However, there are some exceptions to the general rule which are usually invoked by the "exigent circumstances" confronting the officer when he executes the warrant. In the following cases, the courts dealt with the "exigent circumstances" exception.

The defendant was charged with buying merchandise with stolen checks. A search warrant was issued to recover the checks and a television and tape recorder which were bought with the checks. The defendant was arrested on his front porch. The officers then executed the search warrant, and as a result of their search seized a shotgun and pipe bomb which were found in an upstairs closet. The court held the gun to be inadmissible because there was no danger of the defendant reaching it. However, the bomb was held to be admissible, because there were ten people in the building at the time and the object was a hazard to them. This was an exigent circumstance.[31]

Officers executing a valid search warrant on the defendant Bell's premises saw the defendant drive up in his car and park it about 5 feet from the house. The officer showed Bell his identification and approached the car, whereupon he observed Bell take an object from his right-hand pocket. Thinking the object was a gun, the officer drew his own gun and ordered Bell to drop the object. Bell, who was on the left side of the car, dropped a gun on the rear seat within his reach. The door was open and the officer saw that the gun was within Bell's reach, so he reached into the car and seized the weapon. The court said that it was reasonable and necessary, under these "exigent circumstances," to take swift action to recover the weapon from the car and neutralize the threat of harm it posed to the officer and others.[32]

Police had a valid search warrant to search the premises of Stewart for narcotics. They knocked, announced their presence, and after the door was not opened, forced entry and apprehended Stewart as he attempted to escape through a bedroom window. Narcotics were found in the bedroom. Other officers entered the living room where a visitor, Johnson, was seated on the couch. A purse on the coffee table in front of the couch was searched, revealing narcotics, and Johnson was arrested. The evidence was admitted because of the circumstances which confronted the officers.[33]

Other cases have approved the use of evidence gained under exigent circumstances when the search related to the execution of a valid warrant. In one case, the court approved the seizure of a weapon from the person in charge of the premises, reasoning that under the exigent circumstances "the officers necessarily had to take the weapon for their own safety."[34] In another case, the court held that officers executing a valid search warrant had the authority to check the contents of a bag which a person standing on the front porch of the house to be searched held in his hand.[35] Any officer executing a valid search warrant who, because of evidence found during his search, realizes that a crime is being committed in his presence may arrest the person committing the crime and may search incident to the arrest. The incidental search will be discussed later in this chapter.

RETURN OF THE SEARCH WARRANT

All states have statutory provisions regulating a search with a valid search warrant. These statutes also include provisions for the return of the warrant, inventory of items seized, sale of confiscated contraband, and other matters. The officer must be familiar with the pertinent statutes in his state so that he can properly carry out their commands. As a general rule, a valid return must be made by the officer or officers who execute the warrant.

GENERAL FORM OF AFFIDAVIT AND SEARCH WARRANT

The following general forms for an affidavit and search warrant, or similar forms, are used extensively, since they have been found by the various courts to be quite legal and proper. They are provided here for the purpose of demonstrating the application of issues previously discussed. Each step in the process is self-explanatory and when followed, would result in a valid warrant issued upon proper affidavit.

AFFIDAVIT FOR SEARCH WARRANT*

STATE OF ______________________________

COUNTY (or city) OF ______________________________

This day personally appeared before me, the undersigned judicial officer of said jurisdiction, ______________________,
______________________, ______________________,
and ______________________, known to me to be credible persons, who, after having been first duly sworn, depose and say:

1. That affiants have good reason to believe and do believe that certain things hereafter described are now being concealed in or about the following place in this County:
(here particularly describe the place to be searched.)
together with all approaches and appurtenances thereto.

2. That the place described above is occupied and controlled by:
(The person or persons' name who is in control of the premises would appear here; if it is unknown then so state—UNKNOWN.)

3. That said things are particularly described as follows:
(here describe the thing or things to be seized, taking care to describe only those things which affiants have probable cause to believe and do believe are concealed at the place described above, and with enough particularity to insure that an uninformed officer will not seize one thing under a warrant de-

scribing another. Certain things subject to search and seizure include, in addition to the specific subjects enumerated in the code, all contraband; instrumentalities used in the commission of a crime; and books, writings, pictures and prints adjudged in a proper proceeding by a proper court to be obscene.)

4. That possession of the above described things is in itself unlawful in that said things are:
or
The public has a primary interest in, or primary right to possession of, the above described things:
(here state briefly the use or intention for use of the specified things, citing the appropriate Code section or Ordinance being violated and charging its violation, and a brief narrative account of the offense being committed.)

5. The facts tending to establish the foregoing grounds for issuance of a Search Warrant are shown on a sheet headed "Underlying Facts and Circumstances" which is attached hereto, made a part hereof and adopted herein by reference. (the attached sheet must contain enough of the underlying facts and circumstances to enable the issuing officer to fairly ascertain that probable cause exists for the issuance of the warrant. All persons having knowledge of the facts should sign the affidavit and attached sheet, be identified throughout by name, and appear before the issuing officer for examination. Information obtained from informants must be described as reliable and the informants identified as credible persons. It is not absolutely essential that the identity of the informants be disclosed, but there must be shown enough of the underlying facts and circumstances from which the affiants conclude that the informants are credible and their information reliable. Avoid vague recitals such as "suspect was observed" and "the sheriff's office received information." Use factual recitals showing names, places, times and dates, in commonsense, non-technical language. Be specific and give the information in detail.)

6. WHEREFORE, affiants request that a search warrant issue directing a search of the above described place and seizure of the above described things.

____________________	____________________
affiant	affiant
____________________	____________________
affiant	affiant

SWORN TO AND SUBSCRIBED before me, the ________ day of ________________________, 19________.

____
Signature of Judicial Officer

(SEAL)

SEARCH WARRANT*

STATE OF ____________________

COUNTY (or city) OF ____________________

TO ANY LAWFUL OFFICER OF ____________________

WHEREAS ____________________, ____________________, ____________________, and ____________________, known to me to be credible persons, have this day made complaint on oath before me as follows:

1. That affiants have good reason to believe and do believe that certain things hereafter described are now being concealed in or about the following place in this County:

together with all approaches and appurtenances thereto.

2. That the place described above is occupied and controlled by:

3. That said things are particularly described as follows:

4. That possession of the above described things is in itself unlawful (or the public has a primary interest in, or primary right to possession of, the above described things) in that said things are:

5. The facts tending to establish the foregoing grounds for issuance of a Search Warrant are shown on a sheet headed "Underlying Facts and Circumstances" which is attached to the affidavit for Search Warrant.

6. This court, having examined and considered said affidavit, and also having heard and considered evidence in support thereof from the affiants named therein does find that probable cause for the issuance of a search warrant does exist.

THEREFORE, you are hereby commanded to proceed at any time in the day or night to the place described above and to search forthwith said place for the things specified above, making known to the person or persons occupying or controlling said place, if any, your purpose and authority for so doing, and if the things specified above be found there to seize them, leaving a copy of this warrant and a receipt for the things taken; and bring the things seized before this court instanter; and prepare a written inventory of the items seized, and have then and there this writ, with your proceedings noted thereon.

7. Do not interpret this writ as limiting your authority to seize all contraband and things the possession of which in

itself is unlawful which you find incident to your search, or as limiting your authority to make otherwise valid arrests at the place described above.

WITNESS my hand this, the ________ day of ____________________, 19________.

____
Signature of Judicial Officer

(SEAL)

RETURN OF WARRANT*

I received this warrant on the ________ day of ____________________, 19________, and have executed it as follows:

On the ________ day of ____________________, 19________, at ___________ .m., I searched the place described in said warrant and I left a copy of the warrant with ____________________, the person occupying and controlling said place, together with a receipt for the items seized.

The following is an inventory of the things taken pursuant to the warrant:
(here list the things seized, being careful to describe them with sufficient clarity.)

This inventory was made in the presence of ____________________, ____________________, and ____________________.

I swear that this inventory is a true and detailed account of all the things taken by me on the warrant.

____
Signature of Seizing Officer

SUBSCRIBED AND SWORN to and returned before me this ____________ day of ____________________, 19 ________.

____
Signature of Issuing Officer

(SEAL)

SEARCH INCIDENT TO A LAWFUL ARREST

An area of major importance to the law enforcement officer is the search incident to a lawful arrest. The officer will probably make more use of this exception to the warrant requirement than any other, because he usually makes arrests daily in the course of his work. The officer has a very definite right to search incident to an arrest for either a felony or misdemeanor. This authority is not granted because of the nature or severity of the crime; rather, it is based on the officer's right to protect himself. In 1950, the United States Supreme Court gave the officer a general rule to follow. The court stated:

> It is the unreasonable searches that are prohibited by the Fourth Amendment . . . . The right to search a person incident to the arrest has always been recognized in this country and in England . . . . Why is a search of the arrested person permitted? For two reasons: First, in order to protect the arresting officer and deprive the prisoner of potential means of escape, and secondly, to avoid destruction of evidence by the arrested person.[36]

This justification for the search incident to an arrest has been recognized by most since the *Rabinowitz* case, and few attorneys have questioned the officer's authority to make such a search. In February, 1974, two companion cases were decided by the United States Supreme Court which reiterated the *Rabinowitz* rule with approval.

The first case, *United States* v. *Robinson,*[37] involved the search of a traffic offender after his arrest. Officer Jenks observed the defendant driving an automobile. As a result of previous investigations which indicated that the defendant's operator's license had been revoked, Jenks ordered the defendant to stop. He then informed him that he was under arrest for illegal operation of a motor vehicle. In accordance with proper police procedures, Jenks started to search the arrestee and felt an object in the breast pocket of the defendant's coat. He could not tell its size or what it was, so he reached into the pocket and pulled out a crumpled cigarette pack which contained gelatin capsules of white powder, which later was found to be heroin. The evidence was admitted. The Court said that the search did not violate the Fourth Amendment, because a search incident to a lawful arrest is a traditional exception to the warrant requirement of the Constitution. Under this exception, the arrested person may be searched and the immediate area within his control may also be searched.

After an arrest, it is permissible to search for weapons which might be used to harm the officer or to effect an escape, since otherwise the officer's safety might be endangered. A peace officer empowered to arrest must have the authority to disarm; if he is entitled to disarm, he must be allowed to search for concealed weapons. Since the search is lawful, he may seize what he finds if it is connected with the crime.

An officer's decision to search the arrested person is a quick ad hoc determination and does not depend on the probability that weapons will be found. As the Court said in *Robinson:*

> The lawful arrest determines the authority to search, and a full search is reasonable under the Fourth Amendment. It is of no moment that Jenks did not fear the defendant or that he did not himself suspect that the defendant was armed. Having come upon the cigarette package, he had a right to inspect it, and when he saw heroin, he could seize it as the fruits of criminal conduct.

In the other case, *Gustafson* v. *Florida,*[38] a uniformed officer in a marked cruiser observed a car weaving on the highway. The officer saw the occupants look back, and when they saw the police car, they drove to the rear of a grocery before heading for another town. The officer stopped the car and found that the driver did not have an operator's license in his possession as required by Florida statute. The defendant was arrested and searched. As a result of the search, a cigarette box containing marijuana was found in the defendant's coat pocket.

The defense claimed that this was a trivial offense; that it carried no mandatory sentence as did the offense in *Robinson;* that no police regulation required the defendant to be taken into custody; and that there was no regulation requiring a full search at the arrest scene. The Court in *Robinson* stated that "It is the fact of the lawful arrest which establishes the authority to search," and in this case said:

> The authority to search rests as much on the need to disarm the suspect in order to take him into custody as it does on the need to preserve evidence on his person for later use at trial.
>
> While as here the officer was not required to take the defendant into custody by police regulations, and there was no police directive as to a full body search on arrest in the field, these factors do not raise a constitutional issue.
>
> The authority to search incident to a valid arrest is based on the need to disarm and to discover evidence and does not depend on what a court may later state was the probability that in a given arrest case, weapons would be found.
>
> The fact that the officer did not fear the defendant or that he did not suspect that he was armed is of no importance. The officer was justified in making the search and when he came across what appeared to be contraband, he was entitled to seize them as instrumentalities probative of criminal conduct.

In these recent Supreme Court decisions, we see a reaffirmation of the police officer's absolute right to search incident to a lawful arrest. In addition to having authority to search for his own protection, the officer may also look for fruits of the crime, means of committing a crime, and articles which may be used in order to effect an escape, and, under the previously cited decision of *Warden v. Hayden,* can seize "mere evidence." However, the officer should always rely on his basic reason first, that of searching for his own protection, since this would justify a search in many instances when the other reasons may not.

EFFECT OF THE LAWFULNESS OF THE ARREST

The effect of the lawfulness of the arrest may be simply stated: "If an arrest is unlawful, then the search is unlawful and the evidence obtained in the search is not admissible."[39] When a person is arrested under the provisions of a valid warrant and is searched incident thereto, since the arrest is lawful, the search incident thereto is likewise lawful and the evidence obtained is admissible.[40] For example, many times the officer will stop a person on a street or highway, search his person or vehicle, find a concealed weapon, and arrest him for that offense. He goes to trial, loses the case, and then wonders why. Actually, the reason why the case would be dismissed is obvious. The officer had no legal right to search the vehicle or person for the weapon in the first place. One may not base his arrest on what a subsequent search discloses under these circumstances.

The officer should also realize that the arrest must be made in good faith and may not be used as a means to an end. For example, if officers heard that the suspect of a crime which they had been investigating was about to leave town, and they arrested him for the sole purpose of preventing him from leaving and without proper probable cause for doing so, the arrest would not have been made in good faith and would not be valid. Therefore, any evidence uncovered in an incidental search would be inadmissible.[41]

TIME OF THE INCIDENTAL SEARCH

Although the officer has valid authority to search incident to a lawful arrest, the search will not be valid unless it is substantially contemporaneous with the arrest. "Contemporaneous" means existing, occurring, or originating during the same time. Does this mean that the officer is allowed to search an instant before the arrest is formally made? Or does this mean he must wait until after the formal arrest and, if so, how long may he wait? To answer these and other pertinent questions, we must examine several court decisions.

In one Supreme Court case,[42] officers entered an apartment without a warrant to make an arrest for which they had sufficient probable cause. In justifying the entry without warrant, the Court said, "Suspects have no constitutional right to destroy or dispose of evidence, and no basic constitutional guarantees are violated because an officer succeeds in getting to a place where he is entitled to be more quickly than he would had he complied with warrant requirement." Because of the circumstances, the officers conducted their search prior to making the arrest. The Court seemed to be saying that when an officer has reasonable grounds to believe and does honestly believe that to delay his search might be dangerous, a search made immediately prior to the arrest may be valid.

Generally speaking, however, the search incident to the arrest should be made immediately following the arrest. The rationale is that the basic reason to search stems from the officer's right to protect himself and when he does not promptly utilize this authority he implies that no danger existed at the time. For example, in *Preston* v. *United States,*[43] three suspicious men were arrested in a car believed to have been stolen. They were taken to jail and the car was searched after it had been removed to a garage. Guns were found in the glove compartment and other evidence of crime was found in the trunk. After the search, one of the defendants confessed that they intended to rob a bank. In answering the question of the legality of the search, the Supreme Court stated:

> . . . either because the arrests were valid or because the police had probable cause to think the car stolen, the police had the right to search the car when they first came on the scene. But this does not decide the question of the reasonableness of a search at a later time and at another place. The search of the car was not undertaken until petitioner and his companions had been arrested and taken in custody to the police station and the car had been towed to the garage. At this point there was no danger that any of the men arrested could have used any weapons in the car or could have destroyed any evidence of a crime . . . . We think that the search was too remote in time or place to have been made as incidental to the arrest . . . .

In still another case, *Lane* v. *Commonwealth,*[44] the officer stopped a car and arrested the defendant for a traffic violation. The officer placed the accused in the police vehicle after he had searched him, and they both talked for a few minutes while sitting in the car. Afterwards, the officer returned to the defendant's car, searched it, and found whisky, the possession of which was illegal in that jurisdiction. The court ruled that the search of the car was not substantially contemporaneous with the arrest, and that therefore the evidence was inadmissible.

The *Lane* case presents a problem of serious concern to every law enforcement officer. An officer cannot safely allow an offender to stand immediately behind him as a search of the vehicle is made. The officer must, by necessity, handcuff the arrestee and confine him in the police vehicle in order to prevent an attack by the offender. The courts have consistently held that when the officer follows this procedure and immediately returns to the violator's vehicle in order to search safely, the delay is reasonable and the search is contemporaneous with the arrest.

EXTENT OF THE INCIDENTAL SEARCH

The general rule is that the area which is under the control of the arrestee is subject to an incidental search. However, since there may be exceptions in dealing with the person, vehicle, or premises, we shall consider each separately.

Searching the Arrested Person. There is no doubt that any officer who makes a valid arrest has the authority to search the person arrested. This right has been upheld in numerous cases. The officer may also "frisk" persons who are not under arrest if the prevailing circumstances justify it. (This issue will be discussed in detail later in this chapter.)

Searching the Premises. In *Harris* v. *United States,*[45] officers obtained an arrest warrant for Harris' arrest on the basis of his alleged involvement in the cashing and interstate transportation of forged checks. He was arrested in the living room of his four-room apartment, and in an attempt to recover two canceled checks believed to have been used in the crime, officers undertook a thorough search of the entire apartment. The officers found altered selective service documents, sealed in an envelope, inside a desk drawer. The Supreme Court upheld the search as incident to the arrest of Harris. *Harris,* however, is an exception to the general rule, as we will see later. Normally, the officers would have been restricted to the immediate area under Harris' control.

In another decision, the Court stated:

> When an arrest is made, it is reasonable for the arresting officer to search the person arrested in order to remove any weapons that the latter might seek to use in order to resist arrest or effect his escape. Otherwise, the officer's safety might well be endangered, and the arrest itself frustrated. In addition, it is entirely reasonable for the arresting officer to search for and seize any evidence on the arrestee's person in order to prevent its concealment or destruction. And the area into which an arrestee might reach in order to grab a weapon or evidentiary items must, of course, be governed by a like rule. A gun on a table or in a drawer in front of one who is arrested can be as dangerous to the arresting officer as one concealed in the clothing of the person arrested. There is ample justification, therefore, for a search of the arrestee's person and the area "within his immediate control"—construing that phrase to mean the area from within which he might gain possession of a weapon or destructible evidence.
>
> There is no comparable justification, however, for routinely searching rooms other than that in which an arrest occurs—or, for that matter, for searching through all the desk drawers or other closed or concealed areas in that room itself. Such searches, in the absence of well-recognized exceptions, may be made only under the authority of a search warrant.[46]

Let us consider a situation in which the defendant is arrested in the living room and leads the officers to a bedroom to get his coat before being taken to jail. Would a search of the bedroom now be incident to the arrest? Perhaps the following cases will answer the question:

> . . . we cannot construe *Chimel* to mean that the area is confined to that precise spot which is at arm length from the arrestee at the moment of his arrest. He may well lunge forward or move backward or to the side and thus into an area in which he might grab a weapon or evidentiary items then within his reach before the officer could, by exercise of reasonable diligence, restrain him . . . .
>
> It would seem that a seizure of a weapon or destructible evidence in a locked drawer in the immediate presence of the arrestee in the literal sense would be beyond the permissible scope of a search.[47]

Officers went to a motel and approached the room of a suspected bank robber. The door was open and they saw a man who fit the description of the suspect. The officers knocked on the door, and the suspect answered and gave his correct name. He was then arrested. The suspect was seated in a chair in the middle of the room, approximately 6 feet from the closet. He asked the officer to get some clothing from the closet. The officer went to the closet, saw a box which he thought might contain a gun, and seized it. The box contained stolen money orders. The court in its decision said, "there was probable cause for the arrest . . . [The fact] that the defendant had been convicted of armed robbery, that he was seated only 6 feet from the closet, the general experience of the officer, and the suspicion that the box contained a gun made the seizure valid."[48]

After a burglary was committed, officers arrived at the apartment of the defendant, armed with an arrest warrant. When the officers entered, the defendant moved on her own volition to a point between the dining room and kitchen. The officers went to the kitchen, noticed a folder in a cabinet, seized it, and obtained incriminating evidence. The court stated that the kitchen was in the immediate control of the woman and the entry into the kitchen by police was proper to insure their safety.[49]

The victim reported to the police that the defendant Gamble had robbed and assaulted him, and a warrant for defendant's arrest was issued. After knocking and announcing their purpose, the police heard a rustling noise and forcibly entered the premises. Gamble and a woman came from the bedroom into the kitchen, where another woman was seated. Gamble was arrested and searched. One officer searched the bedroom and found an unregistered firearm. The court said that the search of the bedroom was invalid because there were no special circumstances justifying a search beyond the arrestee or the immediate area within his control. The rustling noise was insufficient to justify an extended search.[50]

The defendant was arrested for a parole violation in an upstairs hallway of his residence. He was wearing shorts and returned to his room to get clothing. He was not handcuffed but was ordered to sit on the bed. A closet containing clothing was about 3 feet away. The defendant got up from the bed, reached for underwear near the closet, and then moved toward the closet to get his trousers. The officers ordered him away from the closet, reached in and felt the trousers and other clothing. A bump felt in a bag turned out to be $30,000 in bills. The court said that this was not a search for evidence but was a search for the protection of the officers. Apparently the officers were surprised by the move of the defendant toward the closet, and they could have reasonably suspected that another person was hiding there, or that a weapon was in the closet.[51]

Searching the Outside Premises. The same general rule applies when an arrest is made outside a building as in other instances. For example, if the arrest is made outside a residence, the officer cannot, unless exigent circumstances exist, search the residence as incident to the arrest. Again, several cases will be noted to show the varying circumstances which may confront the officer and how the courts have evaluated them.

The accused was outside a building, and after being lured into the building by misrepresentation was arrested. These acts were done for the sole purpose of searching and the court held that a search under these circumstances was unreasonable and excluded the evidence.[52]

Officers had a particular building under surveillance when they saw a bootlegger emerge from a room with illegal liquor to make a sale. The officers made the arrest outside; however, the court held that a search of the room from which he had brought the contraband was justified as incident to the arrest.[53]

Donald Vale was arrested as he reached the front steps of a house. Because of circumstances leading to the arrest, the officers informed Vale that they "were going to search the house." The search of a rear bedroom revealed a quantity of narcotics. The Supreme Court stated:

> A search may be incident to an arrest "only if it is substantially contemporaneous with the arrest and is confined to the immediate vicinity of the arrest." If a search of a house is to be upheld as incident to an arrest, that arrest must take place inside the house, not somewhere outside—whether two blocks away, twenty feet away, or on the sidewalk near the front steps. Belief, however well founded, that an article sought is concealed in a dwelling house furnishes no justification for a search of that place without a warrant.[54]

The defendant was arrested on the third floor of a hotel while standing by the elevator. A search of his person revealed a room key. He was taken to the room, which was 30 feet away from the site of the arrest. The room was searched and a gun was found. The court held the search to be unreasonable and not incident to the arrest.[55]

Searching the Vehicle. As a general rule, in most jurisdictions an officer, as incident to a misdemeanor arrest, may search the person arrested and the area inside the vehicle which is under his immediate control. In most instances, this would include the area on the seat, under the seat, above the sun visors, on the floor, under the floormat, and inside the glove compartment. However, the glove compartment, if locked, a locked suitcase on the back seat, the trunk compartment, a camper attached to a pickup, and other areas not within the arrestee's immediate reach would not come under this general rule. Usually, when the arrest is for a felony, the officer is allowed to search the entire vehicle. However, since no definite rule has been established for vehicle searches, we should examine some court decisions.

In one case, the court has said that a permissible area of search would include any area into which the arrested person might leap or lunge in order to gain a weapon or destroy evidence.[56]

Officers arrested Hogan upon finding him in an intoxicated condition. They searched him, the interior of his car, and a briefcase which lay unlocked on the rear seat of the vehicle. In the briefcase they found intoxicants, the possession of which was illegal in that jurisdiction. The court stated in its decision:

> . . . it was not unreasonable to search the interior of the automobile, including the briefcase which lay upon its rear seat. Intoxicants are outlawed in Rankin County and there they constitute contraband. The search might have revealed the presence of weapons or intoxicants . . . . It was necessary that the officers take the automobile . . . temporarily into their charge . . . .[57]

Defendant Powers was arrested for speeding and for driving while his license was revoked. At the time of the arrest, the state highway patrolman noticed that the vehicle identification number was missing from the door post. A search was made for the confidential vehicle number underneath the car in a remote and barely accessible place. This search was conducted without a warrant. The court stated that when the arresting officer noticed that the vehicle identification number was missing from the door post, he had reason to be suspicious. This fact created a need for further investigation and furnished the officer with a legitimate reason for checking the confidential number. Where there is a legitimate reason for identifying a motor vehicle, inspection of its confidential number is not an unreasonable search.[58]

An officer was chasing a speeding car when the latter hit the sidewalk. The driver fled the scene, leaving the motor running and the lights on. The driver was not apprehended at the time. The officer took the keys from the car and opened the trunk compartment where he found contraband. In its decision, the court said that the automobile was abandoned and that the defendant's rights to Fourth Amendment protections ended when he abandoned the car.[59]

While driving his car, the defendant Berryhill was stopped and arrested under provisions of a warrant. His wife was sitting on the front seat with him. The officer noticed a paper sticking out of the wife's pocketbook, and since he knew that Berryhill was usually armed, he opened the pocketbook and took the contents. The court held the search of the pocketbook to be reasonable, on the theory that since all companions of an arrestee who are within the immediate vicinity are capable of assaulting the officer, they are constitutionally subject to a "pat-down" search so the officer can make sure that they are not armed.[60]

The defendant was arrested for a traffic violation; a search of his person revealed no weapons. His car was searched and cigarette wrapping paper and a matchbox were found in the glove compartment. The matchbox was opened, revealing marijuana. The trunk compartment was then searched, and more marijuana was found. The court stated that such common items as a matchbox and cigarette wrappings do not, per se, indicate a narcotics violation. Since the officers had no valid reason for opening the matchbox, the evidence from the trunk was also inadmissible.[61]

At 2:00 A.M., officers saw a speeding auto fail to stop for a stop sign. Officers pursued the car, and when it stopped, they saw the driver pull something from his belt and place it under the seat. The officer used his P.A. system to order the defendant from the car. He was frisked, but nothing was found. The officer entered the car through the open door, searched under the seat, and found a pistol. The court stated that the officers had a reasonable basis for believing they were in danger. The search was directed toward the danger at hand and was not exploratory. A search under the seat of an open car to which the driver would return is a search of an area under his immediate control.[62]

A post office was robbed. Three days later, an FBI agent recognized a car about which he had confidential information that it had been used in a post office robbery six months earlier and that it contained burglar's tools. He also knew that there was an outstanding felony warrant for the arrest of one Chapman, who looked like the man he saw approach the car. He followed the car, recognized Chapman, and arrested him. After frisking Chapman, the agent found a pistol on the front seat. He then took the keys, opened the trunk compartment, and found burglar's tools and other evidence. The court said, "The car was stopped on a highway; a valid arrest was made under a warrant; the immediate inspection showed a handgun; and the information that the car had been used in a burglary six months earlier provided probable cause and "exigent circumstances" for the search of the car without a warrant.[63]

SEIZURE RESULTING FROM A STOP AND FRISK

Under appropriate circumstances, an officer who is confronted by persons believed to be involved in criminal activity may stop such persons, identify himself, and conduct a "pat down" or "frisk" in order to discover weapons which might be used to harm him or others. This pat down or frisk must be restricted to a simple touching of the *outside* of the garments; the officer cannot intrude into the inner garments and pockets. If he discovers a weapon in a pat down, he may then make an intrusion in order to retrieve the weapon. Here, the officer must remember that the stop and frisk is allowed solely for his protection and the frisk can only be made to discover weapons which might be used to harm him. He cannot use the frisk as a pretext to search for mere evidence of a crime on which to base an arrest. However, if he in good faith believes himself in danger and in frisking for weapons, finds other evidence, this evidence will generally be admissible. For example, the officer approaches two suspicious persons who are standing in the doorway of a jewelry store at 2:00 A.M. The officer honestly believes that criminal activity is afoot and that the two may be armed and dangerous. He approaches the two, identifies himself, pats one down, and feels a pistol in his pocket. As he reaches into the pocket and pulls the pistol out, two marijuana cigarettes fall to the pavement. The two marijuana cigarettes would probably be admissible evidence, since they were gained incident to the officer's lawful actions.

It was not until 1968 that the officer gained this definite authority to stop and frisk. It has now been granted by statute in some states, and in others, by court decision. In any case, the rule seems to be well established. In the landmark decision of *Terry* v. *Ohio,*[64] the basic facts of the case were: Officer McFadden was patrolling in plain clothes in downtown Cleveland, when he noticed Terry and another man standing on the corner of Huron Road and Euclid Avenue. He had been a policeman for 39 years and he spent 35 of those years as a detective assigned to patrol the same area for shoplifters and pickpockets. His interest aroused, the officer took up a post of observation in the entrance to a store 300 to 400 feet away from the two men. He saw one leave the other and walk past some stores on Huron Road. The man paused for a moment and looked in a store window, then walked a short distance, turned around and walked back toward the corner, pausing once again to look in the same store window. He rejoined his companion at the corner, they conferred briefly, and then the second man went through the same series of motions. The two men repeated this ritual alternately between five and six times apiece. At one point, a third man approached the two at the corner and they conversed briefly. Afterwards, the first two men walked away together, following the same path taken earlier by the third.

Officer McFadden followed Chilton and Terry and saw them stop in front of Zucker's store to talk to the same man who had conferred with them earlier. He suspected the men of "casing a job—a stick-up," and he feared they might have a gun. He approached the three men, identified himself as a police officer, and asked for their names. When the men "mumbled something" in response, Officer McFadden grabbed Terry, spun him around so that they were facing the other two, with Terry between McFadden and the others, and patted down the outside of his clothing. He felt a pistol inside the left breast pocket of Terry's overcoat and reached inside after it but was unable to remove the gun. At this point, keeping Terry between himself and the others, he ordered all three to enter Zucker's store. As they went in, he removed Terry's overcoat and retrieved the weapon and ordered all three to face the wall with their hands raised. He patted down the other two and found another gun in the outer pocket of Chilton's overcoat. He took all three to the police station and charged Chilton and Terry with carrying concealed weapons.

In its decision, the United States Supreme Court stated:

> We conclude that the revolver seized from Terry was properly admitted in evidence against him . . . . Officer McFadden had reasonable grounds to believe that petitioner was armed and dangerous, and it was necessary for the protection of himself and others to take swift measures to discover the true facts and neutralize the threat of harm if it materialized . . . . Each case of this sort will, of course, have to be decided on its own facts. We merely hold today that where a police officer observes unusual conduct which leads him reasonably to conclude in light of his experience that criminal activity may be afoot and that the person with whom he is dealing may be armed and presently dangerous; where in the course of investigating this behavior he identifies himself as a policeman and makes reasonable inquiries; and where nothing in the initial stages of the encounter serves to dispel his reasonable fear for his own and other's safety, he is entitled for the protection of himself and others in the area to conduct a carefully limited search of the outer clothing of such persons in an attempt to discover weapons which might be used to assault him. Such a search is a reasonable search under the Fourth Amendment, and any weapons seized may properly be introduced in evidence against the person from whom they were taken.

In another case, defendant Williams was convicted of both illegal possession of a handgun found during a "stop and frisk" and possession of heroin that was found during a full search incident to his weapons arrest. A person whom Sgt. Connolly knew approached his cruiser and informed him that an individual who was sitting in a nearby vehicle was carrying narcotics and had a gun at his waist. After calling for assistance, Sgt. Connolly approached the vehicle to investigate the informant's report. He tapped on the window and asked Williams to open the door. When Williams rolled down the window instead, the officer reached into the car and removed a fully loaded revolver from Williams' waistband. The gun was found precisely where the informant indicated it would be. A search incident to the arrest disclosed other weapons and substantial quantities of heroin.

The defendant claimed that the initial seizure of his pistol, upon which the later search and seizure of other weapons and narcotics was based, was not justified by the informant's tip to Sgt. Connolly. He claimed that absent a more reliable informant or some corroboration of the tip, the officer's actions were unreasonable under the standards set forth in *Terry* v. *Ohio.* However, in regard to this claim, the Supreme Court stated:

> . . . we reject respondent's argument that reasonable cause for a stop and frisk can only be based on the officer's personal observation, rather than on information supplied by another person . . . . Once Sgt. Connolly had found the gun precisely where the informant had predicted, probable cause existed to arrest Williams for unlawful possession of the weapon . . . . This tended to corroborate the reliability of the informant's further report of narcotics . . . . Under the circumstances . . . the arrest was lawful. The fruits of the search were therefore properly admitted at Williams' trial . . . .[65]

At 10:15 P.M., an officer working in a park saw a car parked with two men in front and two females in the back. Several rapes had recently occurred in the same area. The officer flashed his light on the car and noticed that the girls appeared to be frightened. He asked the driver for identification, and after checking, discovered that he had recently been convicted of car theft and that the registration plate on the vehicle was illegal. The men were removed from the car, whereupon the officer flashed his light through an open door and saw a gun, which he seized. The court said that the investigatory stop was justified, and that the limited intrusion was reasonable under the circumstances.[66]

The defendant's husband was to be arraigned on a felony charge. The defendant, carrying a large bag, entered the courtroom where the arraignment was to be held and sat on the aisle where her husband was to be brought from the lockup. There had been a rumor of an attempted escape. The United States attorney directed a marshall to search the bag, and as a result a firearm was found. The court said that the marshall's intrusion was necessary to protect the courtroom from violence and that the search was therefore reasonable.[67]

In another case, police were executing a valid search warrant when Peep entered the premises with another person. Peep was not named in the warrant as one to be searched. One of the officers observed a large bulge in Peep's front pants pocket. He reached over to pat it in order to determine if it was a weapon, and as he did so, Peep slapped his hand away. At this point, Peep's hands were seized and another officer reached into Peep's pocket and removed a large roll of money. A more thorough search revealed two matchboxes containing narcotics.

The court held that the pat down which produced the large roll of currency was justified as a weapons search under the stop and frisk doctrine of *Terry* v. *Ohio.* When the large roll of money was found, police had probable cause to believe that Peep was part of the narcotics ring, thereby justifying an arrest. The search which produced the matchboxes was incident to a lawful arrest.[68]

As one can see from these cases, our courts do not hesitate to uphold the pat down of a person who is suspected of being involved in criminal activity and who may be armed and presently dangerous. There is no doubt that an officer has the right to protect himself and others when the circumstances indicate a danger of harm from weapons possessed by those who confront the officer.

SEIZURE BY A PRIVATE PERSON

Since Fourth Amendment prohibitions operate only against unreasonable searches and seizures by governmental officials, it has generally been held that one who does not act as a governmental official, or one who does not act as a result of collusion with an official, may seize evidence, even illegally, and present it to an officer, and that such evidence may be used for prosecution purposes. For example, if a private person sees illegal contraband, takes it illegally, and turns it over to an officer, the evidence may generally be used to prosecute those who possessed the contraband, provided there was no collusion between the citizen and the officer. Now we will look at some specific cases.

Jones, who was using a credit card in the name of Peters, attempted to cash a postal money order in Tennessee at an A & P store. The store manager found that the money order was stolen and retained it. He later turned it over to the police. The court said that this seizure was not prohibited by the Fourth Amendment and that therefore the money order was admissible evidence.[69]

Shelton, the manager of an apartment complex, was robbed by two armed men whose faces were masked by stockings. Approximately one month later, an apartment under Shelton's management, which was leased to the defendant's wife, was gutted by fire. Shelton entered the apartment to ascertain the extent of damage, saw a photograph of the defendant, whom he recognized as his assailant, and took it and turned it over to police. The photograph was admitted in evidence, and the defendant was convicted of armed robbery. The court held that the Fourth Amendment was not violated, since Shelton had a right to be in the apartment when he saw the photograph.[70]

In another case, the police responded to a telephone call indicating a possible fight. Upon arrival at the scene, they found Mrs. Williams, who had called police, standing near the defendant's truck. Mrs. Williams opened the truck door, reached in, and handed the officer a pistol. While the door was open, the officer saw a shotgun, which he removed. The court said that the guns were admissible because they were seized as a result of a search by a private party and the Constitution does not protect against searches by private parties.[71]

The officer should remember that if he in any way influences the actions of the private party in order to persuade the latter to seize evidence, this may constitute collusion between them and may taint the evidence seized by the private party. If the private party should act as a result of an officer's suggestions, his actions would be governed by the same rules which apply to official actions.

THE CONSENT SEARCH

As with other constitutional rights, the right against unreasonable searches and seizures guaranteed under the Fourth Amendment may be waived. Like other waivers, the consent to a search must be voluntary and given without force, duress, or compulsion of any kind. It should be remembered that the prosecution has the burden of proving that the consent was voluntary. However, the courts have not yet established guidelines as specific as those announced in *Miranda* v. *Arizona* relating to waivers of Fifth and Sixth Amendment rights. In other words, a signed waiver is not always necessary to show that voluntary consent was obtained. Of course, if the officer acquires a signed waiver, he will certainly not damage his case. Since many questions often arise with a consent search, the following issues are discussed separately.

AREA COVERED BY THE CONSENT

Generally speaking, an officer may search only those places specified by the person giving his consent to search. For example, if a person tells the officer he can search the living room of his apartment, the officer would be estopped from searching any other room of the apartment unless he found something during his search of the living room which would give probable cause to search other portions of the apartment without consent.

The majority opinion is that one who consents to a search may withdraw such consent at any time during the actual search. However, it would seem that once incriminating articles are found, consent could not be revoked. Since there is some difference of opinion about this issue, the officer should examine the applicable rule in his particular jurisdiction.

CAPACITY TO CONSENT

When two or more persons commonly use or equally possess a particular premises, either may generally give a consent to search the premises. However, this rule is not firmly established in every jurisdiction. It seems that many attorneys and some courts have a tendency to confuse property law with criminal law, in the sense that they put too much emphasis on who actually owns the property. In one case, the court said, "The rule seems to be well established that where two persons have equal rights to the use of occupancy of the premises, either may give consent to search, and the evidence thus disclosed can be used."[72]

The key question in this situation seems to be whether the persons mutually use or control the thing or premises to be searched. A landlord would certainly own his leased property, but he could not give a consent to search against his tenant. This rule would likewise cover a guest in a hotel or motel or a roomer in a boardinghouse and would extend to "tenants at sufferance," who are tenants who are not paid up on the rent but are allowed to remain in occupancy. For example, the desk clerk of a motel could not give the officer consent to search a room occupied by a paying guest or a guest who is allowed to occupy the room even though he has not paid. On the other hand, let us assume that Joe and Sally are sharing a motel room; they are not married and Joe pays all the bills. Even though Sally has expended no money, she could consent to a search of the room which would be valid against Joe, because she does share control over it.

In one case, the defendant shared an apartment with Stupke and another person. Officers approached Stupke and advised him that he was not compelled to allow them to enter. Stupke invited them in and took them to the refrigerator where contraband was found. The court found that the consent was valid, that Stupke had the right to use and occupancy of the premises, and that he had access to the refrigerator.[73]

In another case, the defendant was a tenant in an apartment on a weekly basis. The landlord was told by other tenants that the defendant had moved out. The landlord went to the apartment and through the open door saw explosives in plain view. He called police, who came and seized the explosives. The evidence was suppressed in the district court on the ground that the defendant had not been evicted, that he had the right of possession, and that he could object to the search.

The court of appeals reversed and said that the proper test for abandoned property is whether the complaining party retains a reasonable expectation of privacy in the articles alleged to be abandoned. When the defendant left the lodgings leaving the door open and the rent unpaid, he should not have been surprised at the landlord's visit. The explosives were in plain view, and there was other evidence of abandonment. Resumption of control by the landlord was reasonable, and the seizure was valid.[74]

In *United States* v. *DeMarco,*[75] another consent issue was raised. At about 7:00 P.M., police officers observed an overloaded rental van on a back road. The truck was stopped, and the driver walked back to the officers. The officers found that the driver had no operator's license, nor did he have a registration for the truck. The DeMarco brothers, who were in the cab, and the driver stated that they had been hired to drive the truck a short distance.

The police asked the driver to allow them to look in the truck. The driver opened it, revealing 30 rolls of copper wire. All the men were taken to the station in order to "clear up the mess." A check was made, and the 30 rolls of copper wire were found to have been missing from an interstate shipment. The defense claimed that the driver was not told that he could refuse to open the truck, and that this invalidated his consent to search.

The court held that the arrest took place at the police station and that the search of the trucks had been made by consent in a noncustodial situation. "In these cases, a person's knowledge of his right to refuse is one factor to be considered among the totality of circumstances."[76] In this case, the driver was not informed of his rights at the time of the search, but the record showed a lack of coercion in the searching of the truck. The judge properly rejected claims of coercion and ruled that the driver freely opened the truck.

CONSENT OF PARENT

There is some disagreement over whether a parent may give a consent to search which is valid against his child. However, the majority opinion is that the parent can authorize a search of any area which is commonly used by the family. In one case, the court stated:

> The general rule is that a minor child's right in the premises is only a possessory right which he derives from the parent and the parent may authorize a search which would be valid against the child. However, as a rule a minor child cannot give consent that is valid against the parent.[77]

Another case dealt with the consent of a brother. Agents searched the basement of a dwelling occupied by the defendant and his brother, with the consent of the defendant's brother. Items from a bank robbery were seized. The court held that the items seized were properly admitted, since the basement area was not specifically set aside for the use of the defendant and the defendant's brother was therefore fully competent to consent to the search.[78]

The facts in another case were that the defendant lived with his mother and paid her $10 per week for room and board. He shared a bedroom with his brother, and the bedroom closet was used by his mother, who had access to the room. After being informed that she could refuse, the mother gave consent to search the room in the presence of the defendant, who made no objection to the search.

The court held the consent to be valid, stating that "the mother was the householder and could give her consent." The fact that the defendant paid rent to the mother, that he shared the room with the brother, and that the mother had access to the closet indicated that the defendant did not have exclusive possession of the bedroom. The defendant might have considered the room to be "his," but the police must be allowed to rely on the word of the householder and the general circumstances confronting them."[79]

Generally, a minor child cannot give a consent to search which would be valid against a parent in any jurisdiction. In one case, the father was arrested for the murder of his wife and placed in jail. Officers then returned to the home and were allowed to search for the murder weapon by a minor child. The weapon was admitted into evidence at the trial in the lower court. However, on appeal it was excluded, the court holding that the minor child could not consent to the search against the parent and that the weapon was therefore the fruit of an unlawful search.[80]

CONSENT OF SPOUSE

In most states, a husband and wife are said to be "joint tenants in common." This means that they both share equally the use and occupancy of the premises shared by them. The majority rule is that each may consent to a search of those premises that are commonly used by both of them. In one case, the court stated, "Our holding that a wife can consent to a search of the premises she shares with her husband is limited to those premises under mutual control."[81]

In a 1971 decision, the defendant was arrested and keys found on his person were given to his wife, but not at the direction of the defendant. On the key ring was a key to a garage in which the household goods of the defendant and his wife were stored. The defendant kept the only key to the garage in his possession. The wife gave the police permission to search the garage, whereupon they entered and found a gun used in the commission of the robbery for which the defendant was charged. The court said that the consent of the wife was invalid, since there was no suggestion that the defendant authorized his wife to do so. The right to consent is derived from the consenting party's equal right to possess or control the same premises. Here the wife did not have equal access to the garage, and therefore the consent was invalid.[82]

A 1973 Seventh Circuit decision held that "where two people have equal rights to the use or occupation of premises, either may give consent to a search and the evidence thus disclosed can be used against either."[83] In a 1973 Sixth Circuit decision, the court upheld the rule that "where a husband and wife have equal right of occupancy of the premises, either may give a consent to search which would be valid against the other." In this case, the husband was charged with the rape of his wife's sister. The court stated that even though the couple were having marital difficulties, the consent was still valid.[84] It would seem logical that the co-occupant rule established in these cases would apply to any situation where a male and female are living together even though they are not married, and, in fact, this theory was upheld by the United States Supreme Court in April, 1974.[85]

OTHER CONSENT SEARCHES

The general rule governing third-party consent searches is that the person who has control over an article left in his exclusive care may consent to a search of that article. For example, the owner of a house was visited by the defendant and a companion who brought a suitcase full of counterfeit money into the house. The owner informed police and gave them permission to search the house. In the bathroom the officers found counterfeit money. The court held this search to be valid because the bathroom was a communal part of the house used by all.[86]

The officer should understand that if a third party has possession of goods for a limited purpose only, a consent search may not be valid. Under this theory, a bailee who holds goods of another could not consent to a search of those goods since his possession is for a limited purpose. It is said that a bailee cannot waive the constitutional rights of an owner.[87]

Another area of concern is the search of school lockers by consent of the school authorites. There is no definite rule, but the controlling factor seems to be whether the school has charged a maintenance fee or has actually rented the locker to the student. If the school charges a maintenance fee for the locker and allows the student to use it for a limited purpose, it would seem that the school authorities, who are custodians of the locker, could give consent to search whenever suspicion of illegal use arose. On the other hand, if the school authorities rent the locker to the student, a landlord-tenant relationship is established which would normally preclude the school authorities from giving consent to search the locker. In any case, a search warrant would be desirable if time permits.[88]

THE PLAIN VIEW DOCTRINE

If an officer who is where he has a right to be sees illegally possessed articles in plain view, without searching for them, he may seize the articles. It is said that the eyes cannot trespass, and the officer is not required to turn his head the other way or close his eyes to things that offend the law. However, if the officer does any overt act, such as opening a bag, moving a garment, opening a drawer, or bending over to look under the seat of a car, in order to find the illegally possessed article, he would be searching and the plain view doctrine would not apply.[89] In one case, the court held the use of binoculars to be permissible under this doctrine, and in another case, the use of a flashlight at night was held not to violate the Fourth Amendment privilege against unreasonable searches and seizures.

Since the officer has occasion to use the plain view doctrine almost daily, the following cases are discussed to give a fuller understanding of the court's attitude toward such seizures.

In the early morning hours, police stopped a speeding vehicle and as they approached the car, their flashlight beam revealed the barrel of a rifle. The car was then searched and the gun seized. The court held that to flash a light into an auto is not a search, and that the barrel of the gun was in plain view. Therefore, the search was not unreasonable.[90]

A defendant, who was under surveillance for suspected auto theft, was stopped by officers when he was seen driving a car with expired license plates. Defendant told the officers that his license was in the trunk of the car. He opened the trunk and withdrew an attaché case; the officers seized the case, fearing that it might contain weapons. The officers opened the case and handed the defendant his wallet. The open case revealed a fictitious license and an identification card bearing the defendant's picture and a different name. He was arrested when he could not produce ownership papers for the car. The court held that the articles were in plain view, since the officers had a right to be where they were and to do what they did.[91]

A roof repairman reported to police that an illegal drug laboratory was being operated in a house where he had been doing repairs. The police went to investigate, knocked on the door, but received no response since no one was home. While there, the police looked through a partially covered window and observed oxygen tanks, beakers, white powder on the floor, and other paraphernalia. Upon checking, the officers found that a neighbor had kept a record of chemicals brought to the house. The parties were later arrested while leaving the house. The court held that the police were where they had a right to be and that what they saw through the window was in plain view.[92]

Suspecting that the defendant's property was being used for operation of an illegal moonshine still, officers went there and observed the defendant drive up and go inside the residence. One officer approached the house in order to question the defendant. Receiving no answer at the front door, he proceeded to the back of the house. As he passed the defendant's truck, he smelled liquor and looked through a small crack between the rear doors; he saw a large quantity of gallon jugs containing clear liquid. He then entered the truck and found that the jugs contained moonshine, which he seized. The court held that when the officer looked through the crack between the doors he conducted a search, and although he was lawfully on the premises, the contents of the truck were not in plain view. The truck had been parked near the defendant's residence, and he therefore had an expectation of privacy.[93]

THE *CARROLL* DOCTRINE

The rule seems to be well established that when an officer has probable cause for believing that a vehicle is carrying articles which offend the law, such as contraband or illegal merchandise; when it is impossible for the officer to obtain a search warrant before the vehicle leaves his jurisdiction; and when the vehicle is moving or is about to be moved, the officer may search the vehicle without a warrant or consent. This rule does not hinge upon the right to arrest; it is dependent on the probable cause the officer has for believing that the automobile contains contraband. However, the officer must understand that this doctrine cannot be used as an excuse to search every car he observes, for he must have probable cause and the vehicle must be moving or about to be moved.

In the 1925 landmark decision of *Carroll* v. *United States*[94] the Supreme Court stated:

> . . . the true rule is that if the search and seizure without a warrant are made upon probable cause, that is, upon a belief, reasonably arising out of circumstances known to the seizing officer, that an automobile or other vehicle contains that which by law is subject to seizure and destruction, the search and seizure are valid. The Fourth Amendment is to be construed in the light of what was deemed an unreasonable search and seizure when it was adopted, and in a manner which will conserve public interests as well as the interests and rights of individual citizens.

The rule was restated in 1970, when the Court said:

> We have made a somewhat extended reference to these statutes to show that the guaranty of freedom from unreasonable searches and seizures by the Fourth Amendment has been construed, practically since the beginning of the Government, as recognizing a necessary difference between a search of a store, dwelling house or other structure in respect of which a proper official warrant readily may be obtained, and a search of a ship, motor boat, wagon or automobile, for contraband goods, where it is not practicable to secure a warrant because the vehicle can be quickly moved out of the locality or jurisdiction in which the warrant must be sought.
>
> The measure of legality of such a seizure is, therefore, that the seizing officer shall have reasonable or probable cause for believing that the automobile which he stops and seizes has contraband . . . therein which is being illegally transported.
>
> The right to search and the validity of the seizure are not dependent on the right to arrest. They are dependent on the reasonable cause the seizing officer has for belief that the contents of the automobile offend against the law.[95]

In a later, Fifth Circuit decision, the court stated that the numerous search and seizure decisions handed down since *Carroll* have not affected its validity. The circumstances which furnish probable cause to search a particular auto for particular articles are most often unforeseeable; moreover, the opportunity to search is fleeting since a car is readily movable. Where this is true, as in the *Carroll* case, if an effective search is to be made at any time, either the search must be made immediately without a warrant, or the car itself must be seized and held without a warrant for whatever period is necessary to obtain a warrant for a search.[96]

INVENTORY OF AN IMPOUNDED VEHICLE

The general rule regulating seizures made while the officer is inventorying an impounded vehicle was established in *Cooper* v. *California.*[97] The rule is that where state statutes or departmental rules provide for the seizing of any vehicle used to transport things which offend the law, inventory of the impounded car is not unreasonable if carried out within a reasonable time.

In order for an officer to be able to use this method of seizing evidence, he must first have a valid impoundment of the vehicle. If he does not have a statute or departmental rule allowing or providing for the impounding of certain vehicles, he would be estopped from using this method. If the officer uses this method as an excuse or subterfuge, and the defense can prove that he did so, any evidence gained would probably be inadmissible. For example, an officer impounds a vehicle as a result of a traffic arrest, but there is no statute authorizing such impoundments. During an inventory of the vehicle, the officer finds contraband. The contraband would probably be inadmissible, since the officer had no authority to impound the vehicle.

Perhaps a look at case decisions will help to clarify this rule. In one case, the defendant's car was impounded under state statute after he had been arrested for refusal to return his suspended registration plates. During inventory of the impounded car, officers found boxes containing marijuana. The court held this evidence to be admissible.[98]

In another case, the defendant was arrested for leaving the scene of an accident and for driving under the influence of alcohol. The arresting officer checked the car tag number through the National Crime Information Center (N.C.I.C.) and found that the car was stolen. The car was impounded, and the F.B.I. was called but did not inventory the car until the next day. The court held the inventory of the impounded car the next day to be reasonable since the car was an integral part of a crime.[99]

In a Montana case, the defendant was unable to post bond on a traffic arrest. His car was impounded and an officer inventoried the contents according to police procedure. Watches and a gun were found as a result of the inventory. The court stated that since the car was lawfully impounded, the action of collecting the valuable property in plain view was reasonable.[100]

In another case, the defendant and his brother, who were fugitives from Georgia, were arrested outside a Florida motel. A search at the police station produced a set of car keys. The car was found at the motel and was brought to the police station where its contents were inventoried. A bomb and several weapons were found. The court stated that:

> When the police take custody of any sort of container, be it an automobile, suitcase, or any other thing in which property may be stored, it is reasonable to search the container to itemize the property to be held by the police. The Fourth Amendment is not violated when police take custody of property of persons they arrest to store that property for safekeeping.[101]

The Third and Sixth Circuits have also upheld the rule allowing inventory of the impounded vehicle, especially when the vehicle is an instrumentality of a crime. Other courts have held that inventories are reasonable and necessary to protect the property and to protect the police from charges that they have lost or stolen the property.

EMERGENCY OR EXIGENT CIRCUMSTANCES

Within the past few years, many cases have been decided in which the courts have taken special notice of an emergency which may have confronted the officer. In these cases, the courts have been very liberal in their application of rules governing search and seizure. Several cases will be cited here in order to acquaint the officer with the courts' present attitude toward such circumstances.

Responding to a call that a man was "down" in a hallway of a hotel, two officers found the defendant lying on a landing in the hotel. Attempting to wake him, they shook him and stood him on his feet. He was disoriented and incoherent but did not smell as if he had been drinking. When he could not answer questions as to his identity, the officers searched him and found packets of marijuana in his pocket. The court said that although there was no danger to the officers, it was important that they learn his identity, since he could have been diabetic or had another serious illness. This was an emergency situation involving the defendant's safety, and therefore the search for identification was proper and the evidence admissible.[102]

The crime of rape was committed. Officers, knowing the description of the car used and having a good description of the rapist, spent the better part of a night intensively investigating. Upon arriving at the defendant's home, they saw a car answering the description. They entered, arrested the defendant, and searched the car. The court held that the officers had probable cause and the search of the car was justified by exigency, because the defendant's wife could have driven it away before police could have obtained a warrant.[103]

In another case, the defendant was living in a truck, which had been parked for several days on the property of his employer. The employer's wife suspected that the truck was stolen and called police, who came and searched the truck. The court held that a warrant is required in this type of situation, except when exigent circumstances exist. However, here the officers had no reason to believe that such circumstances existed. The mere fact that the object to be searched is a motor vehicle does not, ipso facto, create exigent circumstances. The search was held to be illegal.[104]

An undercover agent called police and said that he was at the defendant's house and had evidence. Officers went there, knocked, waited 15 to 20 seconds, heard barking dogs, and fearing that the undercover agent might be harmed, forcibly entered. The defendant and others were arrested for possession of heroin. The court stated that in the ordinary case, officers might be expected to wait more than 15 to 20 seconds after demanding entrance, but under the circumstances which existed here, including the dangerous position of the undercover agent, it was of paramount importance that quick entry be made.[105]

Often routine police work will create emergency situations, as it did in the following case. Officers who were investigating abandoned cars knocked on the door of an apartment to inquire about cars abandoned nearby. The door was answered by a small child who told the officers that the parents were not at home. The officers waited several minutes and knocked again, and again the small child answered. The officers asked the child to open the door, and they entered and found a five-year-old girl and a two-year-old boy. One of the children, apparently intrigued by the officer's gun, showed them a pistol and marijuana, which were seized. In deciding the case, the court said that unattended children of tender years create an emergency, permitting an officer to enter private property. With the possibility of danger, he may act. Generally, a person who leaves children of tender years at home with no provision for their safety is neglectful.[106]

ARTICLES ABANDONED IN OPEN AREAS

Generally speaking, articles of evidence which are abandoned and those which are placed in "open fields" on property not owned or controlled by the defendant may be seized without violating the Fourth Amendment or state constitutional provisions concerning search and seizure. However, some states do not recognize the open field doctrine while they do recognize the abandonment theory. The officer should study his own state court decisions in addition to the cases which follow.

In one case, in which the charge was possession of stolen goods, an officer on the street saw an empty carton with an I.B.M. card attached to it, lying next to two garbage cans adjacent to the curb. In deciding the case, the court held that the property was not part of the curtilage of the defendant's premises. The property was knowingly exposed to the public and could be treated as abandoned property.[107]

In a robbery case, the defendant went to the police station, admitted that he was involved in the robbery, and then took the police to an open field where he pointed out the location of a hat and gun which were concealed in some bushes. The court held that the evidence was admissible since the defendant did not own or control the bushes where the hat and gun were found.[108]

A New York court held the evidence to be admissible when a railway express policeman checked trash barrels outside the defendant's home during an investigation and found the evidence. The court reasoned that the defendant had abandoned the property when he left it for trash pickup.[109]

In a California case which dealt with narcotics smuggling, a Volkswagen bus was seen leaving the road into a densely wooded area which on occasion was used as a campsite. The officers observed the men take two large boxes from the bus, place them in the grove, and depart. The officers examined the boxes and found marijuana. A stakeout observed other men take the contents of the boxes and place them in duffle bags, whereupon they were arrested. The defense claimed invasion of privacy. The court held that although the police knew that the boxes in the grove may not have been abandoned, the question was whether there was any expectation of privacy. The outdoor area was not adjacent to a house, and there was no evidence to show that the site was being used as a camp. Any casual passerby might have found the boxes and examined the contents. The bus occupants' only expectation of privacy was that the boxes would be secure only as long as they remained undiscovered. The search was therefore legal.[110]

Agents of the Alcohol, Tobacco and Firearms Division of the I.R.S. entered defendant's premises in North Carolina, walked to within a few feet of the barn, and detected an odor of fermenting mash or fruit. They then left to go before a magistrate to obtain a search warrant. As a result of a search with the warrant, the defendant was convicted of violating federal alcohol laws. The court held that when there is no entry upon a constitutionally protected area, there can be no search within the meaning of the Fourth Amendment. The defendant's expectation of privacy did not include open fields around a barn.[111]

WHO MAY CHALLENGE A SEARCH

In many states, one who stands to be affected by an illegal search and seizure may challenge it. In other jurisdictions, one must have some possessory interest in the premises in order to have a standing to challenge the search. For example, under the latter rule, a person arrested while visiting another in the other's premises would have no standing to challenge an illegal search of those premises. Again, the officer should check the applicable rule in his own jurisdiction.

In *Jones* v. *United States,*[112] the Supreme Court stated the following general rule:

> In order to qualify as a person aggrieved by an unlawful search and seizure one must have been a victim of a search or seizure, one against whom the search was directed, as distinguished from one who claims prejudice only through the use of evidence gathered as a consequence of a search or seizure directed at someone else.

In a 1973 Arizona case, heroin was seized at the Douglas, Arizona, point of entry from an auto owned and driven by Joe Santillanes. The Felixes were was in or near the car or the customs inspection station; they did not claim ownership of the car or the contraband, nor were they in possession of it, and they were not the persons against whom the search was directed. However, the evidence seized was admitted against Candido and Gloria Felix, resulting in their conviction. On appeal, the court held that the trial court had properly ruled that the Felixes did not have standing to object to the search. The court further stated that when an accused is not on the premises where the search occurred, his arrest did not stem from possession of contraband, and the search was directed against someone else, the accused does not have standing. Here the defendants were aiders and abettors in the importation of heroin, and possession of contraband was not an essential element of the offense.[113]

In a Georgia case, a husband attacked the affidavit of a search warrant, alleging that the police arrested his purported wife without probable cause. The court held that the husband lacked standing to attack the basis of the warrant.[114]

In another Fifth Circuit decision, the court found that the defendants, who were convicted of knowingly and intentionally conspiring to import marijuana into the United States from Mexico, lacked standing to object to a search which produced incriminating evidence. The court stated:

> There is no standing to contest a search and seizure where as here, the defendants: (a) were not on the premises at the time of the contested search, (b) allege no possessory or proprietary interest in the premises, and (c) were not charged with an offense that includes as an essential element of the offense charged possession of the seized evidence at the time of the contested search.[115]

SUMMARY AND APPLICATION

As times and people change, so do our court decisions, especially those dealing with search and seizure. In order to be effective, the officer of today must keep himself informed of the changes which occur in the application of our laws. Again we will use the problem method, and again the officer should recognize more issues than before.

PROBLEM I

An arrest warrant was served on the defendant at 4:00 A.M. The defendant answered the door dressed in pajamas. The officers suggested that she might get dressed to accompany them to jail. The officers followed the defendant to a bedroom, where she reached for a dresser drawer in order to get her stockings. The officers stopped her and opened the drawer themselves. In the drawer, they saw a pistol and a bag of marijuana. At this time, the defendant stated that the marijuana was not hers and that it belonged to her roommate, but there was no apparent evidence that anyone else occupied the apartment.

Would the weapon be admissible? What about the marijuana? Would both the weapon and marijuana be admissible, and if so, what reason would be given for their seizure? If the defendant did, in truth, have a roommate, could the roommate challenge the search if she was charged with possession of marijuana?

PROBLEM II

Sexy Sally, who was defendant Jones' girlfriend and shared an apartment with him, was arrested and taken to jail. Jones was also in custody at the time, charged with armed robbery. During questioning, Sexy Sally, desiring to help the police, told them that Jones had a gun hidden in the apartment and that she believed it was the one used in the armed robbery. The officers accompanied Sally to the apartment, where she unlocked the door and told them it was all right to search. The officers did not have a search warrant, but they did search and found the gun. Would the weapon be admissible at the trial of Jones? What theory should be used in determining this issue?

PROBLEM III

A police officer stops a speeding car at 2:25 A.M., and as he approaches the vehicle, he observes the passenger put something under the front seat. Upon looking into the stopped vehicle from a standing position outside the car, he sees part of a butcher knife under the seat. When he reaches for the knife, he finds a sawed-off shotgun which he seizes. The defendant is charged with violation of the federal Firearms Act of 1968. Would the shotgun be admissible? How could it be seized properly?

PROBLEM IV

A car is stopped for running a stop sign. As the officer approaches the car, he observes on the front seat a cleaning kit for a 45-caliber firearm and what appears to be an ammunition clip for a Thompson submachine gun. The driver is arrested for the traffic violation, and the interior of the vehicle is searched for the officer's protection. However, no weapon is found. The driver is asked to open the trunk of the car, which he does, and there the officer finds a submachine gun. Would the submachine gun be admissible. If it is, how was it gained legally?

PROBLEM V

An eye-witness gave police the tag number and description of an auto used in a kidnapping. This information was broadcast via the radio network of the state highway patrol. The auto was registered to the defendant who was well known to state patrolman Smith. Smith saw the defendant later that night and arrested him on the aforementioned charge. At the time of arrest, the defendant was driving another car. After placing the defendant in jail, the patrol officer, accompanied by a city police detective, went to defendant's home which was located 1 mile outside the city, found the auto in question, and impounded it. Two days later, the auto was searched by a deputy sheriff, without a warrant, and fingerprints of the kidnap victim and the defendant were lifted from inside the car. Would the fingerprints be admissible or not? What theory should be used to arrive at the correct answer?

PROBLEM VI

An auto was impounded by police officers, following the arrest of the driver. A private wrecker was called and the car was stored at a place used for storing vehicles by the wrecker company. To determine ownership and who would pay for the towing, the wrecker owner looked through the car and found a bag containing a grassy substance which he could not identify. He called the police officer, who came to the wrecker company, searched the car, and found marijuana. The owner of the car (the defendant) now objects to the search made by the officer and disclaims any knowledge of the marijuana. Would the marijuana be admissible or not? Would the defendant have standing to challenge the search?

PROBLEM VII

You are the officer in this case. You are patrolling on a cold, wet, winter night when suddenly you see a car parked in the middle of a busy street. You park your patrol vehicle near the curb and turn on the emergency lights before approaching the illegally parked vehicle. The defendant is unconscious and slumped over on the passenger side of the front seat. The vehicle is parked in a very dangerous spot, so you decide to get in and drive to the curb in order to prevent someone from crashing into it. As you get behind the steering wheel, you notice a small brown paper bag stuffed into the ashtray. The bag is open and with the dome light on you can see that it contains heroin, which you seize. The defendant is arrested for possession of heroin. Would the evidence be admissible? On what theory would the seizure be based?

PROBLEM VIII

Police are checking driver's licenses and tags at a roadblock. An older model vehicle pulls into the block, and one officer requests to see the operator's license which the driver produces. He has a valid New York operator's license, but the vehicle tag is Alabama issue. The officer then requests the registration for the vehicle, but the driver has none and cannot explain the difference in the tag and license. The officer opens the door in order to check the vehicle identification number affixed to the door post. After a check through N.C.I.C., the car is found to be stolen and the driver is arrested. Did the act of opening the door violate the defendant's right against illegal search and seizure? Why?

PROBLEM IX

Officers have a valid search warrant for moonshine whisky. They proceed to the premises described therein and gain entry. During their search, they find narcotics stored in a kitchen cabinet under the sink. However, no moonshine is found. Would the narcotics be admissible? On what theory would the seizure be based?

PROBLEM X

Sadie's Fish Sandwich Shop is located at the bottom of a hill on a dead-end street. For years, Sadie has been selling whisky and beer without a license, but police have been unable to build a case against her. On numerous occasions, search warrants have been executed on her premises, but officers have been unable to find any evidence, since she always observes them approaching down the hill. One determined officer hides at the top of the hill, and with the aid of binoculars, looks through an open window and door and sees Sadie selling whisky and beer. He then signals a companion who drives down the hill. Sadie sees the police car and hides the evidence under a board in the floor, all of which is seen by the officer with the binoculars. Both officers enter the premises immediately, seize the evidence, and arrest Sadie. Would the evidence be admissible? Was the procedure used both correct and legal?

REFERENCES

1. *Boyd* v. *United States,* 116 U.S. 616 (1886).
2. *Weeks* v. *United States,* 232 U.S. 383 (1914).
3. *Wolf* v. *Colorado,* 338 U.S. 25 (1949).
4. *Stefaneli* v. *Minard,* 342 U.S. 117 (1951).
5. *Rea* v. *United States,* 350 U.S. 214 (1956).
6. *Elkins* v. *United States,* 364 U.S. 206 (1960).
7. *Mapp* v. *Ohio,* 367 U.S. 643 (1961).
8. *O'Bean* v. *State,* 184 So.2d 635 (1966).

9. 68 Am. Jur. 2d 700, Search and Seizure, Sec. 47.
10. *Warden, Maryland Penitentiary* v. *Hayden*, 387 U.S. 294 (1967).
11. *United States* v. *Petrucci*, 486 F.2d 329 (1974).
12. *Dumbra* v. *United States*, 268 U.S. 435 (1925).
13. *Aguilar* v. *Texas*, 378 U.S. 108 (1964).
14. *Nathanson* v. *United States*, 290 U.S. 41 (1933).
15. *United States* v. *Chavez*, 482 F.2d 1268 (1974).
16. *Armour* v. *Salisbury*, 492 F.2d 1032 (1974).
17. *Barker* v. *State*, 241 So.2d 355 (1970).
18. *Coolidge* v. *New Hampshire*, 403 U.S. 443 (1971).
19. *Mason* v. *State*, 32 So.2d 140 (1947).
20. *United States* v. *Tranquillo*, 330 F. Supp. 871 (1972).
21. *United States* v. *Rytman*, 475 F.2d 192 (1973).
22. *Taylor* v. *Minnesota*, 466 F.2d 1119 (1973).
23. *Claunch* v. *State*, 45 So.2d 581 (1950).
24. *Keys* v. *State*, 124 So. 789 (1929).
25. *Jenkins* v. *State*, 42 So.2d 198 (1949).
26. *Riley* v. *State*, 37 So.2d 768 (1948).
27. *Harris* v. *United States*, 331 U.S. 145 (1947).
28. *Walker* v. *State*, 115 So.2d 159 (1959).
29. *Jones* v. *State*, 155 So. 430 (1934).
30. *Monette* v. *Toney*, 81 So. 593 (1919).
31. *United States* v. *Harrison*, 319 F. Supp. 888 (1971).
32. *Bell* v. *State*, 452 F.2d 783 (1972).
33. *United States* v. *Johnson*, 475 F.2d 977 (1973).
34. *Curtis* v. *United States*, 263 A.2d 653 (1970).
35. *Clay* v. *United States*, 246 F.2d 298 (1957).
36. *United States* v. *Rabinowitz*, 339 U.S. 56 (1950).
37. *United States* v. *Robinson*, 14 Cr. L. 3043 (1974).
38. *Gustafson* v. *Florida*, 14 Cr. L. 3056 (1974).
39. *Smith* v. *State*, 87 So.2d 917 (1956).
40. *Shay* v. *State*, 90 So.2d 209 (1956).
41. *United States* v. *Pampinella*, 131 F. Supp. 595 (1955).
42. *Ker* v. *California*, 374 U.S. 23 (1963).
43. *Preston* v. *United States*, 376 U.S. 364 (1964).
44. *Lane* v. *Commonwealth*, 386 S.W.2d 743 (1965).
45. *Harris* v. *United States*, 331 U.S. 145 (1947).
46. *Chimel* v. *California*, 395 U.S. 752 (1969).
47. *Scott* v. *State*, 256 A.2d 384 (1969).
48. *United States* v. *Wysocki*, 457 F.2d 1155 (1972).
49. *United States* v. *Patterson*, 447 F.2d 424 (1972).
50. *United States* v. *Gamble*, 473 F.2d 1274 (1973).
51. *United States* v. *Mulligan*, 488 F.2d 732 (1974).
52. *United States* v. *Alberti*, 120 F. Supp. 171 (1954).
53. *Clifton* v. *United States*, 224 F.2d 329 (1955).
54. *Vale* v. *Louisiana*, 339 U.S. 30 (1970).
55. *United States* v. *Kwitek*, 433 F.2d 18 (1971).
56. *In re Kiser*, 419 F.2d 1134 (1969).
57. *Hogan* v. *State*, 235 So.2d 704 (1970).
58. *United States* v. *Powers*, 439 F.2d 373 (1971).
59. *United States* v. *Edwards*, 441 F.2d 749 (1971).
60. *United States* v. *Berryhill*, 445 F.2d 1189 (1972).
61. *Pace* v. *Beto*, 469 F.2d 1389 (1973).
62. *United States* v. *Green*, 465 F.2d 620 (1973).
63. *United States* v. *Chapman*, 474 F.2d 300 (1973).
64. *Terry* v. *Ohio*, 392 U.S. 1 (1968).
65. *Adams* v. *Williams*, 92 S.Ct. 1921 (1972).
66. *United States* v. *Wickizer*, 465 F.2d 1154 (1973).

67. *United States* v. *Miller,* 468 F.2d 1041 (1973).
68. *United States* v. *Peep,* 490 F.2d 903 (1974).
69. *United States* v. *Jones,* 457 F.2d 697 (1972).
70. *United States* v. *Parish,* 468 F.2d 1129 (1973).
71. *United States* v. *Maxwell,* 484 F.2d 1350 (1974).
72. *United States* v. *Sferas,* 210 F.2d 69 (1954).
73. *People* v. *Potter,* 317 N.Y.S.2d 81 (1971).
74. *United States* v. *Wilson,* 472 F.2d 901 (1973).
75. *United States* v. *DeMarco,* 488 F.2d 828 (1974).
76. *Schneckloth* v. *Bustamonte,* 412 U.S. 218 (1973).
77. *United States* v. *Roberts,* 179 F. Supp. 478 (1950).
78. *United States* v. *Mojica,* 442 F.2d 920 (1971).
79. *United States* v. *Di Prima,* 472 F.2d 550 (1973).
80. *May* v. *State,* 199 So.2d 635 (1967).
81. *United States* v. *Thompson,* 421 F.2d 373 (1970).
82. *United States ex rel. Cabey* v. *Mazurkiewicz,* 431 F.2d 839 (1971).
83. *United States* v. *Stone,* 471 F.2d 170 (1973).
84. *McCravy* v. *Moore,* 476 F.2d 281 (1973).
85. *United States* v. *Matlock,* 14 Cr. L. 3108 (1974).
86. *Leeper* v. *United States,* 446 F.2d 281 (1972).
87. *Commonwealth* v. *Storck,* 275 A.2d 362 (1971).
88. *People* v. *Overton,* 249 N.E.2d 366 (1969).
89. *United States* v. *McDaniel,* 154 F. Supp. 1 (1957).
90. *United States* v. *Boaker,* 461 F.2d 990 (1972).
91. *United States* v. *Mahanna,* 461 F.2d 1110 (1972).
92. *United States* v. *Hirsch,* 464 F.2d 228 (1973).
93. *United States* v. *Bradshaw,* 490 F.2d 1097 (1974).
94. *Carroll* v. *United States,* 267 U.S. 132 (1925).
95. *Chambers* v. *Maroney,* 399 U.S. 42 (1970).
96. *United States* v. *Roberts,* 434 F.2d 1016 (1970).
97. *Cooper* v. *California,* 386 U.S. 58 (1967).
98. *Jackson* v. *State,* 243 So.2d 396 (1971).
99. *United States* v. *Hathorn,* 451 F.2d 1337 (1972).
100. *United States* v. *Mitchell,* 458 F.2d 960 (1972).
101. *United States* v. *Gravitt,* 484 F.2d 375 (1974).
102. *People* v. *Smith,* 265 N.E.2d 139 (1971).
103. *Carlton* v. *Estelle,* 480 F.2d 759 (1973).
104. *United States* v. *Young,* 489 F.2d 914 (1974).
105. *Alonzo* v. *United States,* 439 F.2d 991 (1971).
106. *People* v. *Somas,* 327 N.Y.S.2d 779 (1972).
107. *United States* v. *Stroble,* 431 F.2d 1273 (1971).
108. *Watkins* v. *Gagnon,* 432 F.2d 1220 (1971).
109. *United States* v. *Dzialak,* 441 F.2d 212 (1971).
110. *United States* v. *Pruitt,* 464 F.2d 494 (1973).
111. *United States* v. *Brown,* 487 F.2d 208 (1974).
112. *Jones* v. *United States,* 362 U.S. 257 (1960).
113. *United States* v. *Felix,* 474 F.2d 610 (1973).
114. *United States* v. *Altizer,* 477 F.2d 846 (1973).
115. *United States* v. *Sullivan,* 488 F.2d 138 (1974).

CHAPTER V

FELONIES AND MISDEMEANORS

In this chapter, most major felonies will be discussed, including the necessary elements of each. Because of the frequency with which they occur, several misdemeanors will likewise be discussed. The officer should be most concerned with learning the essential elements of each crime, so that he will be able to recognize exactly which crime, if any, has been committed when he is confronted by a situation. Although he should not be concerned with the penalty a guilty person might receive, the officer should know whether a particular crime is a felony or a misdemeanor because, as stated in Chapter II, the arrest procedure would differ somewhat, particularly in the amount of force which may be used. As in previous chapters, the officer should familiarize himself with the pertinent statutes in his own state, as the discussion here will, by necessity, be more general.

SECTION 1: CONSPIRACY AND ACCESSORIES

1-1: CONSPIRACY

A conspiracy takes place when two or more persons conspire to commit a crime, to do any unlawful act, to accomplish any unlawful purpose, or to accomplish a lawful purpose by any unlawful means. There can also be a conspiracy to commit an act injurious to the public health or to prevent another from exercising a lawful trade or calling. This crime is usually punishable as a felony; however, in some states, it is punished as either a felony or a misdemeanor, depending on the seriousness of the act.

1-2: ACCESSORY AFTER THE FACT

An accessory after the fact is one who, having full knowledge that a crime has been committed, conceals, harbors, assists, or protects the person who is charged with or convicted of a crime. In the majority of states, this crime is only applicable to felonies and is punishable as a felony.

1-3: ACCESSORY BEFORE THE FACT

An accessory before the fact is one who, being absent when the crime is committed, yet assists, procures, counsels, incites, induces, encourages, or commands another to commit a felony. Unlike an accessory after the fact, an accessory before the fact would be punished as a principal, that is, as one who actually committed the crime. For example, one who is an accessory before the fact of murder would, if found guilty, be punished for the crime of murder. Theoretically, an accessory before or after the fact could be tried and found guilty of that crime, even though the principal was found innocent or was not even indicted. However, in actual practice, when the principal is found not guilty, the case against an accessory would seldom be pursued.

Often confused with the crime of being an accessory after the fact is the crime of misprision of a felony. Misprision of a felony is committed when one who has knowledge that a particular person has committed a felony fails to report or give that information to the authorities, whereby the felon is concealed from the authorities. Under federal statute, misprision is a felony. However, many states do not have such a statute, and in those states, the offense would be punishable as a misdemeanor under common law.

SECTION 2: CRIMES AGAINST PERSONS

2-1: ASSAULT AND BATTERY

An assault is an intentional, unlawful threat to do, by force, corporal injury to the person of another. The circumstances must be such that a well-founded fear of immediate danger is created in the mind of the victim, and the offender must have the present ability to carry out the threat. A battery is any unlawful beating or other wrongful physical attack on another human without his consent. The threat to use force against another is assault, and the actual use of force is battery, which would always include an assault; hence the two are often combined under the term "assault and battery." In almost every jurisdiction, this crime may be either a felony or a misdemeanor, depending on the seriousness of the act.

Throughout the states, there are many variations of assault and battery, such as simple assault, aggravated assault, assault with intent to do another crime, assault and battery with intent to ravish, and assault and battery with intent to kill. In a majority of states, the intentional pointing or aiming of a firearm at or toward another is an assault and battery punishable as a misdemeanor, and if someone is injured thereby it becomes a felony.

In determining whether an assault and battery is felonious, one must first ascertain the intentional degree of injury which results from the attack. However, one must not overlook the fact that if the act of attacking was wrongful, then the intent must necessarily have been wrongful for the act to have taken place in the beginning. Therefore we might suggest that at least some intent must have been applied to the act of attacking (the assault) as well as to the result of the attack (the battery). Intent is the main ingredient of the offense, and the intent must be actual, not conditional. When the intent to kill is conditioned upon the occurrence of a particular event, which fails to take place, intent to kill is non-existent.

In order to charge a person with assault and battery with intent to kill, the means or force used must at least be capable of causing death. Some decisions have held that the hands or feet may be a means or force likely to produce death; however, this would of course depend on the circumstances of the case. Generally, the use of a deadly weapon in an assault and battery would be prima facie evidence of an intent to kill. Common instruments, other than firearms, may be considered deadly, depending on the circumstances in which they are used. However, one who holds an axe in his hands could not be justly convicted of assault and battery with intent to kill if he was not within striking distance of the other.

2-2: HOMICIDE

Homicide may be defined simply as the killing of one human being by another. This act may or may not constitute a crime. Most homicides fall into two general catagories: murder and manslaughter. Some states have statutory degrees of murder, others do not. Manslaughter may also be divided into two general classifications: voluntary and involuntary.

2-3: HOMICIDE—VOLUNTARY MANSLAUGHTER

Voluntary manslaughter is homicide committed voluntarily or intentionally in the sudden heat of passion. The heat of passion should not be confused with sexual excitement; it is anger or rage resulting from provocation. For example, two persons suddenly quarrel; a fight ensues and one kills the other. There was no malice aforethought, but there was felonious intent and the act was done in the heat of passion.

2-4: HOMICIDE—INVOLUNTARY MANSLAUGHTER

Involuntary manslaughter occurs when a person, in committing an unlawful act which is not felonious per se and which does not tend to do great bodily harm, or in committing a lawful act without proper caution, negligently and unintentionally kills another. For example, a motorist who ran a stop sign, hit another vehicle, and killed the driver would have committed involuntary manslaughter.

2-5: *JUSTIFIABLE HOMICIDE*

Most states have statutes which provide that a homicide may be justifiable if it was neccesarily committed in resisting an attempt to unlawfully kill the person or to commit any felony upon the person (i.e., in self-defense); when necessarily committed by any officer in keeping and preserving the peace; or when necessarily committed by any officer in the service of lawful process issued by a competent court. Some of these statutes also cover persons who aid or assist an officer of the law in necessarily killing another. It has also been defined as a homicide which "is committed intentionally, but without any evil design, and under such circumstances of necessity or duty as render the act proper, and relieve the party from any shadow of blame."[1] In either case, a homicide would be considered justifiable if it was *necessarily* committed by any law officer in the discharge of his legal duty.

2-6: *EXCUSABLE HOMICIDE*

Under some statutes, excusable homicide is defined as true self-defense. For example, some statutes provide that a homicide is excusable if committed upon sudden and sufficient provocation, without any dangerous weapon being used, and not done in a cruel or unusual manner. Others provide that a homicide is excusable when committed by accident and misfortune in a sudden heat of passion or when committed by accident and misfortune in lawfully correcting a child. *Black's Law Dictionary* defines an excusable homicide as "the killing of a human being, either by misadventure or in self-defense."[2]

2-7: *HOMICIDE—MURDER*

Murder has been defined as "the unlawful killing of a human being by another with malice aforethought, either express or implied."[3] As stated earlier, some states have statutory degrees of murder, such as first degree murder, which generally covers those murders committed by "poisoning, lying in wait, and other killings committed in pursuance of a deliberate and premeditated design, and to those which accompany the commission of some of the more atrocious felonies, such as burglary, arson, rape, and robbery; while murder in the second degree occurs where there is no such deliberately formed design to take life or to perpetrate one of the enumerated felonies as is required for the first degree."[4]

Recently, many states have enacted new capital murder statutes because of the United States Supreme Court decision which made the death penalty unconstitutional for violations of the existing state murder statutes. The Mississippi capital murder statute is presented here; it might be noted that there are presently two cases pending which challenge its constitutionality.

MISSISSIPPI CODE OF 1972,
REVISED AND ANNOTATED–SECTION 97-3-19

The killing of a human being without the authority of law by any means or in any manner shall be murder in the following cases:

(a) When done with deliberate design to effect the death of the person killed, or of any human being;

(b) When done in the commission of an act eminently dangerous to others and evincing a depraved heart, regardless of human life, although without any premeditated design to effect the death of any particular individual;

(c) When done without any design to effect death by any person engaged in the commission of any felony other than rape, kidnapping, burglary, arson or robbery, or in any attempt to commit such felonies.

The killing of a human being without the authority of law by any means or in any manner shall be capital murder in the following cases:

(a) Murder which is perpetrated by killing a peace officer or fireman while such officer or fireman is acting in his official capacity or by reason of an act performed in his official capacity, and with knowledge that the victim was a peace officer or fireman . . .;

(b) Murder which is perpetrated by a person who is under sentence of life imprisonment;

(c) Murder which is perpetrated by use or detonation of a bomb or explosive device;

(d) Murder which is perpetrated by any person who has been offered or has received anything of value for committing the murder, and all parties to such murder are guilty as principals;

(e) When done with or without any design to effect death, by any person engaged in the commission of the crime of rape, burglary, kidnapping, arson or robbery, or in any attempt to commit such felonies;

(f) Murder which is perpetrated by the killing of any elected official of a county, municipal, state or federal government with knowledge that the victim was such public official.

2-8: KIDNAPPING

Generally, kidnapping is the intentional, forcible seizing or confining of another, against his will. In most instances, the consent of one so kidnapped may not be used as a defense, unless it is shown that the consent was not extorted by threats, force, or violence. Since the Lindberg kidnapping case many states have enacted statutes which make it a capital crime to kidnap any child under 10 years of age. Some of the more recently enacted statutes provide for the death penalty in cases in which someone is killed in the commission of the kidnapping.

2-9: MAYHEM

Persons are seldom charged with mayhem, possibly because many prosecutors are unfamiliar with the crime. A person who, from any premeditated design, intentionally mutilates, disables, destroys, or disfigures the eye, nose, lip, tongue, or any other limb or member of another is guilty of mayhem. In the majority of states, this crime is punishable as a felony. However, in some states, it may be punished as a misdemeanor, depending on the severity of the injury.

2-10: RAPE

Rape is defined as "the unlawful carnal knowledge of a woman by a man forcibly and against her will."[5] In some states, because of the wording of the statute, it must be accomplished without the victim's consent and she must fully resist the attack. Under some statutes, carnal knowledge of any female under the statutory age of consent is termed "statutory rape."

To understand the crime of rape, one must understand the meaning of "carnal knowledge." "Carnal knowledge is said to mean coitus; copulation; the act of man in having sexual bodily connection with a woman; sexual intercourse. There is carnal knowledge if there is the slightest penetration of the sexual organ of the female by the sexual organ of the male. It is not necessary that the vagina be entered or that the hymen be ruptured; the entering of the vulva or labia is sufficient."[6] Most statutes provide that when the female is of "tender years," proof of penetration of the female's private parts is not necessary when it is shown that they were lacerated or torn in an attempt to have carnal knowledge of her.

Other rape statutes, which primarily deal with those females over the age of consent, make it mandatory that the injured female be of "chaste character." Chaste character denotes a purity of mind or innocence of heart. As used in most statutes it means actual chastity. This requirement may be met by one who was formerly unchaste but is now reformed. For example, a female who was formerly a prostitute may now be of chaste character.

Many rape statutes, other than those dealing with statutory rape, require that the victim's testimony be corroborated. In many instances, the crime of rape goes unreported or unprosecuted because of the victim's fear of publicity and embarrassment. Rape is a felony in every state, and in most it is one of the crimes enumerated in felony murder statutes. For example, when someone is killed in the commission of or attempted commission of rape, the person committing the crime is guilty of murder. If found guilty and sentenced under the new capital murder statutes, the penalty would be death.

2-11: ROBBERY

Robbery is the felonious taking of the personal property of another, from the other's presence or from his person and against the other's will, by violence or by putting the victim in fear of some immediate injury. In practice, it is necessary to allege that the victim was actually attacked or that he was put in fear of injury; otherwise the crime committed may not be robbery.

Robbery may also be committed if property is taken as a result of a threat to injure the person or his relative at another time. In some states, robbery is termed "extortion" when the property or money is obtained by the sending of a threatening letter. When any deadly weapon is used in the commission of the crime, it is called "armed robbery." Robbery is a felony in all states, and like rape, it is included in most felony murder statutes.

It might be helpful to cite a mistake sometimes made in charging the commission of "strong-armed robbery." Three persons enter a liquor store which is operated by one person. Two of the men lure the store operator to the back of the store while the third takes the money from the cash register. The three leave without any further confrontation. This is not robbery because no force or threat of force was used nor was the money taken in the operator's presence. The crime committed here is larceny, which will be discussed later in this chapter.

2-12: CHILD MOLESTING

A child molester is usually a male person over the age of eighteen who, as one statute states, "handles, touches or rubs with his hands or any part of his body or any member thereof," any child of tender years, for the purpose of "gratifying his lust, or indulging his depraved, licentious sexual desires." The statutes of each state specify age requirements for the victim and the perpetrator. This crime is a felony.

SECTION 3: CRIMES AFFECTING ADMINISTRATION OF JUSTICE

3-1: BRIBERY

Bribery is the offering, giving, receiving, or soliciting of anything of value in order to influence the action, judgment, vote, or opinion of any officer, either elected or appointed, on any matter which is pending or which may, at a future time, be subject to such officer's vote, opinion, judgment, or action, or in any way influence the officer's action in the discharge of a legal or public duty. This crime is generally a felony, and if the officer, or his wife with his knowledge and consent, accepts any gift, offer, or promise, which is so offered, he is likewise guilty of a felony. Some statutes provide, in addition to the felony charge, that the officer who accepts such bribe shall forfeit his office.

Bribery statutes do not deal solely with governmental officials; they also may apply to one who bribes a juror, arbitrator, or a referee in a sports event. In addition, persons who offer and those who accept rewards for compounding or concealing a crime may be charged with bribery.

3-2: ESCAPE OF ARRESTED PERSONS

Since each state has many different statutes which deal with the crime of "escape," it would be impossible to state other than a general rule here. As a rule of thumb, one who is being held for a felony and escapes is guilty of a felony. One who is being held for a misdemeanor and escapes without using bodily force against another is usually guilty of a misdemeanor. However, if the misdemeanor offender does use bodily force in order to escape, most statutes make the offense a felony.

This general rule also applies to those who aid, assist, or abet another in escaping and would apply regardless of where or by whom the prisoner was held. These statutes include not only those who aid, assist, or abet, but also any officer or private person who allows an escape. In most states, harboring or concealing an escaped prisoner, knowing him to be an escapee, is a separate crime and is a felony regardless of the escapee's crime.

3-3: OBSTRUCTING JUSTICE

Obstructing justice has been defined as "impeding or obstructing those who seek justice in a court, or those who have duties or powers of administering justice therein . . . . The act by which one or more persons attempt to prevent, or do prevent, the execution of lawful process. The term applies also to obstructing the administration of justice in any way—as by hindering witnesses from appearing."[7]

Some statutes state that if a person, by force, threats, or abuse, attempts to or does intimidate or otherwise influence a judge, juror, witness, defense or prosecuting attorney, or any other officer in the discharge of his duties, or obstructs or impedes the administration of justice in any court, he may be found guilty of a misdemeanor or a felony.

In the application of such statutes, most courts have employed the Latin phrase *ejusdem generis,* which literally means "of the same kind, class, or nature." Therefore the words "threats or abuse, . . . or otherwise" would take on the same meaning as the word "force." An understanding of the court's interpretation of these terms is necessary to enforce the statutes properly. For example, one who makes threats or is speaking abusively to an officer may not be violating a statute of this kind if such threats or abuse is not accompanied by some overt act to carry them out. In other words, a threat unaccompanied by an attempt to carry out the threat would not violate the statute.

In one case involving the application of a similar statute, the court stated, "Merely protesting to the arresting officer that another should not be arrested as he had done nothing, without threats, show of force, or abuse, does not violate the section."[8] In another case, the court said, "There was no violation of the section where the accused gave to the sheriff investigating a crime a false statement which was calculated to mislead the officer, but which was not accompanied by force, threats or abuse."[9]

3-4: RESISTING AND OBSTRUCTING ARREST

Very similar to and often confused with obstructing justice is the crime of resisting arrest or obstructing the arrest of others. This crime is sometimes referred to as "interfering with an officer in the line of duty." In criminal law, resisting arrest has been defined as "the offense of obstructing, opposing, and endeavoring to prevent (with or without actual force) a peace officer in the execution of a writ or in the lawful discharge of his duty while making an arrest or otherwise enforcing the peace."[10]

Like the Mississippi statute, many statutes state that "it shall be unlawful for any person to obstruct or resist by force, or violence, or threats, or in any other manner, his lawful arrest or the lawful arrest of another person." In the majority of states, this crime is punishable as a misdemeanor, and, like obstructing justice, it is strictly applied by the courts. Generally speaking, a person would not be convicted of resisting arrest unless he actually used force. That is to say, he could not, by words alone, resist the officer's actions in making an arrest. And, as the following state court decisions point out, one may use reasonable force to resist an unlawful arrest:

> An owner of the premises may use reasonable force to resist an officer attempting to search the premises without a valid warrant.[11]

> Where the sheriff and deputy sheriff were unlawful in arresting a person without a warrant for an alleged misdemeanor not committed in their presence and were unlawful in invading the home of the owner, the acts of the owner in resisting entry were not unlawful.[12]

> Where an officer made an arrest for a misdemeanor not committed in his presence and without having a warrant in his possession, the charge that the defendant resisted arrest cannot stand for he had a right to resist in a reasonable manner the unlawful arrest.[13]

One of the most frequent instances of misuse of this type of statute occurs when an officer stops a vehicle in order to issue the operator a traffic citation. The driver and officer are outside their vehicles when one or more passengers get out of the violator's vehicle and approach the two, but stop 8 feet away from the officer and violator. One or more of the party start to openly accuse the officer of mistreating the violator by issuing the citation and state that the driver did not do anything wrong and that the "fuzz" or "pigs" are always harassing everyone. What may the officer do in this situation? Could he possibly cite or arrest the passengers for interfering with him in the line of duty? Probably not, because no overt act or open threat has taken place as yet. Could the officer possibly order the passengers back into the violator's vehicle in order to avoid a confrontation? The answer here would be entirely dependent on whether there was an existing statute which would allow him to do so. Without such a statute, the officer could not legally order the passengers back into the car, since they have as much right to be where they are as the officer does, unless they are obstructing traffic. In that case, the officer could legally order them to move without statutory authority to that effect, because the officer's primary function is to preserve the safety of the public.

3-5: PERJURY

Simply stated, perjury is lying while under oath. Technically defined, it is "the willful assertion as to a matter of fact, opinion, belief, or knowledge, made by a witness in a judicial proceeding as part of his evidence, either upon oath or in any form allowed by law to be substituted for an oath, whether such evidence is given in open court, or in an affidavit, or otherwise, such assertion being material to the issue or point of inquiry and known to such witness to be false."[14]

The crime of perjury is a felony and a convicted perjurer may be forever barred from giving testimony in any matter then or thereafter pending unless and until his conviction is reversed. Another crime often associated with the crime of perjury is subornation of perjury, which is the inducing of another to commit perjury. The penalty for this crime is usually the same as that for perjury.

3-6: FAILURE OF OFFICERS TO PERFORM DUTIES

Among the criminal statutes of most states are laws which require all officers to perform their prescribed duties. In most states, the failure to do so is a misdemeanor, and in some states, one who violates these statutes may also be removed from office at the discretion of the court having jurisdiction. Not only do these statutes provide for punishment of those who fail to do their duty, but they also provide penalties for those who fail to return offenders or those who absent themselves, knowing a crime is being committed, in order to avoid taking action against the one committing the crime.

SECTION 4: CRIMES AGAINST PROPERTY

4-1: ARSON

Arson is the wilful and malicious burning of property. In the majority of states, there are different degrees of arson, such as first, second, and third, and all are punished as felonies. However, in a few states, there are statutory provisions which provide that those who by their own negligence, but without wilful and malicious design, allow a fire started by them to burn the woods, marsh, or field of another are guilty of a misdemeanor.

First degree arson usually deals with the burning or aiding or procuring of the burning of a dwelling, whether occupied, unoccupied, or vacant, and any outbuildings. In some states, a state-supported school building would also be included in the first degree arson statute. And in those states with such statutes, one who accidentally sets fire to a state-supported school building and who fails, wilfully, to sound the general alarm, may also be punished for the commission of a felony.

Second degree arson, a felony, is the burning or procuring of the burning of any building or structure which is not enumerated in the first degree arson statute. While third degree arson statutes cover personal property in general, these statutes usually place some minimum value on the personal property burned and provide in addition that the property must belong to someone other than the one charged.

Fourth degree arson is the *attempt* to burn any of the property described in the first, second, and third degree arson statutes. This would include any preliminary act, such as the placing or distribution of any flammable, explosive, or combustible material or substance in any arrangement with the intent to eventually set fire to or burn property. Other arson statutes make it a felony to burn property in order to collect insurance on it. Arson is one of the crimes enumerated in most felony murder statutes.

4-2: BURGLARY

Burglary is the breaking and entering of a building or structure with intent to commit a crime within. This crime is often charged as "breaking and entering" or "B and E." However, in some states, this may be somewhat of a misnomer because of the wording found in the statutes. Some statutes begin, "Every person convicted of breaking and entering . . . shall be guilty of burglary." At present there are several cases on appeal which challenge the validity of a conviction founded on an indictment alleging that the crime was breaking and entering. To be safe, the charge should be written as burglary, and then the actual breaking and entering can be established during the trial.

Most states have various statutes to cover the many different ways to commit burglary. For example, there are those which deal with breaking and entering a dwelling, breaking in at night while armed with a deadly weapon, breaking out of a dwelling, breaking an inner door of a dwelling by one who is lawfully in the house, and breaking into other containers which are located inside a dwelling. However, in all these statutes, the essential elements of the crime remain the same.

Other statutes cover burglary of buildings other than dwellings, and these usually specify that the burglary be done "with intent to steal." In the statutes which deal with the burglary of dwellings, an intent to commit any crime within is usually sufficient, while in the statutes covering non-dwellings, a specific intent to steal would be required. In addition to buildings, the latter type of statute also covers ships, boats, railroad cars, automobiles, trucks, and trailers in which any valuable things are kept, used, or stored. For example, one who breaks into a locked automobile and steals a tape player should be charged with burglary and not larceny, as so often happens. In this instance, the burglary would be a felony, while larceny would probably be a misdemeanor because of the value of the item stolen.

Closely related to burglary is the crime of possession of burglar's tools. In most states, it is a crime to possess implements, tools, or instruments designed to aid the commission of a burglary. This generally is a felony, and the concealed carrying of such implements, tools, or instruments which are peculiarly adapted to burglary by one who does not customarily use them in the normal course of his business would constitute prima facie evidence of an intention to use them for an unlawful purpose. Likewise, burglary with the aid and use of explosives is also covered by statute. Burglary is another of the crimes enumerated in felony murder statutes.

4-3: LARCENY

A person commits larceny when he takes and carries away the personal property of another with intent to convert it to his own use. Any act which lacks any of these essential elements cannot be larceny. Larceny can be a felony or a misdemeanor, depending on the value of the property taken. State statutes specify a certain monetary value, and the taking of anything worth more than that would be grand larceny, a felony, and of anything worth less than that would be petit larceny, a misdemeanor.

Specific larceny statutes deal with, among other things, stealing dogs, livestock, or vehicles, and severing crops, produce, or parts of improvements on real estate. Cattle theft is another term frequently used in lieu of larceny of livestock, and in the last few years it has occurred with much greater frequency in the rural areas of the United States. High meat prices have also caused the rate of cattle theft crimes to rise in the large metropolitan areas.

4-4: LOOTING

At common law, looting was defined as the plunder or taking of goods in time of war; however, through usage and by statute its meaning has been broadened. Today looting occurs when a person or persons, knowingly and without lawful authority or consent, enter any premises in which normal security is lacking because of a hurricane, storm, or fire, or other *vis major* (overwhelming force) which was created by a riot, mob, or other human agency, and carry away, injure, or exert control over the premises or property within. Looting is punishable as a felony.

4-5: MALICIOUS MISCHIEF

This crime has often been used, and abused, as a catchall by officers who were not familiar enough with the laws they were obligated to enforce, and for this reason its use is discouraged in some areas today. If used properly, however, it could be an asset, rather than a liability, to the modern law enforcement officer.

Black's Law Dictionary defines malicious mischief as the "willful destruction of personal property, from actual ill will or resentment towards its owner or possessor." Most statutory definitions include real as well as personal property and make the crime a misdemeanor. Some statutory penalties are unique in that they provide for a fine of twice the value of the property injured or destroyed. Another unusual feature of this crime is that one may be an accessory before the fact in the commission of it if one, by any word, deed or act, instills in the mind of another the will to so act.

4-6: POSSESSION OF STOLEN OR EMBEZZLED PROPERTY

This crime is often charged as "receiving" stolen or embezzled goods, but either charge, receiving or possessing, is usually held valid by our courts. In some instances, however, the officer will make this charge when he lacks sufficient evidence to support a conviction. In order for the defendant to be found guilty of the charge, the prosecution must prove four basic elements: (1) that the property was stolen or embezzled by a person other than the one charged; (2) that the accused actually received the property in question and concealed it; (3) that the accused actually knew the property was stolen or embezzled at the very time he received it; and (4) that he received the property for his own gain.

As stated earlier in Chapter IV, this crime is very difficult to prove, and the officer should remember that possession alone will not sustain a conviction.

4-7: TRESPASS

> Trespass, in its most comprehensive sense, signifies any transgression or offense against the law of nature, of society, or of the country in which we live; and this, whether it relates to a man's person or to his property. In its more limited and ordinary sense, it signifies an injury committed with violence, and this violence may be either actual or implied; and the law will imply violence though none is actually used, when the injury is of a direct and immediate kind, and committed on the person or tangible and corporeal property of the plaintiff. Of actual violence, an assault and battery is an instance; of implied, a peaceable but wrongful entry upon a person's land.[15]

In all states except one, the simple trespass is considered a misdemeanor. In that one state, as a result of a lawsuit stemming from a trespass where the violator was injured, the legislature of that state revised all the trespass statutes, making them felonies. Since a person may use deadly force in resisting a felony, some feel that this threat of injury or death has been a deterrent to potential trespassers.

Most states have many statutes which deal with different kinds of trespass. For example, there could be a trespass by going upon enclosed lands of another, a trespass which is wilful or malicious, a trespass by carrying away vegetation, a trespass by entering upon posted lands of another, a trespass by destroying or altering notices on posted lands, a trespass by going into or upon or remaining in or upon buildings or premises of another after being forbidden to do so and inciting or soliciting other persons to do so. All of these acts, for the most part, are misdemeanors and most are petty in nature. Some states have statutes which make it a felonious trespass to go into or upon premises where nuclear-powered machinery, equipment, or vessels, or rockets, missiles, propulsion systems, explosives, or other dangerous devices are stored, used, or kept with the intent to commit a crime.

SECTION 5: FALSE PRETENSE

5-1: FALSE PRETENSE—BAD CHECKS

Every state has statutory provisions concerning the issuance of bad checks. Most of these statutes provide that it shall be unlawful for any person, with fraudulent intent, to issue, for money or any article of value, a check or draft, knowing at the time the check or draft is written that there are insufficient funds available to cover it. Many statutes provide that when payment is refused, such refusal, whether because of insufficient funds or because there is no bank account at all, is prima facie evidence of the intent to defraud. One indispensable element of the crime is that the one who issues the check or draft must receive something of value at the very time the check or draft is delivered. Issuing bad checks, often called "uttering," is punishable as either a misdemeanor or a felony, depending on statutory provisions. Some statutes make the first and second offense a misdemeanor when the amount or value of the check is below that specified in the statute. A felony would be charged for the third offense or whenever the amount or value of the check is over that stated in the statute.

As an example, let us suppose that a person does credit business with a certain store and has allowed his account to run for several months without paying for the items received. The store owner finally demands payment in the amount of $400, which makes the buyer angry. In his anger, he writes a check for $400, knowing that he has no funds available to cover it. Could he be convicted of the crime of false pretense? Probably not, because he did not receive the thing of value for which the check was written at the same time the check was delivered to the merchant. However, the merchant may have an action at law for recovery of the goods, or he may ask for a judgment and recover the price of the goods. Since these statutes vary a great deal from state to state, the officer should study his own state's statutes.

5-2: UNIFORM CREDIT CARD ACT

Most states have adopted fairly uniform statutes to deal with crimes committed with credit cards. These statutes cover acts such as procuring the issuance of a credit card by a false statement; theft of a card; unlawful sales and purchases by use of a card; forgery, signing, or use of a card with intent to defraud; and counterfeiting cards for illegal purposes. In a few instances, an offense under these statutes might be a felony, but most are misdemeanors.

5-3: FORGERY AND COUNTERFEITING

Forgery is defined as "the false making or material altering, with intent to defraud, of any writing which, if genuine, might apparently be of legal efficacy or the foundation of a legal liability."[16] To counterfeit is defined as "to forge; to copy or imitate, without authority or right, and with a view to deceive or defraud, by passing the copy or thing forged for that which is original or genuine. Most commonly applied to the fraudulent and criminal imitation of money."[17]

In common criminal practice, forgery usually involves some private writing or instrument, such as a check, will, deed, note, or other instrument requiring a signature, while counterfeiting usually denotes the fraudulent imitation of money, stocks, bonds, or other negotiable instruments. Both forgery and counterfeiting are statutory offenses, usually punishable as felonies. However, we should keep in mind that counterfeiting of money is a federal offense, as is forgery of government documents or checks. For these federal crimes, the officer should contact the local office of the United States Secret Service, since they have jurisdiction over these matters.

SECTION 6: CRIMES AFFECTING BUSINESS AND PROFESSIONS

6-1: EMBEZZLEMENT

Embezzlement is the fraudulent appropriation of the property of another to one's own use without authority or permission after a fiduciary relationship has been established. For example, the bank teller has a legal right to handle a depositor's money and to do with it whatever is permitted under law; however, he does not have a legal right to convert it to his own use without authority or permission. Another good example is a person who rents a car and then sells it. He does have a legal right to the use and control of the vehicle, but he does not have a right to convert it to his own use, as by selling it.

The crime of embezzlement may be committed by an agent, bailee, trustee, servant, or generally, by any party to a fiduciary relationship. One should also remember that, subject to statutory provisions, the buying or receiving of embezzled goods is a crime. While most state statutes make embezzlement a felony, some statutes make it a felony or misdemeanor, depending on the amount or value of the goods involved. Since embezzlement is actually an extension of common law larceny to include those cases in which the property originally came into the defendant's possession without a trespass, some states rely heavily upon the larceny statutes in convicting and sentencing embezzlers.

6-2: SHOPLIFTING

Shoplifting is another crime which was derived from the crime of larceny. A shoplifter is a person who wilfully and unlawfully takes possession of any goods, wares, or merchandise owned or held by and offered or displayed for sale by any store or other mercantile establishment with the intent to convert the goods, wares, or merchandise to his own use without paying the purchase price. Shoplifting has become a widespread crime in the United States, and many use it as their only means of support. Whether one who is convicted of shoplifting is punished for a felony or a misdemeanor generally depends upon the amount or value of the goods taken and whether it is the first, second, or third offense.

The Mississippi statute provides:

> If any person shall willfully conceal unpurchased goods, wares or merchandise owned or held by and offered or displayed for sale by any store or other mercantile establishment, whether such concealment be on his own person or otherwise and whether on or off the premises of said store or mercantile establishment, such concealment shall constitute prima facie evidence that such person intended to convert same to his own use without paying the purchase price therefore . . .; and the finding of such unpurchased goods, wares or merchandise concealed upon the person of or within or among the personal effects or belongings of such person shall constitute prima facie evidence of willful concealment; and if such person conceals, or causes to be concealed, such unpurchased goods, wares or merchandise upon the person or within or among the belongings or personal effects of another, the finding of same shall also be prima facie evidence of willful concealment on the part of the person so concealing such goods, wares or merchandise.[18]

Other statutes have been written to protect from civil suits those who stop and question suspected shoplifters. The following is an example of such a statute:

> If any person shall commit or attempt to commit the offense of shoplifting, . . . or if any person shall willfully conceal upon his person or otherwise any unpurchased goods, wares or merchandise held or owned by any store or mercantile establishment, the merchant or any employee thereof or any peace or police officer, acting in good faith and upon probable cause based upon reasonable grounds therefore, may question such person, in a reasonable manner for the purpose of ascertaining whether or not such person is guilty of shoplifting . . . . Such questioning of a person by a merchant, merchant's employee or peace or police officer shall not render such merchant, merchant's employee or peace or police officer civilly liable for slander, false arrest, false imprisonment, malicious prosecution, unlawful detention or otherwise in any case where such merchant, merchant's employee or peace or police officer acts in good faith and upon reasonable grounds to believe that the person questioned is committing or attempting to commit the crime of shoplifting.[19]

The officer who is assigned to such detail should use extreme caution in confronting or accusing a suspected shoplifter because the nature of the conversation is privileged; that is to say, only those having an interest in the conversation may hear it without the questioner's incurring civil liability. Therefore, it is suggested that the suspected shoplifter be taken to a private place, such as an office or other room of the store, before any questions are asked or any accusations made. By doing so, the possibility of civil liability is avoided.

Another question often asked is whether the suspect should be allowed to exit the premises before any confrontation is made. To answer properly, one would, by necessity, be forced to examine the applicable statute in a particular jurisdiction. However, in the absence of such specific knowledge, it is generally wise to give the suspect the benefit of the doubt and allow him to at least pass the check-out point, but not necessarily pass out of or off the premises. In this way, there would be no doubt as to the suspect's intent to leave the store without paying the purchase price for the goods.

6-3: UNLAWFUL RESTRAINT OF TRADE—BOYCOTTS

Many states have statutes which make it a misdemeanor for any person to unlawfully restrain another from trading, doing business, or practicing a profession of his choice. However, it should be noted that those statutes which were written for the primary purpose of preserving segregation of the races have been held to be unconstitutional by the Supreme Court of the United States. Therefore, it is suggested that specific statutes be examined in order to determine whether they were intended to prohibit unlawful actions or whether they were directed toward a particular class of persons.

SECTION 7: OFFENSES AGAINST PUBLIC MORALS AND DECENCY

7-1: ADULTERY AND FORNICATION

Adultery has been defined as "voluntary sexual intercourse of a married person with a person other than the offender's husband or wife."[20] Fornication is "unlawful sexual intercourse between two unmarried persons. Further, if one of the persons be married and the other not, it is fornication on the part of the latter, though adultery for the former."[21] Such statutes still remain in the criminal codes of most states, although they are now seldom enforced. These two crimes are usually punishable as felonies.

7-2: BIGAMY—POLYGAMY

Black's Law Dictionary defines bigamy as, "the criminal offense of willfully and knowingly contracting a second marriage (or going through the form of a second marriage) while the first marriage, to the knowledge of the offender, is still subsisting and undissolved." This crime is a felony in all states.

7-3: *INCEST*

Incest is described as sexual intercourse or cohabitation between a male and female who are related to each other within the degrees wherein marriage is prohibited by law. Often this crime is charged as incestuous adultery, which is the same as incest.

7-4: *OBSCENITY—IN GENERAL*

Obscenity, in general, is "the character or quality of being obscene; conduct tending to corrupt the public morals by its indecency or lewdness."[22] Obscene means:

> . . . offensive to chastity of mind or to modesty, expressing or presenting to the mind or view something that delicacy, purity, and decency forbids to be exposed; offensive to modesty, decency, or chastity; impure, unchaste, indecent, lewd; offensive to senses; repulsive; disgusting; foul; filthy; calculated to corrupt, deprave, and debauch the morals of the people, and promote violation of law; of such character as to deprave and corrupt those whose minds are open to such immoral influences; calculated to lower the standard which we regard as essential to civilization or calculated, with the ordinary person, to deprave his morals or lead to impure purposes; licentious and libidinous and tending to excite feelings of an impure or unchaste character; having relation to sexual impurity; tending to stir the sex impulses or to lead to sexually impure and lustful thoughts; tending to corrupt the morals of youth or to lower the standards of right and wrong especially as to the sexual relation.[23]

7-5: *OBSCENITY—INDECENT EXPOSURE*

Almost every state has a statute like Mississippi's which makes it a misdemeanor for a person "to willfully and lewdly expose his person, or the private parts thereof, in any public place, or in any place where others are present, or to procure another to so expose himself."

7-6: *OBSCENITY—OTHER OFFENSES*

Other state statutes make it a crime to exhibit obscene or immoral motion pictures; to distribute, advertise, or show obscene photographs, pictures, or indecent articles; or to publish, sell, or distribute obscene printed or written material.

Until recently, the burden of deciding whether something was obscene fell upon the officer's shoulders. Therefore, the laws dealing with obscenity were not uniformly enforced, because each officer had different opinions as to what was or was not obscene. Mistakes were made in apprehending violators of the obscenity laws, and many went free to commit the crime again while others received the maximum penalty provided for in the statutes. Finally, the issues were brought before the United States Supreme Court and it too seemed to have some problem in formulating a definite answer. The following article, written by Charles Marx, Assistant Attorney General for the State of Mississippi and attorney for the Mississippi Highway Safety Patrol, is reprinted here by express permission in an attempt to show the officer what is required of him today.

OBSCENITY–THE POLICEMAN'S ROLE IN ENFORCEMENT

On June 21, 1973, the United States Supreme Court announced its decision in *Miller* v. *California,* 37 L.Ed. 2d. 419, and immediately there arose a hue and cry across the nation from those who would call upon the local police agency to use this decision to rid their respective communities of all types of offensive material and chastise those responsible for its presence. Equally heard were those who protest the slightest real or imagined invasion of constitutionally protected rights such as the first amendment freedoms. Meanwhile the policeman on the street is, as always, expected to appease both groups. The problem is how to enforce laws dealing with obscenity and not violate laws dealing with the rights of individuals.

Under *Miller* the Court drew the line that is to be followed with relative certainty using this language:

> Under the holdings announced today, no one will be subject to prosecution for the sale or exposure of obscene materials unless these materials depict or describe patently offensive "hard core" sexual conduct specifically defined by the regulating State law, as written or construed. We are satisfied that these specific prerequisites will provide fair notice to a dealer in such materials that his public and commercial activities may bring prosecution. (Slip opinion, p. 12.)

That statement means many things to many people but for sure it says to the policeman that "no one will be" prosecuted for obscenity offenses unless they are "hard core" and very specifically drawn. Each officer . . . knows that all crimes must be specifically defined and has no quarrel with that. What, however, is "hard core" and what was the Court driving at? Perhaps an example would give a clue. Section 2290, Mississippi Code of 1942 [Mississippi Code of 1972, Revised and Annotated, Section 97-29-31] has been codified under the heading "Obscenity–exposure of person." It reads as follows:

> A person who willfully and lewdly exposes his person, or private parts thereof, in any public place, or in any place where

> others are present, or procures another to so expose himself is guilty of a misdemeanor, and, on conviction, shall be fined not exceeding fifty dollars, or be imprisoned not exceeding twenty days in the county jail, or both.

Under this statute Mrs. Roy C. Pendergrass was indicted, tried and convicted in the George County Circuit Court. She appealed and her case was reversed. What were the facts? The indictment was couched in language to establish the fact that the indecent exposure was committed on public road 307 in front of the Salem Missionary Baptist Church and in the presence of Rev. Dennis McDonald and his two young sons. Mr. Pendergrass owns the property across 307 from the church. Do you begin to get a picture? A little country church along the side of a local highway and maybe a spiteful witch living across the road—made an appearance at every service when they park all over the place. Wrong picture, let me paint with a cleaner brush.

Laura B. and her husband, Roy C. Pendergrass, are residents of East Mass Point, Mississippi. They own a fourteen and one half acre tract of undeveloped land on the north side of public road 307 with the Salem Missionary Baptist Church occupying a tract on the south side of the road. The Pendergrass property is undeveloped and, except for a small clearing, it is in its natural wooded state. The cleared area is not visible whatsoever from public road 307 or Salem Church. The private "tow path" road off public road 307 is posted with "No Trespassing" signs. A short distance to the north traveling along the private road turns to the right or eastwardly. Shortly thereafter the road is crossed by a large barrier gate in the form of a counter-balanced 2" x 12" board painted white, approximately eighteen feet long, extending across the road. Clearly visible on the barrier in the center is a sign which says "Blow your horn to enter." On each side thereof is a "Posted" sign as well as similar posted signs on the trees to which the gate barrier is attached. One end of the barrier is fastened to a tree with 24" hinges. The free end of the barrier is chained around a post. After leaving the barrier the road proceeds five hundred to six hundred feet where a slight brush obstruction is present, and the road then turns northwardly again for an additional fifty to sixty feet and thence turns back westwardly an additional thirty to forty feet. At the end of the road is the cleared area where the alleged exposure took place. Looks rather different from here, doesn't it. The case was *Pendergrass* v. *State,* 193 So.2d 126.

Any officer reader will be relieved to know that the indictment was returned upon the testimony of the good reverend and no law enforcement officer was shown by the record to have participated in cracking this case. (No pun intended.)

The Mississippi Supreme Court held in *Pendergrass* that willfully and lewdly must be shown for the offense described to have been committed. They also foreshadowed the United States Supreme Court's ruling in *Stanley* v. *Georgia,* 394 U.S. 557, when they ended the opinion with a Latin phrase "De gustibus non disputandum" meaning there's no disputing tastes, or to each his own.

The *Pendergrass* facts were given as an example of what the Court was driving at when it sought to limit the direction of enforcement efforts. *Stanley* held that a citizen has a right to privacy in the home and a correlative right to possess obscene material within that zone of privacy.

In questions of obscenity control as in regard to all other matters of special concern to the criminal law, the officer's role should be that of an objective, knowledgeable, highly skilled and independent collector of facts needed to establish a violation of law and identify the offender. Determinations as to what acts should be punishable as crimes must be made by legislators, not officers, because the police function is limited to execution of the laws. However, the recent shift in interpretation of obscenity law by the Supreme Court has made it essential for officers to be aware of the revised elements in order to remain objective and independent while enforcing the law and to avoid the danger of being influenced by nonauthoritative subjective definitions and assessments of obscenity.

In *Miller* v. *California* the Court held that the basic guidelines for the trier of fact (the jury) must be: Whether "the average person, applying contemporary community standards" would find that a work, taken as a whole, appeals to the prurient interest in sex; portrays, in a patently offensive way, sexual conduct specifically defined by the applicable state law; and taken as a whole, does not have serious literary, artistic, political, or scientific value. (Slip opinion pp. 9–10).

What does the average person think "obscene" means? The dictionary defines obscenity as "The state or quality of being obscene." The definition of obscene is then given as "offensive to one's feelings, or to prevailing notions, of modesty or decency; lewd; disgusting; repulsive." Maybe the word "pornography" would bring about a clearer picture. This word is defined to include "writings, pictures, etc. intended primarily to arouse sexual desire; and, the production of such writings, pictures, etc." In *Williams* v. *State,* 94 So. 882 (1923), the Mississippi Supreme Court adopted the following language in defining the word obscene: "The word 'obscene' means offensive to senses; repulsive; disgusting; foul; filthy; offensive to modesty or decency; impure; indecent; lewd . . ." (citations omitted). With these definitions in mind then what should an officer do? Let's look at a couple of cases.

McGrew v. *City of Jackson,* 307 F. Supp. 754 (1969), and *Hosey* v. *City of Jackson,* 307 F. Supp. 527 (1970), are companion cases for our purposes. Both cases involve a challenge to Section 2286, Mississippi Code of 1942, which is entitled by the codifiers as "Moving Pictures–obscene and immoral exhibition of." This section makes it unlawful to show or exhibit to public view any obscene, indecent, or immoral picture and prescribes a penalty of not less than $25.00 nor more than $100.00 or sixty days or both. This statute has been construed to read "obscene, indecent and immoral." The charge must be that the picture is obscene, indecent and immoral, *Anderson* v. *City of Hattiesburg,* 94 So. 163 (1922).

The factual situation in both federal cases is strikingly similar although the movies are different. *McGrew* involved the motion picture "The Fox" while *Hosey* was about the showing of the movie "Candy." What was "Candy" about? The film depicts illicit sexual intercourse between Candy, an unmarried female, and a gardener, a photographer, a hunchback and a guru; unnatural sexual gratification between Candy and a doctor and between a drunken poet and a doll, mistaken for a girl, and the incestuous relationship of Candy with her father and uncle. The other film "The Fox" was dealing with the sex life of a lesbian, her lover and the lover's male love. The three-judge court called it, ". . . a classic case of hard core pornography wherein sex is pondered solely for profit." Without pointing out minor differences the facts are as follows: At least two police officers bought tickets and as paid guests viewed the public showing of the film in question; and at the conclusion of the showing, the officers arrested the individuals involved–the projectionist, the theater manager and ticket seller–and seized the entire film without any warrant of seizure or arrest. Both courts noted Section 2470, Mississippi Code of 1942, and said, "Accordingly, these police officers duly arrested the plaintiffs for this misdemeanor committed in their presence after viewing the entire film, and seized the film as an instrument or vehicle of the offense for violating this statute" (Section 2286). The individuals were charged in criminal court and brought an action against the City and its officers in federal court seeking to have the statute declared unconstitutional on its face or as it had been applied. A three-judge court was impaneled and in both cases denied the relief sought. There was different reasoning as to the legal arguments presented in either case but as to the policeman's actions, they were together. The Supreme Court of the United States reversed these cases for other reasons (401 U.S. 987, 1971).

Four days after *Miller* the Supreme Court announced another obscenity decision, or rather two such decisions, both dealing with movies and having an effect on the action to be taken by an officer. These two were *Heller* v. *New York,* 37 L.Ed. 2d. 745, . . . and *Roaden* v. *Kentucky,* 37 L.Ed. 2d. 757 . . . . In *Heller* a judge viewed the entire film and signed a warrant for seizure and for arrest of the movie theater manager on the grounds the film was obscene. [The Supreme Court stated:]

> Here seems to be the answer, where a film is seized for the bona fide purpose of preserving it as evidence in a criminal proceeding, and it is seized pursuant to a warrant issued after a determination of probable obscenity by a neutral magistrate, and following the seizure a prompt judicial determination of the obscenity issue in an adversary proceeding is available at the request of any interested party, the seizure is constitutionally permissible. On a showing to the trial court that other copies are not available for exhibition, the court should permit the seized film to be copied so that exhibition can be continued pending judicial resolution of the obscenity issue in an adversary proceeding. Otherwise, the film must be returned. With such safeguards, a pre-seizure adversary hearing is not mandated by the First Amendment. (Slip opinion, pp. 4–10.)

In *Roaden* the sheriff viewed the film and seized it and arrested those responsible for its showing. This was held unconstitutional—seizing a film, then being exhibited to the general public, presents essentially the same restraint on expression as the seizure of all the books in a bookstore. The High Court noted *Hosey* and then stated that here "nothing prior to seizure afforded a magistrate an opportunity to 'focus searchingly' on the question of obscenity."

Most everyone is familiar with the old adage, "take a kid fishing"; here the Court seems to say, "take a judge to the movies." This at least is the safe way for the policeman to step out of the middle. None of these cases provide all the answers and likely there will never be such a case. For now however, all of them suggest that the policeman not take it upon himself to decide what is and what is not obscene. The *Miller* case provides the elements that must be met:

(1) The scope of regulation must be confined to depiction or description of sexual conduct;

(2) The conduct must be specifically defined by State law as written or authoritatively construed;

(3) The regulation of obscene works must be limited to those which:

a. taken as a whole, appeal to the prurient interest in sex;

b. portray sexual conduct in a patently offensive way; and

c. taken as a whole, do not have serious literary, artistic, or scientific value.

Other cases concerning obscenity law enforcement decided the same day as the *Miller* case are:

(1) *Paris Adult Theater I* v. *Slayton,* 37 L.Ed. 2d 446, stating the rule that "States may regulate commerce in obscene material including public display in 'adults only' theaters."

(2) *United States* v. *Orito,* 37 L.Ed. 2d 513, and *United States* v. *12 200 ft. Reels of Film,* 37 L.Ed. 2d 500, stating the rule that "Congress has power to prevent obscene material from entering the stream of commerce whether the transportation is for commercial or private purposes."

(3) *Kaplan* v. *California,* 37 L.Ed. 2d 492, which stated the rule, "A State may control commerce in obscene material in book form whether or not it contains pictorial content in addition to text."

Earlier the Court had pointed out that the right recognized in *Stanley* was a limited one. In *United States* v. *Thirty-seven Photographs,* 402 U.S. 363, the Court held that the protected right to possess obscene material in the privacy of one's home does not give rise to a correlative right to have someone sell or give it to others.

The plethora of case law in the area of obscenity and its lack of an absolute definition has prompted one writer to comment, "What is the reason for this multiple sclerosis of the judicial faculty? It is due to the fact . . . that obscenity is a matter of taste and social custom, not of fact." Brant, *The Bill of Rights* (1965) pp. 491–492.

May we close with certain knowledge that obscenity, like the poor, we will have with us always. The first reported case involving obscene conduct was not until 1663. There, the defendant was fined for "shewing himself naked in a balkony, and throwing down bottles (pist in) vi et armis among the people in Convent Garden, contra pacem, and to the scandal of the Government." *Sir Charles Sydlyes Case,* 83 Eng. Rep. 1146 (K.B. 1663). The latest case may very well be when someone brings charges against this paper.

7-7: EXAMPLE OF NEW OBSCENITY STATUTES

The following is the City of New Orleans, Louisiana, ordinance which was amended and adopted on September 4, 1973. It provides an example of how many jurisdictions are amending their existing statutes in order to comply with the United States Supreme Court guidelines.

> SECTION I. THE COUNCIL OF THE CITY OF NEW ORLEANS, HEREBY ORDAINS, That Section 42–46 of Ordinance Number 828 M.C.S., known as the Code of New Orleans, relative to "Obscenity—Offenses defined and prohibited," be, and the same is hereby amended to read as follows:
>
> Section 42–46 Sale and Distribution of Obscene Material
>
> It is unlawful for any person to knowingly send or cause to be sent, bring or cause to be brought into the Parish of Orleans for

sale or distribution, or in this Parish prepare, publish, print, exhibit, distribute or offer to distribute, or have in his possession with intent to distribute or to exhibit or offer to distribute any obscene material.

Definitions:

A. "Obscene" means that:

(1) the average person, applying contemporary community standards, would find that the work, taken as a whole, appeals to the prurient interest; and

(2) the work depicts or describes actual or simulated acts of human sexual intercourse, sodomy, bestiality, oral copulation, masturbation, excretory functions or lewd exhibition of the genitals; and

(3) the work, taken as a whole, lacks serious literary, artistic, political or scientific value.

B. "Material" means any book, magazine, newspaper, or other printed or written material, or any picture, drawing, photograph, motion picture or other pictorial representation.

C. "Person" means any individual, partnership, firm, association, corporation or other legal entity.

D. "Distribute" means to transfer possession of, whether with or without consideration.

E. "Knowingly" means having general knowledge of or having reason to know or a belief or reasonable grounds for belief which warrants further inspection or inquiry or both of the character and content of any material described herein which is reasonably susceptible of examination by the defendant.

Section 42-46.1 Public Displays of Explicit Sexual Material

A. Purpose. It is the purpose of this section to prohibit the public display of explicit sexual material, in order to protect persons from involuntary exposure to such materials.

B. Offense Defined. A person is guilty of a misdemeanor if he knowingly fails to take prompt action to remove the public display of explicit sexual material from property in his possession.

C. Definitions:

(1) "Explicit sexual material" means any picture, drawing, photograph, motion picture, or other pictorial representation, which depicts actual or simulated acts of human sexual intercourse, sodomy, bestiality, oral copulation, masturbation, excretory functions, torture in the context of a sexual relationship, or exhibition of the genitals.

(2) "Public display" is material that is visible on a billboard, viewing screen, theatre marquee, newsstand, display rack, window, showcase, display case or other similar area that is visible from a

public street, sidewalk, park or other public place or from the property of others

(3) "Knowingly" means having general knowledge of or having reason to know or a belief or reasonable grounds for belief which warrants further inspection or inquiry or both of the character and content of any material described herein which is reasonably susceptible of examination by the defendant.

Section 42–46.2 Sale and Display of Explicit Sexual Material to Young Persons

A. Purpose. It is the purpose of this section to regulate the direct distribution of certain explicit sexual materials to young persons in order to aid parents in supervising and controlling the access of children to such material.

B. Offenses Defined. A person is guilty of a misdemeanor if he:

(1) knowingly disseminates explicit sexual material, as hereinafter defined, to young persons, or

(2) knowingly displays explicit sexual material in an area to which young persons have access, unless such material, taken as a whole, has serious artistic, literary, historical, scientific, medical, or educational value.

(3) Subsection B does not apply to a parent, guardian or other person acting in loco parentis to the young person.

C. Definitions:

(1) "Young persons" means any unmarried person less than eighteen (18) years of age.

(2) "Explicit sexual material" means:

a. Any picture, drawing, photograph, motion picture or other pictorial representation of uncovered human genitals, of human sexual intercourse, sodomy, oral copulation, bestiality, masturbation or direct physical stimulation of clothed or unclothed genitals, of torture in the context of a sexual relationship, or any description of, advertisement of or offer to sell such pictorial material where such description or advertisement includes such materials; or

b. any *artificial* human penis or vagina or device primarily designed physically to stimulate genitals, or any description, advertisement or offer to sell or distribute such an artificial organ or device where such description or advertisement presents either a pictorial representation or a detailed verbal description of such organ or device or its manner of use; or

c. any book, magazine, newspaper or other printed or written material, which is made up in whole or in dominant part of depiction or descriptions of human sexual intercourse, oral copulation, bestiality, sodomy, masturbation or torture in the context of a sexual relationship.

(3) "Disseminate" means to transfer possession of, whether with or without consideration.

(4) "Knowingly" means having general knowledge of or having reason to know or a belief or reasonable grounds for belief which warrants further inspection or inquiry or both of the character and content of any material described herein which is reasonably susceptible of examination by the defendant.

Section 42-46.3 Obscene Live Conduct

It shall be unlawful for any person to knowingly engage or participate in, manage, produce, sponsor, present or exhibit obscene live conduct, with production, performance or exhibition, when taken as a whole, lacks serious literary, theatrical or artistic value, to be before an audience consisting of at least one person or spectator on any street, sidewalk, park or other public place or in any place exposed to public view, or in any place open to the public or to a segment thereof, whether or not an admission fee is charged or whether or not attendance is conditioned upon the presentation of a membership card.

Definitions:

A. "Obscene live conduct" is:

(1) the actual or simulated performance of acts of human sexual intercourse, masturbation, sodomy, bestiality, oral copulation or excretory functions; or

(2) the actual or simulated touching, caressing, or fondling of the anus, genitals or female breast; or

(3) the actual or simulated displaying of the pubic hairs, anus, vulva, genitals or nipples of the female breast.

B. "Knowingly" means having general knowledge of or having reason to know or a belief or reasonable grounds for belief which warrants further inspection or inquiry or both of the character of any conduct described herein.

7-8: PROFANITY AND PUBLIC DRUNKENNESS

Most states have statutes which make it a misdemeanor to profanely swear or curse, or use vulgar and indecent language, or to be drunk in any public place. Some of these statutes require that two or more persons, other than the violator, be present, and others provide that the vulgar language violation be committed in the presence of a female.

In determining what a public place is, one could say that it is any place which, by general invitation, members of the public attend for reasons of business, entertainment, instructions, or the like, and are welcome so long as they conform to what is customarily done there.[24] In one federal decision, the court said that a highway or street was a public place within the meaning of one state statute, even though the statute required that the offense be done "in the presence of two or more persons," because of the likelihood that two or more people would pass by.[25]

7-9: PROSTITUTION

Prostitution has been defined as "common lewdness of a woman for gain; whoredom; the act or practice of a woman who permits any man who will pay her price to have sexual intercourse with her. The act or practice of a female of prostituting or offering her body to an indiscriminate intercourse with men for money or its equivalent."[26]

The crime of prostitution is a misdemeanor in many states, and in some states it is also a crime to aid or abet prostitution or to procure or solicit, to reside in, or to enter or remain in any place used for the purpose of prostitution. In other jurisdictions, it is a crime to procure a female for the purpose of prostitution or to accept money from a prostitute. In most states where these laws are in effect, they are generally not strictly enforced.

7-10: UNNATURAL INTERCOURSE

If generally applied, this crime would include almost any unnatural sexual act. When narrowly applied, it generally refers to sodomy or bestiality. In any case, these crimes are defined by the prevailing statutes of the particular jurisdiction and are usually punishable as felonies.

7-11: PEEPING TOM

A peeping Tom is "a person who makes it a habit of sneaking up to windows and peeping in, for the purpose generally of seeing the women of the household in the nude."[27] This crime is often referred to as voyeurism in many statutes and is usually punishable as a felony.

Discretion should be used in the prosecution of this crime, because, in order to be found guilty, the person accused must have trespassed on the property of the one offended. In other words, the eyes alone cannot trespass, and if the person is standing on the street or sidewalk or other place where he has a right to be, he cannot be guilty of the offense. Another point of interest is that a female who does not wish to be observed in the nude will usually close the drapes, blinds, or pull the shade in order to cover the open window or other opening, as it is the nature of the male to observe the beauty of the female, especially when the latter is unclothed!

SECTION 8: OFFENSES AGAINST PUBLIC PEACE AND SAFETY

8-1: DISORDERLY CONDUCT

The word "disorderly" is defined by *Black's Law Dictionary* as meaning "contrary to the rules of good order and behavior; violative of the public peace or good order; turbulent, riotous, or indecent," and almost every state and city has a statute or ordinance relating to this misdemeanor offense.

Disorderly conduct is "a term of loose and indefinite meaning (except as occasionally defined in statutes), but signifying generally any behavior that is contrary to law, and more particularly such as tends to disturb the public peace or decorum, scandalize the community, or shock the public sense of morality."[28]

Since the officer deals with this offense very often, he should become fully familiar with the prevailing statutes in his jurisdiction. Among the states, there are various statutes which cover disorderly conduct in general, the use of profane or indecent language in certain places, acts intended to provoke a breach of the peace, interference with business, and failure to comply with requests or commands of police officers and others. In many instances, except for the general disorderly conduct statute, these other related misdemeanors are rarely enforced, possibly because of changing community standards of behavior.

8-2: DISTURBING THE PEACE

Like disorderly conduct, the misdemeanor offense of disturbing the peace is a relatively minor offense which is defined by statute or ordinance. It is generally defined as "any act causing annoyance, disgust, agitation, or derangement to another, or interrupting his peace, or interfering with him in the pursuit of a lawful and appropriate occupation or contrary to the usages of a sort of meeting and class of persons assembled that interferes with its due progress or irritates the assembly in whole or in part."[29] An early common law definition was "a wrong done to an incorporeal hereditament* by hindering or disquieting the owner in the enjoyment of it."[30] Disturbance of the peace is also defined as "interruption of the peace, quiet, and good order of a neighborhood or community, particularly by unnecessary and distracting noises."[31]

With these general definitions in mind, let us now examine the application of disturbing-the-peace and disorderly-conduct statutes. First, it is quite common for an officer to make mistakes while trying to enforce these types of

---

*Hereditaments are those things which are capable of being inherited.

statutes. He usually assumes that they cover any situation in which any person's peace is disturbed or anyone is disorderly and often does not concern himself with *where* these actions take place. For example, officers respond to a domestic disturbance as a result of a telephone call from the wife of the one who is "raising hell." The husband in this instance may not have committed either crime, disturbing the peace or disorderly conduct, if no one other than the wife was affected by his conduct. It is said that "every man's home is his castle," and it would seem that he would have a broad right to the personal enjoyment of his home as long as he does not infringe on the rights of other persons to enjoy their own homes. However, if neighbors or others in close proximity complain, then the officer might be justified in taking the necessary legal actions to quell the disturbance.

This is not to say, however, that an officer who was on the property legally could not make an arrest for other crimes committed in his presence. As stated earlier, the officer may enter the premises legally if he has a valid writ issued from a proper court or if he is invited in by anyone having a possessory right to the premises. He may also enter in order to investigate if he has probable cause to believe that a crime has been or is being committed. However, he should remember that when the crime is a misdemeanor as here, it must be committed in his presence or he must have a proper writ.

Because these statutes are quite general, they are often misunderstood, and, unfortunately, sometimes abused by officers. For example, officers may not use such statutes as a subterfuge to preserve racial segregation of places open to the public; such attempts have been held to be unconstitutional. However, if a group or an individual is attempting, lawfully, to desegregate a public facility, and a breach of the peace is threatened or carried out, it is within the officer's authority to arrest for the unlawful actions involved in the breach of the peace.[32]

Every state and most cities have numerous statutes which deal with disturbances of many different types. Some of the most common are disturbance of the public peace, disturbance in a public place, disturbance of the family, disturbance of worship, and disturbance by explosions, noises, and offensive conduct. In any case, the officer should be completely familiar with the applicable statutes in his jurisdiction, because a major portion of his on-duty time is spent in dealing with this type of offense.

8-3: REGISTRATION OF CONVICTED FELONS

All states have statutes requiring a convicted felon who resides in or enters the state and remains for a specified period to register with a prescribed law enforcement agency. Such registration usually consists of a statement in writing of the information required and the fingerprints and photograph of the person. Such statutes also provide for re-registration if the convicted felon changes his residence while in the state. These registration records are usually forwarded by the law enforcement agency of local jurisdiction to a central records bureau where a permanent, up-to-date file is kept, which is available to any bona fide law enforcement officer or agency. Failure to register is generally punishable as a misdemeanor.

8-4: TRAMPS AND VAGRANTS

At one time, every jurisdiction had some type of statute which made it a misdemeanor for persons to go about as tramps or vagrants, having no visible means of support or livelihood. Today, in our so-called permissive society, many of these statutes are not enforced, in some cases because of their vagueness and in others because of changes in community standards. In other jurisdictions, these statutes have been held unconstitutional, not because they were so on their face, but primarily because some officers used them as an excuse to arrest and hold persons against whom they were prejudiced or to do other acts which the officer had no valid legal basis for doing. For this reason, it is unusual for a person to be charged with being a tramp or vagrant today.

SECTION 9: DEADLY WEAPONS AND EXPLOSIVES

9-1: CARRYING DEADLY WEAPONS

Every state has statutes regulating the carrying of or the use of a deadly weapon in the commission of a crime. The following Mississippi statute is presented as an example:

CHAPTER 37–MISSISSIPPI CODE OF 1972,
REVISED and ANNOTATED

97-37-1. Deadly weapons–carrying deadly weapon and use of imitation firearm prohibited–penalties.

Any person who carries, concealed in whole or in part, any bowie knife, dirk knife, butcher knife, switchblade knife, metallic knuckles, blackjack, slingshot, pistol, revolver, or any rifle with a barrel of less than eighteen (18) inches in length, or any shotgun with a barrel of less than eighteen (18) inches in length, machine gun or any fully automatic firearm or deadly weapon, or any muffler or silencer for any firearm, whether or not it is accompanied by a firearm, or uses or attempts to use against another person any imitation firearm, shall upon conviction be punished as follows:

(a) By a fine of not less than one hundred dollars ($100.00), nor more than five hundred dollars ($500.00), or by imprisonment in the county jail for not more than six (6) months, or both, in the discretion of the court, for the first conviction under this section.

(b) By a fine of not less than one hundred dollars ($100.00), nor more than five hundred dollars ($500.00), and imprisonment in the county jail for not less than thirty (30) days, nor more than six (6) months, for the second conviction under this section.

(c) By imprisonment in the state penitentiary for not less than one (1) year, nor more than five (5) years, for the third or more convictions under this section.

(d) By imprisonment in the state penitentiary for not less than one (1) year, nor more than five (5) years, for any person previously convicted of any felony, who is convicted under this section.

97-37-3. Deadly weapons—forfeiture of weapon.

Any deadly weapon used in violation of section 97-37-1 shall be seized by the arresting officer, introduced in evidence, and in the event of a conviction, shall be ordered to be forfeited, and shall be disposed of as ordered by the court having jurisdiction of such offense.

97-37-5. Deadly weapons—possession by convicted felon as evidence of crime.

The possession of any deadly weapon as described in section 97-37-1 by any person who has been convicted of a felony under the laws of this state, any other state, or of the United States, shall be prima facie evidence of a violation of that section.

97-37-7. Deadly weapons—persons permitted to carry weapons—bond.

It shall not be a violation of section 97-37-1 or any other statute for pistols, firearms or other suitable and appropriate weapons to be carried by duly constituted bank guards, company guards, watchmen, railroad special agents or duly authorized representatives, agents or employees of a patrol service, guard service, or a company engaged in the business of transporting money, securities or other valuables, or persons similarly employed and engaged, while actually engaged in the performance of their duties as such, provided that such persons are under bond in a sum of not less than one thousand dollars ($1000.00) for the lawful and faithful performance of their duties . . . .

97-37-9. Deadly weapons—defenses against indictment for carrying deadly weapons.

Any person indicted or charged for a violation of section 97-37-1 may show as a defense:

(a) that he was threatened, and had good and sufficient reason to apprehend a serious attack from any enemy, and that he did so apprehend; or

(b) that he was traveling and was not a tramp, or was setting out on a journey and was not a tramp; or

(c) that he was a law enforcement or peace officer in the discharge of his duties; or
(d) that he was at the time in the discharge of his duties as a mail carrier; or
(e) that he was at the time engaged in transporting valuables for an express company or bank; or
(f) that he was a member of the Armed Forces of the United States, National Guard, State Militia, Civil Defense Corps, guard or patrolman in a state or municipal institution while in the performance of his official duties; or
(g) that he was in lawful pursuit of a felon; or
(h) that he was lawfully engaged in legitimate sports; or
(i) that at the time he was a company guard, bank guard, watchman, or other person enumerated in section 97-37-7, and was then actually engaged in the performance of his duties as such . . . .

In the application of most deadly weapon statutes, many officers are inclined to place too much emphasis on whether the weapon is concealed or not. The various courts do not place a great deal of emphasis on this issue, and the officer should not either. Most courts have generally held that a deadly weapon creates a danger to the officer whether concealed or not and that the exigency of the situation is the determining issue. Although everyone agrees that a criminal should not be allowed to carry a weapon, there are those who say, "When guns are outlawed only outlaws will have guns." Enforcement of these statutes is not an easy or simple task, since it involves finding the right balance between the individual's right to protect himself and the public's right to safety. In addition, the Second Amendment to the Constitution states that the right of the people to keep and bear arms, shall not be infringed."

With these considerations in mind, it is suggested that the officer seize any deadly weapon found incident to an arrest and charge the person with possession of it. This would include those who are committing and those who are attempting to commit a crime. On the other hand, if an officer had no lawful or valid reason to know or suspect that a person possesses a deadly weapon, he should not be obsessed with the idea that every person he meets on the street has a gun or that the person would use it for anything other than self-protection.

The Federal Gun Control Act of 1968, enacted by Congress on October 22, 1968, repealed the Federal Firearms Act of 1938 and amended the National Firearms Act of 1934. In addition, Title VII of the Omnibus Crime Control and Safe Streets Act of 1968 was amended and included in the Gun Control Act. Although the primary jurisdiction and responsibility for the enforcement of all federal firearms laws is vested in the Alcohol, Tobacco and Firearms Division of the Internal Revenue Service (A.T.&F.), the officer should, at the least, have some basic idea of what the Gun Control Act provides.

Congress declared that the purpose of the act is to provide support to federal, state, and local law enforcement officials in their fight against crime and violence, and not to place any undue or unnecessary federal restrictions or burdens on law-abiding citizens with respect to the acquisition, possession, or use of firearms appropriate for the purpose of hunting, trapshooting, target shooting, personal protection, or any other lawful activity. It is also not intended to discourage or eliminate the private ownership or use of firearms by law-abiding citizens for lawful purposes or to impose by federal regulation any procedures or requirements other than those reasonably necessary to implement and effectuate the act.

The Gun Control Act of 1968 is divided into three titles. Title I requires the licensing of manufacturers, importers, and dealers of firearms and ammunition. However, antique firearms are not included in the act. It does, however, require the licensing of collectors who acquire or dispose of firearms or ammunition as curios or relics in interstate or foreign commerce. A permit from the A.T.&F. is required for the importation of firearms or ammunition, and the importation of all military surplus firearms is prohibited. Firearms imported or manufactured on or after December 16, 1968, are required to have serial numbers. With certain exceptions, the transportation, shipment, or receipt of firearms or ammunition in interstate or foreign commerce by anyone other than federal licensees is prohibited. The act prohibits over-the-counter sales or delivery of rifles or shotguns or rifle or shotgun ammunition to persons under 18 years of age and the sale or delivery of a handgun or handgun ammunition to persons under 21 years of age. The selling, trading, giving, transporting, or delivering of any firearm by a non-licensee to another non-licensee who is not a resident of the same state is prohibited, and the sale or delivery of firearms or ammunition by licensees in violation of state or local law is also prohibited. The shipment, transportation, or receipt of firearms in interstate or foreign commerce by (1) fugitives from justice; (2) convicted felons; (3) persons under indictment for a felony; (4) unlawful users of narcotics or drugs; and (5) persons adjudicated as mental defectives or those having been committed to a mental institution is prohibited. The shipment, transportation, or receipt of stolen firearms or ammunition, or firearms from which the serial number has been removed, obliterated, or altered is also prohibited.

The act permits the renting or lending of firearms to non-residents for temporary use for lawful purposes. It also permits the sale, under sworn statement, of rifles or shotguns to non-residents who are engaged in lawful hunting or organized shooting competitions and whose firearms have been lost, stolen, or become inoperable. The sale of rifles and shotguns to a resident of a contiguous state is permitted, providing the purchaser's state has passed specific enabling legislation which allows it. As of September 1, 1969, only 25 states had enacted such legislation.

An antique firearm is defined in the act as any firearm made in or before 1898, or any replica thereof, if the replica is not designed or re-designed for using rimfire or conventional center-fire ammunition, or uses fixed ammunition no longer manufactured in the United States and not readily available in ordinary commercial channels of trade. Ammunition includes cartridge cases, primers, bullets, and propellent powder. Shot and unprimed non-metallic shot shell cases are excluded.

Title II of the Gun Control Act imposes special occupational taxes on manufacturers, importers and dealers of firearms coming under that title. In addition, the licensing requirement of Title I must also be met. Individuals must pay a making or transfer tax on all firearms included in Title II and must register the firearms with the A.T.&F. The following is a listing of the types of firearms which are included:

1. all fully automatic firearms;
2. all rifles with barrels of less than 16 inches in length or overall length of less than 26 inches;
3. all shotguns with barrels of less than 18 inches in length or overall length of less than 26 inches;
4. any handgun with a shoulder stock;
5. other concealable firearms, except pistols and revolvers;
6. silencers and mufflers for firearms;
7. destructive devices, such as bombs, grenades, bazookas, rockets, mines, and incendiary bombs.

None of these firearms or destructive devices may now be registered, except to bona fide law enforcement agencies. Anyone having such firearms or destructive devices included under Title II who has not previously registered them with the A.T.&F. is subject to imprisonment for not more than 10 years, a fine of $10,000, or both. It would seem that unregistered firearms and destructive devices could be confiscated by the A.T.&F. Persons having registered firearms or devices enumerated in Title II must obtain permission from the A.T.&F. prior to moving them across a state line unless such movement is done in the performance of an official duty as a law enforcement officer.

Title VII of the Safe Streets Act prohibits the transportation, possession, or receipt of *any* firearm in interstate or foreign commerce by (1) convicted felons; (2) persons dishonorably discharged from the Armed Services; (3) persons adjudicated to be mentally incompetent; (4) aliens illegally in the United States; and (5) citizens who have renounced their citizenship.

It should be noted here that any officer who is confronted by any situation in which he believes there may be a violation of the Federal Firearms Act should contact the A.T.&F. office located in his jurisdiction, in addition to charging the violator with a violation of state or local law.[33]

9-2: DEADLY WEAPONS—OTHER VIOLATIONS

Many states have statutes which make it a misdemeanor to exhibit any deadly weapon in a rude, angry, or threatening manner, not in necessary self-defense, or to so exhibit a weapon unlawfully in a fight or quarrel. In a prosecution under such statutes it is not usually necessary to prove or to aver that the firearm so used was loaded or even capable of being fired, since the gist of the offense is the threat of use rather than the actual use of the weapon. Other statutes prohibit students of colleges and universities from possessing deadly weapons on campus. There are statutes which prohibit minors from possessing or carrying concealed weapons, and some of these even provide for punishment of a parent or guardian who knowingly allows such a violation to occur.

9-3: EXPLOSIVES

In addition to federal laws, every state has statutory provisions which make it unlawful to possess or use explosives in the commission of a crime. These crimes are usually serious felonies; however, making a false report of the placing of explosives is generally a serious misdemeanor. The officer should examine the statutes of his own jurisdiction in order to determine what permits are required to use or possess explosives and the safety precautions which must be taken in order to transport them.

SUMMARY AND APPLICATION

Unlike the preceding chapters, which concentrated on law enforcement techniques and criminal procedure, this chapter is mainly concerned with substantive criminal law. In the following hypothetical situations, several, one, or no crimes may have occurred. In order to determine how many and which crimes were committed, the reader must consider the necessary elements of each crime and then see if each is present in the situation described.

PROBLEM I

Frank B. Sott, a drunken bum, entered a bar to buy a drink. After being seated, he was served a double shot of bourbon and a beer chaser. He tendered the bartender a $500 bill in payment. The bartender took the bill, walked approximately 10 feet to the cash register, and suddenly realized that there was not enough money to change the $500 bill. The bartender turned to Honest Everett, who was sitting at the bar having a ginger ale, handed the $500 to him and asked him to go and get it changed. Everett accepted the bill and made his exit without uttering a word, never to return. Everett was not employed at the bar nor did the bartender know him to be honest. What crimes were committed and who committed them? What reasoning should be applied?

PROBLEM II

William Goodnature met Sam Friendlie on the street. Bill was feeling his Cheerios so he attacked Sam with his fists. Sam blocked the blow and hit Bill once, knocking him to the pavement. Bill's head struck the curb, and he was killed instantly. Bill was 6 feet 4 inches tall and weighed 98 pounds. Sam was 4 feet 8 inches tall and weighed 220 pounds. Was there a crime committed? Is weight a determining factor here?

PROBLEM III

Johnnie Walker was taking his usual afternoon stroll in the countryside. It was raining and he wanted to smoke, so he broke into a barn in order to light his pipe. He did no damage in breaking in, but while lighting his pipe, he set fire to the barn and it burned, up or down, and in any event it burned Little Boy Blue to death who was fast asleep in the hay. What crimes were committed by John and what reasoning should be applied?

PROBLEM IV

Judith Cash wanted to give her friends a Christmas present, so she wrote them each a check for $50. The checks were written on the Last National Bank of St. Louis, Indiana Branch, and when her friends attempted to cash the checks they found that Judith had no account at the bank. To say the least, they were deeply hurt and insulted. Was a crime committed? What theory should be applied?

PROBLEM V

Patrick Pigeondrop went to the home of Ezra N. Ernest and told Ezra that he was the lucky winner of first prize in a National Sweepstakes, which was $10,000 worth of furniture, but that he (Ezra) would have to pay the cost of delivery which was $200. Ezra gave Pat the $200. and received a receipt. Pat assured him that the furniture would be delivered just as soon as the moving company could schedule the delivery, probably within four weeks. However, the next day, at the office, Ezra hears that Pat is a crook who has been involved in all kinds of get-rich schemes. You are a police officer and live next door to Ezra. Since you know the law, Ezra comes to you for advice, because he wants Pat to be prosecuted. What advice do you give him?

PROBLEM VI

John Dillinger decided to rob a bank, so he got a plan of the bank, bought a gun, and then "cased the job." He then got in touch with "Baby Face" Nelson and asked him to drive the get-away car for 25 per cent of the "take." While John was in the bank, a policeman approached Baby Face to advise him to move from a "No Parking" zone. Baby Face got nervous, shot the policeman, killing him instantly, then left without John. As John came out of the bank, he was apprehended by other officers who told him what Baby Face had done. He stated that they didn't plan to shoot anyone, and if he had known that it would happen he would have gone to the movies instead. What is the most significant crime committed and who committed it?

PROBLEM VII

Norris Nearsighted, who was somewhat inebriated, pried open a door and entered the wrong house, thinking that he was at his own house and his wife would not let him in. He was arrested inside the house and charged with burglary by local police. Is he guilty of burglary? What reasoning should be applied in arriving at the correct answer?

PROBLEM VIII

Mat Dillon wants to frighten Festus in order to get him to do some work around the jail. While Festus is not looking, Mat quickly checks his "buntline" to make sure it is not loaded. He then screams, points the gun at Festus, and pulls the trigger. Festus is frightened and jumps up from the chair where he was sleeping, hits the gun in Mat's hand, which does fire. The bullet passes through the window, creases Doc's forehead, ricochets and passes through the open door of the Longbranch and strikes Kitty in her left "chest cavity," killing her instantly. What crimes, if any, have been committed? Mat later says that he has been hearing voices and they make him feel confused. Will this affect your answer?

PROBLEM IX

Joe Desperate made plans to murder his business partner and purchased a $500,000 insurance policy on him. He told his secretary, who he had been intimate with, of the plans and asked her to drive him to the murder scene. She did as asked, and both were apprehended after the crime, while hiding in

Joe's mother's wine cellar. Joe's mother was away in Europe at the time, but she had left the butler specific instructions that the two be hidden in the wine cellar. What crimes were committed, by whom, and what theory should be used in reaching a decision?

PROBLEM X

Gail Hungry approached Ima Skinflint while the latter was powdering her nose in the powder room of the Blades Inn. Gail picked up Ima's purse, and Ima said, "That's my purse!" Gail stated, "If you open your mouth I'll tell everything," and then left with the purse, which contained $8.43, two pairs of black lace bikini briefs, and a centerfold from Playgirl magazine. What crime was committed by Gail?

PROBLEM XI

Tess Truelove was living with her friend Clyde in his apartment at the Ritz. While Clyde was away one night attending a burlesque show, Tess broke into Clyde's locked trunk in order to steal some comic books which Clyde had had since he was a small child. However, after opening the trunk, Tess found that the comic books were not there, so she packed her clothes and went to stay with another friend named Bruce. Clyde came home and found the open trunk, and although there was nothing missing, he would like to press charges against Tess. What crime, if any, was committed by Tess? Why?

PROBLEM XII

A 16-year-old boy was driving along a highway with his father. A patrol officer observed their vehicle make a traffic violation. It was night, and the officer immediately gave chase with intent to stop the vehicle and issue a traffic citation for the violation. Upon noticing the officer's flashing "blue lights," the father told his son, "Turn your headlights off, drive as fast as you can, and don't stop for the fuzz!" The young boy did as he was told, and hit another vehicle head-on, killing the occupant of the other vehicle. What crimes were committed and who should be charged?

PROBLEM XIII

Officer Shifty Doright was parked at an intersection, observing the flow of traffic, when another unit called via radio and asked Shifty to stop a red 1970 Ford. About 5 minutes later, Shifty saw the vehicle pass through the intersection. Shifty stopped the car, approached it, and requested to see the driver's operator's license. At this point, T.C. Goodboy, a passenger, got out on the other side of the vehicle and approached Officer Shifty as the latter unsnapped the leather strap on his holster. T.C. said, "Well! It looks like a damn pig has his stinger out. You fuzz always go around putting your hands on people who are afraid of you–why don't you put them on me?" Shifty jerked his weapon from its holster and hit T.C. with it. T.C. then hit Shifty once with his fist, knocking him to the pavement. T.C. took Shifty's gun and blackjack, but did not use either of them against Shifty. T.C. and the driver then left the scene, and returned the weapons to the officer's shift captain the next day. Shifty is 27 years old and weighs 195 pounds. T.C. is also 27 years old but weighs only 175 pounds. What crimes were committed, if any, and what reasoning should be used in arriving at an answer?

PROBLEM XIV

You are the officer assigned to patrol the "midnight" shift. You observe a car parked on the shoulder of the highway which is in your jurisdiction. It is cold and raining. The vehicle is not causing a traffic hazard, but since it appears to be abandoned and the weather is so bad, you decide to stop and check it out. When you look into the car you see Frank Sot passed out drunk on the front seat. The motor is not running, the gear shift is in "park" position, and there is no key in the ignition. Can Frank be charged with a crime? What procedure should be followed in handling Frank?

PROBLEM XV

Bill Neverforget had had a profound dislike for Steve Friendlie ever since they were small boys and neighbors on the same block. Bill's dislike for Steve began when Steve stole Bill's sucker one day when they were playing in a sandbox at age 4. Bill's dislike grew through the years until one day, on their 46th birthday, he took a 12-gauge shotgun and shot Steve four or five times with "00" buckshot. Bill did not intend to kill Steve, only to wound him. Before Steve died, he told the doctor that Bill shot him but he didn't think Bill really intended to kill him. What crime, if any, should Bill be charged with and why?

PROBLEM XVI

You, the officer, stop a motorist, check his driver's license and registration plate, and ask why he ran off the pavement onto the shoulder several times. He explains that hot cigarette ashes dropped on his leg and that he was trying to remove them before the seat was burned. He offers to show you a burned spot on the seat. It is night; you look inside and see the burn, but in your flashlight beam, you also notice a pistol butt protruding from under the seat directly under the burned spot. You pick the weapon up and ask whom it belongs to. The driver states that it is his brother's gun, which he is borrowing for a short time. Explaining further, the driver states that threats were made on his life several months earlier, but that the party who made them had been arrested and was presently in custody. If the driver is charged with possessing a concealed weapon, would the officer likely have a good case?

REFERENCES

1. Black's Law Dictionary, rev. 4th ed., St. Paul, West Publishing Co., 1968, p. 867.
2. Ibid., p. 867.
3. Ibid., p. 1170.
4. Ibid., p. 1171.
5. Ibid., p. 1427.
6. *State* v. *Huggins,* 87 A. 630 (1913).
7. Black's Law Dictionary, rev. 4th ed., St. Paul, West Publishing Co., 1968, p. 1228.
8. *Gaston* v. *State,* 123 So.2d 546 (1960).
9. *Wilbourn* v. *State,* 164 S.2d 424 (1964).
10. Black's Law Dictionary, rev. 4th ed., St. Paul, West Publishing Co., 1968, p. 1474.
11. *Deaton* v. *State,* 102 So. 175 (1924).
12. *Pettis* v. *State,* 48 So.2d 355 (1950).
13. *Smith* v. *State,* 208 So.2d 746 (1968).
14. Black's Law Dictionary, rev. 4th ed., St. Paul, West Publishing Co., 1968, p. 1297.
15. Ibid., p. 1674.
16. Ibid., p. 779.
17. Ibid., p. 420.
18. Mississippi Code of 1972, Revised and Annotated, Sec. 97-23-49.
19. Mississippi Code of 1972, Revised and Annotated, Sec. 97-23-51.
20. *Franzetti* v. *Franzetti,* 120 S.W.2d 123 (1938).
21. *Banks* v. *State,* 11 So. 404 (1892).
22. *State* v. *Pfenninger,* 76 Mo. App. 313 (1898).
23. Black's Law Dictionary, rev. 4th ed., St. Paul, West Publishing Co., 1968, p. 1227.
24. *Nelson* v. *Natchez,* 19 So.2d 747 (1944).
25. *United States* v. *Hathorn,* 451 F.2d 1337 (1971).
26. Black's Law Dictionary, rev. 4th ed., St. Paul, West Publishing Co., 1968, p. 1386.
27. *Browder* v. *Cook,* 59 F. Supp. 225 (1944).
28. Black's Law Dictionary, rev. 4th ed., St. Paul, West Publishing Co., 1968, p. 556.
29. *State* v. *Mancini,* 91 Vt. 507 (1916).
30. 3 Blackstone's Commentaries 235.
31. Black's Law Dictionary, rev. 4th ed., St. Paul West Publishing Co., 1968, p. 563.
32. *Thomas* v. *Mississippi,* 380 U.S. 524 (1965); *Baily* v. *Patterson,* 369 U.S. 31 (1962).
33. Public Law 90-618, 90th Congress, H.R. 17735, October 22, 1968.

CIVIL?
CRIMINAL?

CHAPTER VI

HANDLING JUVENILE OFFENDERS

"One must give something for what he gets."
"Always listen to children, even when they are not talking."

A FATHER

In an eastern state, during the early morning hours, three youthful inmates of a boys' training school attacked a 48-year-old correctional officer while they were attempting to escape. The three youths, Stan, 15, Larry, 17, and Jim, 16, approached the officer from behind as he was sitting at a desk in the dormitory and struck him repeatedly with a desk lamp, broom handle, and their fists. He died approximately two months later from injuries inflicted by the trio.

After beating the officer into insensibility and obtaining his keys, the three boys ran down the stairs only to be apprehended by other officers before they could make their way to freedom. The trio admitted to investigating officers that they had been planning the escape for about a week. Jurisdiction was waived by juvenile court and the three youths were bound over to the superior court to be tried as adults for first degree murder of the officer.

Stan and Larry pled guilty to manslaughter and were sentenced to a maximum term of from 5 to 15 years in prison. It was recommended that Stan be kept in a maximum security cell, and in passing sentence, the judge said, "Although the youngest, he was the ringleader and apparently the most vicious." Jim also pled guilty, but final sentencing was postponed indefinitely.

Were these youths' backgrounds a contributing factor in the commission of the crime? It would seem so in this case, although one cannot conclude that an offender's background is an essential factor in every case. Compare the general background and criminal activities of each youth.

Stan came from a very poor home and has not seen his father since infancy. Both parents were of questionable character and led a nomadic existence, traveling throughout the South. Stan's mother remarried, and both she and her present husband are alcoholics. In 1958, Stan was arrested on twelve charges of housebreaking and was released with only a warning on each occasion. Later, he left home without permission after stealing $100 from his mother, and, after being located, was again placed on probation and released. Numerous arrests were added to Stan's record when he was involved in thefts of motorbikes and automobiles. As a result of an automobile theft, he was placed in an institution in a southern state, but he escaped. Upon apprehension, he was sentenced to confinement in the boys' training school until he reached his twenty-first birthday.

Jim's parents were divorced after years of an "off-and-on" marriage. Both remarried, and Jim went to live with his father and stepmother. He complained that his stepmother did not care for him, and he had considerable trouble with her. Both Jim's parents spent time in correctional or penal institutions and are classed as persons of poor habits and character. Jim reached only the fifth grade in school, and he shows marked feelings of inferiority and insecurity. In 1957, Jim was charged with molesting an 8-year-old girl. Fortunately, a neighborhood woman had noticed that something was wrong and scared him away. He was referred to a state medical clinic; the examiners reported that they "rather doubted that Jim had any sexual aspirations." He was released, and no further action taken. Later in 1957, Jim was arrested approximately 32 times by numerous police agencies, and in December, 1957, he was committed to a state school. He escaped from this institution over 40 times and was an escapee when he and another youth broke into a church and stole $100. Using the stolen money, the youths went to a northeastern state where they committed several burglaries. In February, 1960, Jim was sentenced to the boys' training school.

Although Larry's father died when Larry was 6 years old, his mother was able to provide a very comfortable living for him, because his father had left considerable property. Larry, however, dropped out of school during the tenth grade because of lack of interest and constant truancy. After quitting school, he worked at a filling station and also drove a delivery truck. He began to associate with persons of bad reputation, and this is believed to be the reason for his initial involvement in criminal activities. Larry, along with other companions, stole several automobiles and traveled through many different states, using money obtained from burglaries. Before abandoning these automobiles, they kicked out the dashboards and broke all the windows. Larry was arrested in November, 1969, after being pursued by police into a dead-end street.

In passing sentence on the trio, the judge commented, "The fact that these defendants are young is not a mitigating circumstance as far as their crime is concerned. They are really murderers."

On the afternoon of April 30, 1960, an 80-year-old grocer was killed during the robbery of his store in a northeastern city. Police launched an intensive investigation, and 3 days later, before any suspects could be apprehended, a 64-year-old filling station attendant was shot to death in the same manner. Virgil, aged 16, was picked up as a suspect in the two robbery-killings but was released when his mother stated that he had been at home at the time of the slayings. On May 5, 1960, Virgil and another youth were arrested in a neighboring city for possession of a stolen automobile; both youths had been drinking heavily. They were returned to their home city because the car had been stolen in that area. During questioning, Virgil admitted breaking into a filling station and stealing $15 and a revolver. He then admitted that with the revolver he had shot and killed the 64-year-old filling station attendant after robbing him. He also confessed to shooting the 80-year-old grocer with the stolen gun during the robbery, which netted $29.

After being adjudged sane, Virgil was tried separately for the two murders. On July 31, 1960, he was sentenced to life imprisonment for the murder of the filling station attendant. On October 3, 1960, he was tried for the murder of the grocer, and again was given life imprisonment, the sentences to run consecutively.

What was Virgil's background and prior criminal record? Like many other youthful offenders, Virgil never got along very well with his parents, and it was learned at the trial that his mother had been accused of adultery by her husband, who alleged that Virgil was not his offspring. The husband worked at many different jobs and spent most evenings playing guitar in skid-row taverns.

Virgil got in trouble for the first time in 1955, when he admitted setting fire to a parochial school. He was only 10 years old at the time and set the fire because he didn't like the Sisters who taught there. He was released and no action was taken. Approximately 1 year later, Virgil again was arrested for attempting to set fire to the school. He admitted entering through an unlocked window, ransacking all the desks, and setting fire to the teacher's desk. Virgil was then made a ward of the court and was placed in an orphanage where he remained until 1958. In October, 1958, after his release, Virgil was again arrested and charged with burglary and larceny of a filling station. He also confessed to nine other burglaries. Virgil was sentenced to the state training school for boys and remained in custody until early 1960, when he was released. He was free on parole when he committed the two murders.

Virgil showed no remorse for his crimes and summed up his feelings by stating, "Ain't I a bad boy?" Asked why he stole the gun, Virgil told police, "I intended to use it in an armed robbery." When asked if he had planned to shoot anyone with the gun, he replied, "No, I never thought about that. I'm not looking for pity. Maybe I'd do it again."

During February and March of 1960, 17-year-old William went on a coast-to-coast murder spree, leaving seven persons dead in the wake of his blood and bullets trail. When apprehended, William admitted the cold-blooded murders of the seven, including one person in a southwestern coastal state, three in a southern state, and three in a southeastern state. He preyed upon service station operators, robbing them and shooting them in the head with a .22-caliber pistol. He was captured after shooting and killing a 62-year-old woman. This victim was shot in the head with two slugs from the pistol, which had been stolen by William in a southeastern state before the murder spree began.

William was tried in May, 1960, for the first degree murder of the 62-year-old woman. He was convicted, but the jury recommended mercy and he thus escaped the electric chair. He was sentenced to life imprisonment on May 12, 1960. The state's attorney who prosecuted the case, clearly disappointed in the verdict, stated, "Give William the mercy he gave his 62-year-old victim in her last minutes on earth." An insanity plea was avoided as a result of a psychiatrist's statement that William was perfectly sane. The possibility still exists, however, that William may be tried in other jurisdictions for the murders committed in those areas.

As for William's background, it is very similar to the others discussed previously. He came from a family of 10 children. His mother died when he was very young, and he was reared by his father. A sister told authorities that the father beat all his children, and that prior to his wife's death, she had been partially paralyzed from beatings he inflicted upon her. Reportedly, the father's only interest in the children from the beginning was abusing them. In addition to his brothers and sisters, William had 22 nephews and nieces. During Christmas, 1959, William allegedly had held down two different jobs in order to buy gifts for each of them, as well as his own sisters and brothers. William's family was at a loss to explain his actions and could only conclude that his behavior might be the result of a hit-and-run accident in which he sustained head injuries. William had a juvenile record for breaking and entering a store. According to one of his sisters, William committed that crime because of the father's failure to support the family.

Following his apprehension, William was quoted as saying, "I just don't give a damn. I guess I'll get the chair or life imprisonment. I suppose I'll go to hell." Upon hearing the verdict, one of William's intended victims, a 28-year-old service station operator, who was shot four times but lived to identify his assailant, remarked, "William didn't give me any mercy. He just pumped me full of lead and I was doing everything he said. He left me for dead, and as far as he knew, I was dead." The husband of William's seventh victim said, "Now William can be pardoned and do the same thing again. If kids get away with this kind of stuff, we are in real trouble." During his trial, William became the object of much attention from teen-age girls who stood around the courthouse watching and discussing him. The girls were sympathetic to William, and one father even approached him and asked for an autograph for his daughter.

Joan, aged 16, was at home with her parents in a northeastern state and was examining a box of steak knives she had received for her "hope chest." Her mother, aged 42, and stepfather, aged 62, were resting in adjoining rooms. Joan took a hammer and proceeded to repair a few items in the home. An argument developed when her mother severely reprimanded her for making noise, and this led to accusations by the mother regarding Joan's activities at a recent high school prom. Joan became enraged, and picked up one of the steak knives and plunged it into her mother's back and chest over 10 times. When the stepfather, awakened by the struggle, started toward Joan, she picked up the hammer and threw it at him. The blow from the hammer stunned him and Joan was able to beat him into insensibility with it and then stab him several times with the knife she had used to kill his wife. Joan then left the house, taking the family car. She was picked up several hours later as she drove aimlessly around the countryside. The bodies of her mother and stepfather were not found until the next day when the stepfather failed to report for work.

Joan was tried in September, 1960, for the murder of her mother but was acquitted by reason of "temporary insanity." The entire defense was based on the insanity plea, and great emphasis was placed on the fact that there were constant arguments within the family. Defense witnesses testified about the unrealistic discipline imposed on Joan by her mother, and her constant accusations regarding Joan's morals. Joan was again brought to trial in January, 1961, for the murder of her stepfather. She pled guilty to manslaughter and was sentenced to a year in prison with credit for the time she had spent in jail awaiting trial.

As for Joan's background, she was born out of wedlock in 1943 and lived with her mother and stepfather. The stepfather married her mother when Joan was 2 years old and provided an average middle-class income for the family. When Joan was 13 years old, she ran away from home because of continuous arguments with her mother regarding her actions, friends, and associates. She was found within a short time and was returned to her home. Two years later, Joan again ran away from home because of arguments with her mother. The mother accused Joan of being promiscuous with boys and once even had her examined for pregnancy. Again Joan was located and this time was turned over to a guidance clinic. The clinic found that she was not insane, but that she did have an unstable personality. Her trouble was attributed to her difficulties with her mother and her antisocial attitude. Joan was placed in a foster home for a while, but when this did not prove successful, she was allowed to return home. Joan had no prior criminal record, except for the two instances when she was a runaway and was located by local law enforcement agencies.

On April 30, 1960, the ravished body of a 16-year-old part-time waitress was found on a rain-drenched slope beside a railroad track in a northeastern city. Her face and head were bludgeoned and her clothes had been ripped off and strewn about. She mumbled incoherently before lapsing into a coma as she was rushed to the hospital. The girl never regained consciousness, and she died the next morning.

Raymond, aged 16, a fugitive from a state forestry camp, was immediately suspected. A 1958 model automobile had been stolen in the vicinity of the murder, and Raymond was known to have a preference for that model car, in addition to having a prior record of auto theft. Apprehended on May 2, 1960, while riding in the stolen car, he immediately confessed to the murder.

Raymond told officers that he had known the young girl previously and had arranged to date her after she had finished work. When they met that night, they strolled around and eventually purchased some wine by using his older sister's identification card. They decided to take shelter in a nearby railroad underpass when it began to rain. Because it was too light and people were passing by, they proceeded along the tracks and took shelter beneath some sheds. At that time, Raymond began making advances toward the girl, which she strenuously resisted. Raymond flew into a rage and struck the girl with his fist, kicked her a number of times, and, apparently not satisfied, seized some bricks lying nearby and began bludgeoning her about the head. He was also charged with raping her during the attack. After finding her unconscious, Raymond left the area but returned shortly and took $4 from her wallet. About one block away he found the 1958 model car and drove it away.

The victim suffered fractures of the jaw, extensive facial injuries, and severe lacerations of the scalp. In addition, her left ear was nearly torn off and most of her teeth were knocked loose. Raymond claimed the girl had been drinking wine with him, but a neurosurgeon reported that his examination revealed no trace of alcohol in her system.

Raymond appeared in court on August 22, 1960, and pled guilty to the charge of murder. Before the state could begin introducing evidence, however, Raymond changed his plea to "not guilty." The trial was completed on August 26, 1960, and a guilty verdict was rendered after only 41 minutes of deliberation by the jury. Punishment was fixed at death in the electric chair, but 1 month later an indefinite stay of execution was granted. The final disposition is not known.

Raymond's background differs somewhat from those of the youths discussed previously. Raymond was of average intelligence but was immature, impulsive, and lacking in self-confidence. He had lived at home with his widowed mother and 18-year-old sister before he was incarcerated. Raymond's father died while serving in the Navy during World War II.

Raymond began his criminal career at the age of 10. He was brought to the police station for truancy and curfew violations, but the charges were both adjusted. In January, 1955, he was charged with stealing a bicycle, but this was also adjusted and he was turned over to his mother. The following month, Raymond was placed under the supervision of the family court after a homosexual complaint was filed against him. In August, 1955, he ran away from home and violated curfew again. In February, 1956, Raymond was arrested for burglary and was sent to a school for delinquents, from which he escaped in May. He was arrested on the day of his escape and was returned to the school.

During November, 1957, Raymond was arrested for the larceny of two automobiles and was committed to the state training school for boys. He was paroled in June of the following year. A few days before Christmas, 1958, he and several other boys were arrested while wearing girl's clothing. They told arresting officers that it was just a "lark," but police thought otherwise when one of the older boys was found to be carrying a gun. Raymond was given a psychiatric examination, but was not found to be a "sexually dangerous person." Once again, he was committed to the training school for boys and remained there until August, 1959, when he was paroled.

Not content with his new-found freedom, Raymond stole an automobile in November but was quickly apprehended. The following month, he was recommitted to the same training school, but was quickly transferred to the state industrial school, a maximum security institution. After serving a brief time there, he was transferred to the forestry camp. Believing Raymond to have some semblance of decency left, authorities gave him leave to visit his widowed mother during Easter, 1960. Raymond repaid the kindness by failing to return to the forestry camp. In fact, he was a fugitive from that institution when he bludgeoned the young girl to death.

In a western state, during the evening of September 5, 1960, two young escapees from a county detention home shot and killed an 18-year-old watchman during the commission of a burglary of a large hardware supply store. Apparently, the watchman and a friend had caught two youths, Dan and Marvin, both aged 15, breaking into candy vending machines inside the store. A struggle ensued, and Dan pulled a gun and told the watchman, "Don't do anything, or I'll shoot you." The young night watchman was shot in the back when the youths fled from the store.

Police authorities were immediately notified, and an intensive investigation was launched. The two young criminals were apprehended as they were driving in an automobile just three blocks from the murder scene. A search of the automobile revealed two pistols and two bags of money, and a further check of the auto uncovered items believed to have been taken in a burglary committed two nights before. The murder weapon, a .22-caliber pistol, was found 20 feet from the watchman's body. Two shots had been fired from the weapon, and it was cocked, ready to be fired again. Police believed that the youths obtained the three pistols, one of which was the murder weapon, from the burglary committed earlier that week. Both Dan and Marvin were charged in local district court with first degree murder, and "not guilty" pleas were entered at that time.

Both Dan and Marvin were tried and convicted of first degree murder, but an all male jury's recommendation for mercy spared them the death penalty. The pair were sentenced to the state prison for life at hard labor on December 20, 1960. Because the state in which the offense occurred had no maximum security facility for juveniles, they were sent to another state to be confined until they reached age 21, after which time they were to be sent to a penitentiary in their own state.

Dan, who was only 5 feet 1 inch tall and weighed only 100 pounds, seemed to have a pleasant disposition and to crave recognition and affection. Dan's deceased father had been a poor provider, and apparently his stepfather was not much better. Dan displayed a strong aversion to him, and in previous interviews had said that he preferred foster-home placement to remaining at home with his stepfather. When asked how his stepfather might feel about the burglaries, Dan indicated that his stepfather was not in the least concerned and that on occasion he had even purchased stolen articles from Dan.

Dan's mother had apparently failed miserably in providing love and affection and a stable home environment. She reportedly lived with various men without benefit of marriage and bore five children by different fathers. The mother openly displayed her lack of concern for the welfare of Dan and the other children in the family. Dan, completely bewildered, failed all courses in school and indicated that rather than attend school, he preferred to attend a state vocational training school.

Marvin's background differed somewhat from that of Dan. Marvin did average work in school and was active on the school paper. His record had been good until he started associating with youths who had juvenile records. After his father's death, his school activities decreased, and his mother, who was completely disinterested in Marvin's welfare, left the state.

Dan's official criminal record began in October, 1954, when, at the age of 8, he was placed on official probation for truancy. From that time, at least once each year, he was charged with a crime, including burglary, breaking and entering, theft, and trespass to property. In each instance, he was released and no action was taken. Marvin's record was similar to Dan's. He was arrested for theft, breaking and entering, and similar crimes, but received punishment in only one case, that being restitution for a theft he had committed. At the time of their arrest, both youths were escapees from the county detention home, where they had been held as runaways.

While these two murder suspects were in the county jail, their escape was foiled by alert jailers who found three cell bars partially sawed off. The bars were completely sawed off at the bottom and could easily have been removed. Three hacksaw blades were found, and it was presumed that the blades had been smuggled in by fellow inmates. This case is a classic illustration of the fact that youthful offenders are capable of the most vicious types of crimes and when apprehended can be ingenious and persistent in their escape attempts.

INTRODUCTION

The foregoing cases were presented to illustrate the fact that the officer may be confronted with a juvenile who is entirely capable of committing as heinous a crime as any adult. However, the officer should not allow himself to be so prejudiced by these cases that he will be unable to objectively evaluate the information presented in this chapter. He should also keep in mind from the outset that the causal factors of juvenile delinquency are not dealt with here, since this chapter focuses on the legal aspects of handling the juvenile offender.

The officer should keep in mind that the youths he deals with today will become the adults he will be dealing with for many years to come. His actions and contacts with them now will determine, to a large degree, the success of his future contacts. If a first offender is handled in an improper manner, he may be irreparably harmed rather than benefited. It is essential to recognize the fact that only a small percentage of the several million children who are considered to be "in trouble" have committed serious crimes. Although society obviously must be protected from those who have, others, who are not a threat to society and whose only "crime" may be having parents who neglect them, are all too often treated as hardened criminals. Thousands of children, some as young as 8 or 10, spend weeks or even months behind bars for offenses that would not put an adult in jail for an hour.

Experts who deal with these troubled youngsters have classified them into eight basic, often overlapping, categories. They include: (1) the neglected and battered child; (2) the physically handicapped; (3) the mentally retarded or handicapped; (4) the mentally or emotionally disturbed; (5) children with serious school problems; (6) the one-parent child; (7) youngsters without families who are fighting to survive in slums and other poor environments; and (8) the outright delinquent.

Of course, not all the children in these specific categories are in trouble, but most experts point out that those who are need some type of special help, such as strong adult support and supervision. The same experts tell us that the key to the category into which a child falls generally depends upon who first becomes confronted and concerned with his behavior. What happens to him depends largely on the interest and tolerance of his parents, school officials, neighbors, and others who frequently come in direct contact with the child, such as the police officer.

If a child who is in trouble is first noticed by the police, and there is little interest and support at home, the child may well become delinquent. In many police stations, the child's contact with the police is entered on a permanent record. This contact may result because the child has committed a serious crime or simply because he may have been out past curfew. In some instances, the child's record remains in a permanent file until he becomes 21, when it may then be disposed of; however, in other jurisdictions, this juvenile police record remains in the file indefinitely.

All too often, youngsters receive penalties that are much too harsh for the offense. Children are sometimes taken from basically sound and supportive home environments and placed in institutions where they may become embittered, distrustful, and hostile to authority. As an example, consider Joe, a 13-year-old Negro boy from a rural area. In late January, he was sent by a judge to a state detention home to await an opening in a reform school. Joe had committed no crime, other than skipping school. He had been placed on probation for truancy in the previous spring and was caught skipping school again in the winter. State officials reported that none of his eight brothers and sisters had been in trouble, except for frequent absences from school. The nine children lived with their mother and stepfather in an unpainted, four-room shack on a farm owned by someone else. While they had electricity, there was no inside plumbing, and the only heat in winter was provided by a single, small, woodburning stove. The total income for the family of 11, which was very little, was earned by the stepfather. Joe's mother went only as far as the tenth grade in school.

It was fairly clear why, despite their acute poverty, the children had never been in much trouble. Joe's stepfather was described as "the definite head of the household," a man with "a very warm relationship with his wife and children." The family regularly attended their local church, and the shack in which they lived was located in a wooded area with a stream to fish in and plenty of room for all the children to play.

Often little or no help is provided for children who stumble along the inviting path to delinquency. Action is very seldom taken until it is too late, and parents, police, welfare officers, and school officials often speed up the delinquency process. Jailing homeless or mistreated children is, unfortunately, a practice too commonly resorted to. What is the answer then for the law enforcement officer? If he is knowledgeable in the law and utilizes the proper procedures in handling the youthful offender, his actions can improve the youth's respect for the law and the law enforcement officer instead of destroying it.

A BRIEF HISTORY OF THE YOUTH COURT

Until the early 1900's, little or no distinction was made between the youthful and the adult offender. The juvenile offender could only receive an institutional disposition of his case, since no special juvenile courts existed at that time. In the early 1900's, the first juvenile courts were established by legislation throughout the United States. However, these early acts did very little to establish what we term modern procedures for handling the juvenile offender, although some of these acts did provide for jury trials for the juvenile at the insistence of the parents, guardian, or the courts. In some states, these juvenile acts gave the criminal court jurisdiction over juvenile offenders, unless that court saw fit to assign the case to the youth court. Most youth court acts that are in effect today were created in the mid 1940's and early 1950's, when legislatures recognized the pressing need for a separate court with informal and confidential proceedings for juvenile offenders. Since these original acts were passed, the major change has been in the youth court's jurisdiction. Today almost every state allows its youth courts to handle all cases involving juvenile offenders, except capital cases. In those latter instances, some state statutes provide for certification of the juvenile so that he may be tried as an adult. In other states, a juvenile who is over a certain age (usually 13 years) may be tried in the court of original jurisdiction for such an offense without certification by the juvenile court.

PHILOSOPHY OF THE YOUTH COURT

The philosophy of the youth court is derived from the "parens patriae" doctrine. According to *Black's Law Dictionary,* this Latin phrase means "father of his country; parent of the country. In England, the king. In the United States, the state, as a sovereign–referring to the sovereign power of guardianship over persons under disability . . . such as minors, and insane and incompetent persons. . . ."[1]

This doctrine, which came from early English common law, vests in the state the paramount right and responsibility toward children, superior even to the rights of a parent. There is a great deal of difference between the youth court's purposes and procedures and those of the adult criminal court. The latter's purpose is to convict and sentence criminals, and its procedures are formal and relatively rigid. The youth court represents the power of a particular state to act in behalf of the child as a wise parent would, and its primary responsibility is protecting a child's right to full physical, mental, and moral development. The judge of the youth court in every instance exercises wide latitude in dealing with each child as a distinct and separate individual who needs and is entitled to help and treatment, which is determined by the circumstances of each individual case. The youth court exercises its powers in various ways; for example, by removing a child from a detrimental home environment or by setting standards for parental supervision.

Any successful youth court functions as a sociolegal court which has a basically dual purpose. First, it is a court of law with the general responsibility of protecting the constitutional and other legal rights of both children and their parents or guardian. Second, its purpose is to understand and help, not necessarily to convict and punish. The competent youth court recognizes that the child's home environment, his acquired or inherited traits, and many other factors can combine to influence his behavior. Also, one should not overlook the fact that the child's playmates and associates often have a strong influence upon his actions. The conscientious youth court judge recognizes that all behavior is motivated by underlying causes, and also that only as a court can he get at the causes of delinquency. As the court, with the help of its personnel, begins to outline a plan of help and care that will be in the best interests of the child, it must be recognized that each child is a unique individual and that each case should be considered individually. In regard to the philosophy of the youth court, the officer must keep in mind that the youth court is not basically a social agency, a mental health clinic, or an arm of law enforcement; it is a court of law for children.

JURISDICTIONAL MATTERS

All states have statutes that provide that the youth court, with certain exceptions, has original jurisdiction in all proceedings concerning any delinquent or neglected child residing or present in that particular jurisdiction. In addition, the youth court has jurisdiction over all children and over those adults who have direct control over or influence on a child. However, before continuing with jurisdictional matters, it will be helpful to have a general definition of the word "juvenile."

In the majority of states, a "juvenile" is defined statutorily as a male or female child under 18 years of age. However, in a minority of states, such as Illinois, a juvenile is defined as a person under 21 years of age. Although juveniles are defined chronologically by statute for jurisdictional purposes, we can also provide more specific definitions by classifying juveniles into two general categories: the delinquent child and the neglected child.

THE DELINQUENT CHILD

The term "delinquent child" is synonymous with what is commonly meant by the term "juvenile offender" and generally means a child of not less than 10 years of age (in the majority of states) whose behavior, occupation, environment, or association with persons of poor character or bad reputation are injurious to his welfare or the welfare of other children. This would also include one who deserts his home; one who is habitually disobedient to or beyond the control of his parents, guardian, or custodian; one who, being required to attend school, wilfully absents himself from school or wilfully violates its rules; one who violates any state laws or municipal ordinances; or one who, by reason of his being habitually wayward or habitually disobedient, becomes an incorrigible or uncontrollable child, or who so deports himself as to injure or endanger the health or morals of himself or any other person.

THE NEGLECTED CHILD

In the majority of states, a neglected child is one whose parent, guardian, or custodian, or any person legally responsible for his care and support, refuses or neglects, when able to so do, to provide for him the necessary or proper care and support, or education as required by law, or medical, surgical, or other care that is necessary for his well-being. This category would also include, in most instances, a child who is otherwise without proper care, supervision, support, or custody; or who, for any reason, or as the result of the faults or habits of anyone, lacks the special care he requires because of his mental condition, whether or not he is mentally defective or mentally disordered; or who, for any reason, or as the result of the faults or habits of anyone, lacks the necessary care for his health, morals, or well-being; or who is found in a disreputable place, or who associates with vagrant, vicious, or immoral persons.

Many youth courts are of the opinion that in situations in which the parents, guardians, or custodians of such children are apparently guilty of neglect, neither the youth counselor nor the youth court need be informed of or consulted about the situation, unless it is the opinion of the social worker or welfare department that some legal action might be necessary. In those cases, the youth counselor or the youth court should be contacted so that they can further investigate the situation and take such action as the facts and the law dictate.

In cases in which adults are guilty of gross neglect or contributing to the delinquency of a minor, certainly court action should be taken, either in the youth court or in any court having proper jurisdiction over such criminal acts. Under most statutes, contributing to delinquency is a misdemeanor, and courts other than the youth court may have jurisdiction. Often, such cases are presented to a grand jury so that an indictment can be obtained. Many states have statutory provisions that exempt those allegedly neglected children whose religious faith prohibits them from seeking medical aid. Mississippi has such a statute:

> No child who in good faith is under treatment by spiritual means alone through prayer in accordance with the tenets and practice of a recognized church or religious denomination by a duly accredited practitioner thereof shall, for this reason alone, be considered to be medically neglected under any provision of this act.[2]

The main sources of information in neglect cases are usually relatives, neighbors, school authorities, and local or other law enforcement agencies. In such cases, these sources should be asked to contact the social worker or welfare department so that a thorough investigation can be made. After the investigation, the caseworker would usually have a sufficiently clear picture to decide if any further action is necessary. If there is any doubt, the caseworker should confer with a youth counselor of the youth court, and if doubt still remains, it would be entirely proper to discuss the matter with other interested officials. In the event of a very complicated case, it might be best to contact all agencies which might have an interest in or jurisdiction over the parties. In the majority of states, any child under 13 years of age who commits an offense or violates a state law is classified as a "neglected child" by the youth court. Runaway children might be classified as either neglected or delinquent, depending on the facts of each case. What classification and action would be appropriate would be decided by the person or agency having jurisdiction.

In appropriate cases in which the adult is alleged to have contributed to delinquency, the youth court, or other court having jurisdiction over such offense, may impose certain conditions upon the conduct of those adults guilty of such violations. If this court order is violated, the adult may be held in contempt of court instead of being charged with a new, separate offense. Therefore, it would be wise for the officer, before charging a person with contributing to delinquency, to check the existing records to make sure that there is not an existing court order regulating the conduct of the adult involved.

In determining whether a particular youth court has or can take jurisdiction over the juvenile in question, consideration must be given to: (1) the place of residence of the child; (2) the present location of the child; and (3), in cases involving a violation of law, the place where the violation occurred. When there is more than one court that could hear the case, it is usual in most instances for the case to be returned to the youth's home jurisdiction. Generally speaking, if a child is 13 years of age or older, the youth court may waive its jurisdiction in favor of any other court having secondary jurisdiction of such matters. In most states, this may be done when a state or local law has been violated. Statutes in the majority of states provide that a youth 13 years of age or older who is guilty of a traffic violation may be dealt with in the court having jurisdiction over traffic offenses, without being transferred to the youth court. If the youth is found guilty of the offense in that court, he is subject to the same punishment as an adult would be if tried for the same offense. Other statutes provide for the youth court to take jurisdiction of such traffic cases if the child is a habitual offender, and in some cases, even after conviction and punishment has been set by the other court, the youth court may have the power, by its own motion, to take charge or custody of such a juvenile offender and to direct such punishment as it sees fit.

POLICE PROCEDURES FOR HANDLING JUVENILE OFFENDERS

The law enforcement officer should make as thorough an investigation of cases involving juvenile delinquents as he would make in cases involving adults. The officer should gather evidence, interrogate witnesses, and take statements from juvenile offenders, provided the offenders agree to be questioned and the statements are taken pursuant to the guidelines set down in *In re Gault* (see pp. 55–56). An officer may use his discretion in referring juveniles who have committed first offenses of a minor nature to the youth court. If the officer is uncertain about the need to refer a particular juvenile to the youth court, he should discuss the matter with the youth counselor. In certain cases, the court may request the welfare department or other social agency to make any necessary studies and evaluations of the juvenile offender in preparation for a court hearing. Since definite rules have not been established in many jurisdictions, the following guidelines are offered for the officers benefit.

CASES NOT REQUIRING COURT REFERRAL

The following circumstances would indicate that the child might be released to his parents or guardian without court referral:

1. The offense is minor, and there is no real or apparent need for treatment.
2. The child shows no habitual delinquency pattern.
3. The family situation is generally stable.
4. The relationship between the child and his parents is good, and the parents are aware of the child's problems and are able to cope with them.

The following are suggested referral cases that generally should be handled by an agency other than the youth court:

1. Cases in which the offense committed by the child has not had a serious impact on the community.
2. Cases in which the child and the parents cooperate in a disposition, but no institutional commitment or change of custody is involved.
3. Cases in which the problem indicates a need for a relatively short period of supervision.
4. Cases for which adequate help is available through a public, private, or voluntary agency of the community.

CASES REQUIRING COURT REFERRAL

In selecting the cases which should go to court, the officer or other proper person should seriously consider the following factors:

1. The act allegedly committed by the child is of a serious nature.
2. The act committed is not serious in itself, but the total circumstances indicate the need for some type of protective action.
3. The accused child has a record of repeated delinquency, even though he has not previously been referred to the court.

4. The child and his parents have failed to cooperate with other agencies outside the court.
5. Protective services needed by the child can best be obtained through the court and its probation or parole facilities.
6. The child denies the offense, but the police officer feels the evidence he has is sufficient, and a judicial determination is called for.
7. Treatment is needed and can best be obtained through the court.
8. Any case in which the child is placed in detention by the police.

In the following cases, the juvenile alleged to have committed the act or who is involved should always go before the court:

1. All cases in which it is necessary for a factual determination to be made on the issue of delinquency, dependency, or neglect.
2. All cases that are likely to involve commitment or change of custody.
3. All cases in which either the parent or the child indicates a strong desire to appear before a judge.
4. All cases that tend to have a serious impact on the community.
5. All cases in which the court must determine whether a child who is in custody or who is detained should remain so.
6. All cases in which the child or his parents refuse to give officials any cooperation.
7. All cases in which two or more children are involved in the same act, and it has already been decided that one or more of those who are involved should be referred to the court.

INFORMATION THE OFFICER SHOULD PROVIDE TO THE COURT

Although most law enforcement agencies have their own forms and procedures for reporting juvenile offenses, the following data should be gathered in order to protect the officer and to provide information to the court:

1. All the alleged facts that give the court jurisdiction over the case, plus identifying and other pertinent personal data about the child.
2. All available information about any co-delinquent who may be involved.
3. All available information about the complainant or victim, including a statement regarding the approximate extent of injuries or damages.
4. Any facts which would further explain the reason for the request for juvenile court action (other than the immediate offense), such as previous police contact that did not culminate in a court referral.
5. A brief but adequate summary of any significant factors revealed in the investigation that indicate a need for protective action, such as court records of the parents or other pertinent circumstances.

While the officer has the right and authority to detain a juvenile offender, he should remember that the detention facility must be one which is officially approved for detaining juveniles. However, this is usually a routine matter and generally is handled by the administrative division of a particular department. The officer should also be aware that, in general, a child may be detained for only three reasons: (1) for the child's own protection; (2) for the protection of others; and (3) when it is necessary to assure the child's appearance in court. If a child is detained, he must not be placed in the same cell, ward, or room with an adult offender. A juvenile who is arrested and detained for the commission of an offense for which he is to be tried as an adult may be booked, fingerprinted, and photographed. However, it is generally recommended that a juvenile who is taken into custody for an offense for which he will be handled as a juvenile by the youth court should not be fingerprinted or photographed. Whenever a juvenile is taken into custody, his parents or guardian should be notified as soon as possible, and an officer should never remove a juvenile from his home without first fully explaining to the child and his parents or guardian the purpose and reason for such removal.

It has been said that, in all respects, a juvenile has the same rights as an adult would have under similar circumstances. However, this has been a matter of some dispute, and for this reason, we will examine several court decisions on the rights of the juvenile offender. One of the first cases which dealt primarily with the juvenile and his rights involved the failure of the juvenile court to comply with the required procedures of waiving jurisdiction of the juvenile case to criminal court. Although some of our state supreme courts have subsequently held that the ruling in this case was limited to the construction of a District of Columbia statute and was not directed specifically to the constitutional rights of juveniles, it nonetheless is a good barometer of the Supreme Court's thinking. In *Kent* v. *United States,*[3] the Supreme Court held that:

> . . . a waiver of jurisdiction is a "critically important" action determining vitally important statutory rights of the juvenile. As a condition to a valid waiver order, under the District of Columbia statute, "read in the context of constitutional principles relating to due process and the assistance of counsel," the juvenile is entitled to a hearing, including access by his counsel to the social records and probation or similar reports which presumably are considered by the court, and to a statement of reasons for the juvenile court's decision.
>
> The juvenile court must accompany its waiver order with a statement of the reasons or considerations therefore, and the statement must be sufficient to demonstrate that the statutory requirement of "full investigation" has been met.
>
> Counsel must be afforded to the child in waiver proceedings, and he must have access to the court records including the social records. Counsel's role is not limited to presenting to the court anything on behalf of the child which might help the court in arriving at a decision, but if the staff's reports include materials

> which are susceptible to challenge or impeachment, it is precisely the role of counsel to "denigrate" such matter.

Kent was the forerunner of the *Gault* decision[4] which followed a year later in 1967. The *Gault* decision was not primarily concerned with the pre-judicial or post-adjudicative (dispositional) stages of a juvenile proceeding. The ruling applies only to the adjudicatory proceeding to determine whether a juvenile is a delinquent, with the consequence that he may be commited to a state institution. In *Gault* the Court stated:

> In *Kent* v. *United States,* we considered the requirements for a valid waiver of the "exclusive" jurisdiction of the juvenile court of the District of Columbia so that a juvenile could be tried in the adult criminal court of the District. Although our decision turned upon the language of the statute, we emphasized the necessity that "the basic requirements of due process and fairness" be satisfied in such proceedings. *Haley* v. *Ohio,* 332 U.S. 596 (1948) involved the admissibility, in a state criminal court of general jurisdiction, of a confession by a 15-year-old boy. The court held that the Fourteenth Amendment applied to prohibit the use of the coerced confession. Accordingly, while these cases relate only to restricted aspects of the subject, they unmistakably indicate that, whatever may be their precise impact, neither the Fourteenth Amendment nor the Bill of Rights is for adults alone.

In dealing with the issue of "notice of charges," the Court said:

> Notice, to comply with due process requirements, must be given sufficiently in advance of scheduled court proceedings so that reasonable opportunity to prepare will be afforded, and it must set forth the alleged misconduct with particularity. The "initial hearing" in the present case was a hearing on the merits. Notice at that time is not timely; and even if there were a conceivable purpose served by the deferral proposed by the court below, it would have to yield to the requirements that the child and his parents or guardian be notified, in writing, of the specific charge or factual allegations to be considered at the hearing, and that such written notice be given at the earliest practicable time, and in any event sufficiently in advance of the hearing to permit preparation. It does not allow a hearing to be held in which a youth's freedom and his parents' right to his custody are at stake without giving them timely notice, in advance of the hearing, of the specific issues that they must meet.

On the question of right to counsel, the appellants in *Gault* charged that the juvenile court proceedings were fatally defective because the court did not advise Gerald or his parents of his right to counsel and proceeded with the hearing, the adjudication of delinquency, and the order of commitment in absence of either counsel for the child and his parents or an express waiver of his right to counsel. To this challenge, the Supreme Court answered:

> We conclude that the Due Process Clause of the Fourteenth Amendment requires that in respect of proceedings to determine delinquency which may result in commitment to an institution in which the juvenile's freedom is curtailed, the child and his parents must be notified of the child's right to be represented by counsel retained by them, or if they are unable to afford counsel, that counsel will be appointed to represent the child.

The next issue considered in *Gault* was the juvenile's right to confrontation of witnesses against him, privilege against self-incrimination, and right of cross-examination. The court stated:

> In light of *Miranda* v. *Arizona,* we must also consider whether, if the privilege against self-incrimination is available, it can effectively be waived unless counsel is present or the right to counsel has been waived.
>
> It would indeed be surprising if the privilege against self-incrimination were available to hardened criminals but not to children. The language of the Fifth Amendment, applicable to the States by operation of the Fourteenth Amendment, is unequivocal and without exception. And the scope of the privilege is comprehensive. As Mr. Justice White, concurring, stated in *Murphy* v. *Waterfront Commission,* 378 U.S. 52, "The privilege can be claimed in any proceeding, be it criminal or civil, administrative or judicial, investigatory or adjudicatory. . . . it protects any disclosures which the witness may reasonably apprehend could be used in a criminal prosecution or which could lead to other evidence that might be so used."
>
> With respect to juveniles, both common observation and expert opinion emphasize that the "distrust of confessions made in certain situations" is imperative in the case of children from an early age through adolescence.
>
> The authoritative "Standards for Juvenile and Family Courts" concludes that, "Whether or not transfer to the criminal court is a possibility, certain procedures should always be followed. Before being interviewed, the child and his parents should be informed of his right to have legal counsel present and to refuse to answer questions or be fingerprinted if he should so decide."
>
> Against the application to juveniles of the right to silence, it is argued that juvenile proceedings are "civil" and not "criminal," and therefore the privilege should not apply. It is true that the statement of the privilege in the Fifth Amendment, which is applicable to the States by reason of the Fourteenth Amendment, is that no person "shall be compelled in any criminal case to be a witness against himself." However, it is also clear that the availability of the privilege does not turn upon the type of proceeding in which its protection is invoked, but upon the nature of the statement or admissions and the exposure which it invites.
>
> It would be entirely unrealistic to carve out of the Fifth Amendment all statements by juveniles on the ground that these cannot lead to "criminal" involvement. In the first place, juvenile

> proceedings to determine "delinquency," which may lead to commitment to a state institution, must be regarded as "criminal" for purposes of the privilege against self-incrimination.
>
> We conclude that the constitutional privilege against self-incrimination is applicable in the case of juveniles as it is with respect to adults. We appreciate that special problems may arise with respect to waiver of the privilege by or on behalf of children, and that there may well be some differences in technique—but not in principle—depending upon the age of the child and the presence and competence of parents. The participation of counsel will, of course, assist the police, Juvenile Courts and appellate tribunals in administering the privilege. If counsel was not present for some permissible reason when an admission was obtained, the greatest care must be taken to assure that the admission was voluntary, in the sense not only that it was not coerced or suggested, but also that it was not the product of ignorance of rights or of adolescent fantasy, fright or despair.

As to the issues of appellate review and provision of a transcript of the proceedings, the Court reiterated its holding in *Kent,* saying:

> ". . . it is incumbent upon the Juvenile Court to accompany its waiver order with a statement of the reasons or consideration therefore." As the present case illustrates, the consequences of failure to provide an appeal, to record the proceedings, or to make findings or state the grounds for the juvenile court's conclusion may be to throw a burden on the machinery for habeas corpus, to saddle the reviewing process with the burden of attempting to reconstruct a record, and to impose upon the Juvenile Judge the unseeming duty of testifying under cross-examination as to the events that transpired in the hearings before him.

The 1970 Supreme Court case, *In re Winship,*[5] arose in New York where the pertinent statute required a finding of jurisdiction by the juvenile court based on a preponderance of the evidence. Winship was a 12-year-old boy who allegedly stole $112 from a woman's pocketbook. In accordance with the statute, the juvenile court found that it had jurisdiction, based on a preponderance of the evidence. At the dispositional hearing, Winship was ordered to be placed in a training school for 18 months, subject to annual extensions of the commitment until he reached his eighteenth birthday.

On appeal, the New York Court of Appeals upheld the constitutionality of the statute. However, the United States Supreme Court reversed and noted that although nothing in the Constitution requires the reasonable doubt standard, it is universally applied in all adult criminal courts. In various previous decisions, the Court had held that the reasonable doubt standard was an essential element of due process.

In concurring opinion, Mr. Justice Harlan stated:

> Although there are no doubt costs to society and possibly even to the youth himself in letting a guilty youth go free, I think

> here, as in a criminal case, it is far worse to declare an innocent youth a delinquent. I therefore agree that a juvenile court judge should be no less convinced of the factual conclusion that the accused committed the criminal act with which he is charged than would be required in a criminal trial.

In this decision, the United States Supreme Court held the New York statute to be unconstitutional, and therefore ruled that in the adjudicatory phase of a juvenile proceeding, the quantum of proof necessary to find that the child charged with violating a criminal law is within the juvenile court's jurisdiction is proof beyond a reasonable doubt. In a later 1972 decision,[6] the United States Supreme Court upheld the *Winship* ruling requiring proof beyond a reasonable doubt to convict a juvenile of an act which would be a crime if committed by an adult. In addition, the Court held the rule to be completely retroactive.

A 1971 Supreme Court case[7] involved 16-year-old McKeiver, who had been charged with robbery, larceny, and receiving stolen property. His counsel's motion for a jury trial was denied by the juvenile court, and he was found to be delinquent and was placed on probation. On appeal, the Pennsylvania Supreme Court affirmed the lower court's holding. On appeal to the United States Supreme Court, the case presented the narrow but precise issue of whether the Due Process Clause of the Fourteenth Amendment assures the right to trial by jury in the adjudicative phase of a state juvenile court delinquency proceeding. In answering this question, the United States Supreme Court stated:

> All the litigants here agree that the applicable due process standard in juvenile proceedings, as developed by *Gault* and *Winship,* is a fundamental fairness. As that standard was applied in those two cases, we have an emphasis on fact finding procedures. The requirements of notice, counsel, confrontation, cross-examination and standard of proof naturally flowed from this emphasis. But one cannot say that in our legal system the jury is a necessary component of accurate fact finding. There is much to be said for it, to be sure, but we have been content to pursue other ways for determining facts. Juries are not required, and have not been, for example, in equity cases, in workmen's compensation, in probate, or in deportation cases. Neither have they been generally used in military trials. In *Duncan* the Court stated, "We would not assert, however, that every criminal trial—or any particular trial—held before a judge alone is unfair or that a defendant may never be as fairly treated by a judge as he would be by a jury." . . . And in *Williams* v. *Florida,* 399 U.S. 78 (1970) the Court saw no particular magic in a 12-man jury for a criminal case, thus revealing that even jury concepts themselves are not inflexible.
>
> We must recognize, as the Court has recognized before, that the fond and idealistic hopes of the juvenile court proponents and

early reformers of three generations ago have not been realized. . . .

Despite all these disappointments, all these failures, and all these shortcomings, we conclude that trial by jury in the juvenile court's adjudicative stage is not a constitutional requirement. We so conclude for a number of reasons:

1. The court has refrained in the cases heretofore decided, from taking the easy way with a flat holding that all rights constitutionally assured for the adult accused are to be imposed upon the state juvenile proceeding. . . .

2. There is a possibility, at least, that the jury trial, if required as a matter of constitutional precept, will remake the juvenile proceeding into a fully adversary process and will put an effective end to what has been the idealistic prospect of an intimate, informal protective proceeding.

3. The Task Force Report (President's Commission on Law Enforcement and Administration of Justice, Task Force Report: Juvenile Delinquency and Youth Crime, 1967) although concededly pre-*Gault* is notable for its not making any recommendation that the jury trial be imposed upon the juvenile court system. This is so despite its vivid description of the system's deficiencies and disappointments. Had the Commission thought this vital to the integrity of the juvenile process, or to the handling of juveniles, surely a recommendation or suggestion to this effect would have appeared. The intimations, instead, are quite the other way. Further, it expressly recommends against abandonment of the system and against the return of the juvenile to the criminal courts.

4. The Court specifically has recognized by dictum that a jury is not a necessary part even of every criminal process that is fair and equitable (*Duncan* v. *Louisiana*).

5. The imposition of the jury trial on the juvenile court system would not strengthen greatly, if at all, the fact finding function, and would, contrarily, provide an attrition of the juvenile court's assumed ability to function in a unique manner. It would not remedy the defects of the system. Meager as has been the hoped-for advance in the juvenile field, the alternative would be regressive, would lose what has been gained, and would tend once again to place the juvenile squarely in the routine of the criminal process.

6. The juvenile concept held high promise. We are reluctant to say that, despite disappointments of grave dimensions, it still does not hold promise, and we are particularly reluctant to say, as do the Pennsylvania appellants here, that the system cannot accomplish its rehabilitative goals. . . . We are reluctant to disallow the States to experiment further and to seek in new and different ways the elusive answers to the problems of the young, and we feel that we would be impeding that experimentation by imposing the jury trial. If, in its wisdom, any State feels the jury is desirable in all cases, or in certain kinds, there appears to be no impediment to its installing a system embracing that feature. That, however, is the State's privilege and not its obligation.

7. Of course there have been abuses. The Task Force Report has noted them. We refrain from saying at this point that those abuses are of constitutional dimension. They relate to the lack of resources and of dedication rather than to inherent unfairness.

8. There is, of course, nothing to prevent a juvenile court judge, in a particular case where he feels the need, or when the need is demonstrated, from using an advisory jury.

9. The fact that a practice is followed by a large number of states is not conclusive in a decision as to whether that practice accords with due process, but it is plainly worth considering in determining whether the practice "offends some principle of justice so rooted in the traditions and conscience of our people as to be ranked as fundamental." It therefore is of more than passing interest that at least 29 States and the District of Columbia by statute deny the juvenile a right to a jury trial in cases such as these.

10. Since *Gault* and since *Duncan* the great majority of States, in addition to Pennsylvania and North Carolina, that have faced the issue have concluded that the considerations that lead to the result in those two cases do not compel trial by jury in the juvenile court . . . .

11. Stopping short of proposing the jury trial for juvenile proceedings are the Uniform Juvenile Court Act, the Standard Juvenile Court Act, and the Legislative Guide for Drafting Family and Juvenile Court Acts.

12. If the jury trial were to be injected into the juvenile court system as a matter of right, it would bring with it into that system the traditional delay, the formality, and the clamor of the adversary system and, possibly, the public trial.

13. Finally, the arguments advanced by the juveniles here are, of course, the identical arguments that underlie the demand for the jury trial for criminal proceedings. The arguments necessarily equate the juvenile proceeding—or at least the adjudicative phase of it—with the criminal trial. Whether they should be so equated is our issue. Concern about the inapplicability of exclusionary and other rules of evidence, about the juvenile court judge's possible awareness of the juvenile's prior record and of the contents of the social file; about repeated appearances of the same familiar witnesses in the persons of juvenile and probation officers and social workers—all to the effect that this will create the likelihood of pre-judgment—chooses to ignore, it seems to us every aspect of fairness, of concern, of sympathy, and of paternal attention that the juvenile court system contemplates.

If the formalities of the criminal adjudicative process are to be superimposed upon the juvenile court system, there is little need for its separate existence. Perhaps that ultimate disillusionment will come one day, but for the moment we are disinclined to give impetus to it.

What do these decisions mean to the law enforcement officer on the street? They tell us, first, that a juvenile is entitled to the same due process rights as any adult would be under the United States Constitution and the Bill of Rights. Second, a juvenile has the same right to Miranda warnings as an adult would have. The Uniform Juvenile Court Act, section 27, provides that a confession that would be constitutionally inadmissible in a criminal proceeding would not be admissible against a juvenile. Third, in all probability, a juvenile is entitled to the same protection as an adult against unreasonable searches and seizures. The Uniform Juvenile Court Act, section 27(b), provides that, "evidence illegally seized or obtained shall not be received over objection to establish the allegations made against him." Fourth, the right to counsel would seem to extend to intake and detention hearings, and in all probability, it would be reversible error to deny the right to counsel at these hearings, if it is requested. The Uniform Juvenile Court Act, section 26, provides that the juvenile is entitled to representation by legal counsel "at all stages of any proceeding under this act." And fifth, in the majority of jurisdictions, the juvenile does not have a right to bail. This is generally the result of statutory provisions that allow release to the parents as an acceptable equivalent of bail. Apart from the aforementioned guidelines, most cases involving the rights of juveniles have dealt with the administrative procedures of the juvenile court and have no real bearing on the officer's actions before that point in the process.

NEW LEGISLATION CONCERNING JUVENILES

The following excerpt from the *Congressional Record*[8] describes the objectives and key provisions of the Juvenile Justice and Delinquency Prevention Act of 1974:

> The Juvenile Justice and Delinquency Prevention Act of 1974, S. 821, passed the Senate on August 19, the House of Representatives on August 21 and was sent to the President on the same day. This legislation combines two bills authored by Senator Birch Bayh—the Juvenile Justice and Delinquency Prevention Act and the Runaway Youth Act—to make up a comprehensive juvenile justice and delinquency prevention law. S. 821 is the product of a 3-year bipartisan effort to improve the quality of juvenile justice in the United States and to overhaul the Federal approach to the problems of juvenile delinquency and children in trouble, led by Senator Bayh, as Chairman of the Subcommittee to Investigate Juvenile Delinquency.
>
> The Subcommittee held 10 days of hearings and heard 80 witnesses on S. 821 and S. 3148, a similar bill that Senator Bayh introduced in the 92d Congress. These hearings demonstrated the need for comprehensive changes in Federal Juvenile Delinquency programs combined with assistance to states, local governments, and private agencies to prevent delinquency and to provide community-based alternatives to juvenile detention and correctional facilities.
>
> In 1971, Senator Bayh introduced the Runaway Youth Act and in early 1972 the Subcommittee heard over 20 witnesses

testify about the concerns of runaways and their families. The Senate twice passed Senator Bayh's Runaway Youth Act, once in 1972, and again in June of 1973, which is designed to help the estimated one million youngsters who run away each year.

S. 821 achieves such vital objectives as coordination of Federal delinquency programs; authorization of additional resources to states, localities, and public and private agencies for community-based prevention, diversion, and treatment programs; creation of centralized research, training, technical assistance, and evaluation activities; development of national guidelines for the administration of juvenile justice, including conditions of confinement; provisions for a one-year phasing out of the Juvenile Delinquency Prevention Act; establishment of a National Institute of Corrections within the Federal Bureau of Prisons; establishment of temporary shelter-care facilities for runaway youth; and finally, adoption of basic procedural protections for juveniles under Federal jurisdiction.

This legislation offers a comprehensive response to the juvenile delinquency crisis that sees young people account for more than half the crimes in this country. The court caseloads of juvenile offenders have increased dramatically and the rate of recidivism for persons under 20 is the highest of any age group. Its goal is to make the prevention of delinquency a national priority of the Federal Government and in so doing save tens of thousands of young people from the ravages of a life of crime, while helping them, their families, and society.

KEY PROVISIONS OF THE LAW

1. It creates a new Office of Juvenile Justice and Delinquency Prevention in the Law Enforcement Assistance Administration [LEAA] in the Department of Justice to implement Federal delinquency programs and to administer a new juvenile delinquency prevention, diversion and community-based alternative program and to have policy control over all juvenile delinquency programs funded by LEAA. It is to be headed by an assistant administrator who will be appointed by the President subject to the advice and consent of the Senate.

2. It authorizes substantial block grants to states that submit comprehensive juvenile justice plans and it revises the method for the composition of the existing LEAA state and regional planning agencies to guarantee adequate representation on planning boards, at the state and local levels, of specialists in delinquency prevention, including representatives of public and private agencies involved in this important effort.

3. It authorizes a new set of programs of delinquency prevention, diversion from the juvenile justice system and community-based alternatives to traditional incarceration, all of which are designed to stem the high incidence of juvenile crime and the extremely high incidence of recidivism among juveniles. For these new programs, $75 million is authorized to be spent in the current fiscal year, $125 million for the second year, and $150 million for the third year, with a guaranteed commitment to help support useful programs of private agencies.

4. It requires, in addition to the new programs, that LEAA sustain its present commitment of $140 million a year to juvenile programs, while giving the new assistant administrator, who will run the juvenile justice office, police control over existing LEAA juvenile programs.

5. It provides that 75% of newly authorized state funds must be expended on advanced "techniques" in developing and maintaining services to prevent juvenile delinquency, to divert juveniles from the juvenile justice system and to provide community-based alternatives to juvenile detention and correctional facilities such as:

a. community-based service for prevention and treatment of juvenile delinquency through development of foster care and shelter care homes;

b. youth service bureaus and other counseling and supportive services for delinquents, potential delinquents and their families;

c. comprehensive programs of drug and alcohol abuse education and prevention;

d. education programs or supportive services designed to keep delinquents and to encourage other youth to remain in elementary and secondary schools or in alternative learning situations; and

e. expanded use of probation and probation subsidy programs.

6. It establishes the Coordinating Council on Juvenile Justice and Delinquency Prevention and it creates a National Advisory Committee appointed by the President to advise the LEAA on the planning, operations, and management of Federal juvenile delinquency programs.

7. It authorizes direct special-emphasis grants to agencies to develop new approaches to juvenile delinquency prevention and requires that at least 20% of these funds must go to private nonprofit agencies.

8. It establishes within this same Office a National Institute of Juvenile Justice and Delinquency Prevention to provide ongoing research into new techniques of working with juveniles, to serve as a national clearinghouse for information on delinquency and to offer training in those techniques to personnel who will work with juveniles.

9. It establishes a Federal assistance program for local public and private groups to establish temporary shelter-care facilities for runaway youth and to provide counseling services to facilitate the voluntary return of runaways to their families. Grants would be made on the basis of the number of runaways in the community; the present availability of services for runaways; and priority would be given to private organizations or institutions who have had prior experience in dealing with runaways. This provision is to be administered by the Secretary of the Department of Health, Education and Welfare at an annual authorization of $10 million for the next three years.

10. It provides for a one year extension phase out of the

Juvenile Delinquency Prevention Act administered by HEW, with necessary funding.

11. It improves significantly the Federal procedures for dealing with juveniles in the justice system, with the goal of letting Federal standards serve as a worthy example for improved procedures in the states.

12. It establishes a National Institute of Corrections within the Federal Bureau of Prisons to serve as a center of correctional knowledge for Federal, state and local correctional agencies and programs to develop national policies, educational and training programs and provide research, evaluation and technical assistance. Funds are authorized as may be necessary to carry out the purposes of this provision.

Although this legislation is much needed and its basic concepts are good, there may be unforeseen problems in implementation because of the financial costs involved.

On October 20, 1971, the National Advisory Commission on Criminal Justice Standards and Goals was appointed "to formulate for the first time national criminal justice standards and goals for crime reduction and prevention at the State and local levels." Chairman Russell W. Peterson, who wrote the foreword to one of six reports that resulted from the commission's study, stated in the *Report on Police:*[9]

> Other recent commissions have studied the causes and debilitating effects of crime in our society. We have sought to expand their work and build upon it by developing a clear statement of priorities, goals, and standards to help set a national strategy to reduce crime through the timely and equitable administration of justice; the protection of life, liberty and property; and the efficient mobilization of resources.
>
> Some State or local governments already may have equaled or surpassed standards or recommendations proposed in this report; most in the Nation have not. But in any case, each State and local government is encouraged to evaluate its present status and to implement those standards and recommendations that are appropriate.

At the end of the commission's study, in early 1973, state-level Commissions on Criminal Justice Standards and Goals began to be formed. Membership in these commissions are drawn from the three branches of state and local government, from private industry, and from select citizen's groups. Commissioners are chosen primarily for their working experience and knowledge in the criminal justice area. Police chiefs, sheriffs, judges, correctional officers, and prosecutors are represented. Although the members are appointed by the governor of each state, the Law Enforcement Assistance Administration is charged with the administration of the program by providing assistance and supervision. The hoped-for result is that the standards and goals of the national commission will be accepted, or modified and accepted. By involving many local citizens, the community will become more aware of the need for new legislation and enforcement of existing legislation relating to criminal justice standards and goals.

Standard 9.5 and the commentary on that standard from the national commission's *Report on Police* are reprinted here so that the officer can compare these recommendations with what has been or is being done in his jurisdiction in relation to juvenile operations.

STANDARD 9.5: JUVENILE OPERATIONS

The chief executive of every police agency immediately should develop written policy governing his agency's involvement in the detection, deterrence, and prevention of delinquent behavior and juvenile crime.

1. Every police agency should provide all its police officers with specific training in preventing delinquent behavior and juvenile crime.

2. Every police agency should cooperate actively with other agencies and organizations, public and private, in order to employ all available resources to detect and deter delinquent behavior and combat juvenile crime.

3. Every police agency should establish in cooperation with courts written policies and procedures governing agency action in juvenile matters. These policies and procedures should stipulate at least:

   a. The specific form of agency cooperation with other governmental agencies concerned with delinquent behavior, abandonment, neglect, and juvenile crime;

   b. The specific form of agency cooperation with non-governmental agencies and organizations where assistance in juvenile matters may be obtained;

   c. The procedures for release of juveniles into parental custody; and

   d. The procedures for the detention of juveniles.

4. Every police agency having more than 15 employees should establish juvenile investigation capabilities.

   a. The specific duties and responsibilities of these positions should be based upon the particular juvenile problems within the community.

   b. The juvenile specialists, besides concentrating on law enforcement as related to juveniles, should provide support and coordination of all community efforts for the benefit of juveniles.

5. Every police agency having more than 75 employees should establish a juvenile investigation unit, and every smaller police agency should establish a juvenile investigation unit if community conditions warrant. This unit:

   a. Should be assigned responsibility for conducting as many juvenile investigations as practicable, assisting field officers in juvenile matters, and maintaining liaison with other agencies and organizations interested in juvenile matters; and

b. Should be functionally decentralized to the most effective command level.

Commentary

A juvenile becomes a delinquent when he commits an act which, if he were an adult, would be a crime. The activities of police in connection with juveniles who are not yet delinquent is a matter of controversy and concern. Some believe that the police should have no contact with a juvenile unless he commits a crime. This belief, however, precludes the assistance of law enforcement agencies in the identification of neglected and dependent children; from deterring the delinquency of children who persistently refuse to obey the reasonable directions of parents and school authorities, or are beyond the control of these authorities; or are otherwise in clear and present danger of becoming delinquent.

In California children fitting the latter description are within the jurisdiction of the juvenile court, and may be made wards of the court. This provision of law allows police in California to take an active part in preventing delinquency. Police officers throughout the Nation are in a position to do this, because they confront juvenile problems 24 hours a day and are trained and experienced in those problems.

To suggest that law enforcement abrogate its preventive responsibilities concerning juvenile delinquency is to recommend that police merely enforce the law through the apprehension process.

Every community has special juvenile problems, varying from gang murders to underage youths loitering in pool halls. Rather than merely trying to apply what has been successful in one community to another, juvenile operations should be generated by an evaluation of local needs and local capabilities. Programs may be all-inclusive in smaller communities, and on a neighborhood basis in metropolitan areas.

The police chief executive, after assessing conditions, should write a policy governing the activities of his agency involving juveniles. This policy should be based upon community needs and resources.

Police Training in Juvenile Problems

Each officer must be given adequate training at the entry level to identify neglected and dependent children, detect and deter predelinquent behavior, and develop insight into juvenile crime problems, departmental policy, and available procedures and resources.

The extent of the training will vary according to the community's problems. Cities such as Los Angeles, Calif., and Chicago, Ill., have comprehensive programs in this area; many States, including Michigan and California, have mandated a minimum period of training in juvenile problems.

Training must not stop at the entry level; it should be reinforced periodically through various in-service training techniques. This additional training is needed to maintain awareness of ever-changing problems and to maintain the capability of responding adequately to community needs.

Agencies that choose to assign personnel fulltime to juvenile operations should provide additional training in juvenile activities, preferably at a professional school. Such training is conducted at various times each year at designated locations throughout the country.

Other Agencies and Organizations

Activities focused on juvenile problems do not involve law enforcement agencies alone. Courts, social assistance agencies, schools and governmental counseling agencies, as well as many privately operated agencies, are concerned and involved.

The police agency should make every effort to participate actively with other agencies and organizations whenever practicable, to reduce the duplication of services directed at juvenile problems, and to approach those problems with maximum effectiveness.

Many joint efforts by law enforcement and other community resources have proved effective. Police athletic leagues and junior police and sheriffs' programs are among the most successful.

The Dallas, Tex., Police Department program, in conjunction with the Dallas School District, has had considerable impact in reducing delinquency problems.

In Grand Rapids, Mich., where the police department and other community organizations provide summer camp for deprived children, measurable benefits have been demonstrated.

Cooperation must prevail between the law enforcement agency and the entire community if they are to achieve a lasting effect on juvenile problems. Neither can function adequately in this area without the support of the other.

Written Policies and Procedures

Written juvenile policies and procedures in each law enforcement agency should require constant planning, implementation, program evaluation, and refinement based on changing community needs.

These procedures must incorporate legal methods of discovering situations, activities, and environments that are harmful to juveniles' development, in order to detect and deter conditions that may lead to delinquent behavior. Legal procedures for apprehension and detention of juvenile offenders should also be included. This written policy and procedure should cover at least the following:

- Exerting every possible effort toward discovery of potential delinquents and conditions conducive to delinquent behavior;
- Working closely with other agencies to remove or control environmental conditions conducive to creating juvenile problems;
- Advising and assisting all agencies and organizations concerned

with juvenile problems when the police agency is not directly involved in the activity;

• Using preventive patrol techniques in areas where there is potential for juvenile problems;

• Conducting thorough investigations into delinquency problems that lead to the commission of juvenile offenses. This includes apprehension and prosecution of adults who contribute to, or are involved in, delinquency problems;

• Detecting and apprehending juvenile offenders as prescribed by existing laws and procedures. There should be guidelines for the release of juveniles into parental or guardian custody, or their detention;

• Followup as needed in the referral of the offender, obtaining the necessary legal process, and obtaining the disposition of each action involving a juvenile offender; and

• Retaining prescribed juvenile records as indicated by the courts and required by law.

Juvenile Investigative Capabilities

Every agency with over 15 employees should have specific juvenile investigative capabilities. The extent of these capabilities will depend upon the extent of the juvenile problems within the community and the resources available to the agency. The conditions and the resources may indicate a part-time capability, a regional capability, or the assignment of full-time personnel to juvenile operations.

Personnel assigned specifically to juvenile activities should have the additional responsibility of coordinating with other agencies and organizations within the community. Where personnel are not specifically assigned, even on a part-time basis, followup activities must be the concern of each individual officer.

Establishment of Juvenile Units

A police agency with 75 or fewer personnel should establish a juvenile unit if community conditions warrant; police agencies with more than 75 personnel should provide full-time juvenile investigators unless the community clearly has no juvenile problem. The creation of a juvenile investigation should not relieve the patrol force, or other elements of the agency, of responsibility for juvenile activities.

The responsibility of the juvenile unit should be to conduct as many juvenile investigations as is practicable, to provide assistance to field officers in matters involving juvenile problems, and to coordinate with other agencies. The Kalamazoo, Mich., and Kettering, Ohio, Police Departments have developed effective programs of this type.

Geography and population frequently dictate that operations be decentralized. Juvenile operations should be decentralized to the most effective command level. The Los Angeles, Calif., Police Department is presently implementing decentralized activities including certain juvenile operations.

Several State agencies, including the Michigan State Police,

> have successfully implemented programs that are decentralized in operation and coordinated through a headquarters unit.
>
> The application of police resources to the detection and deterrence of delinquent behavior, as well as the apprehension of juvenile offenders, is of primary concern in communities coast-to-coast. The total resources of the community must be applied to the juvenile problem, and this must include police efforts as well as other agencies and organizations concerned with this problem.[10]

THE JUVENILE'S LIABILITY

At one time or another in every officer's career, he is approached by an irate citizen who demands that he proceed to 10- or 12-year-old Johnny's home and recover money from Johnny's parents for damages which were caused by some act of little Johnny. In dealing with this type of situation, the officer should be very careful in taking any action, because the parents are not generally liable for their child's tort, except where prevailing statutes provide for such liability. In tort law, a child is generally liable for his own actions that are tortious in nature if he knows the difference between right and wrong. In some jurisdictions, children under 7 years of age are conclusively presumed to not know the difference between right and wrong. For children between 7 and 12 years of age, there is a rebuttable presumption that they do know the difference, and for those over 12 years of age, there is a conclusive presumption that they know the difference. Of course, this general rule would not apply to mentally retarded or defective children.

The officer should understand, however, that in many instances, a parent will pay for the damages caused by his child because he feels a moral obligation to do so. Often the parent is not aware of his right to refuse and may feel that he has a legal obligation also.

Many people believe that a child cannot be sued; however, this is a misconception, especially in those jurisdictions where the aforementioned general rules apply. The usual procedure is to sue the child by or through someone else of majority, such as his parent or guardian, sometimes referred to as suing "by and through his next friend." Others feel that it is useless to sue a child, because the child usually has no money or property of his own that may be attached. However, in many jurisdictions, a judgment is enforceable for 7 years, and at the end of that period it may be renewed. In fact, it may be renewed seven times, and so the judgment can remain in force for a total of 49 years.

In some situations, a parent or other adult could be held jointly liable for a tort committed by a child. If the parent or other adult contributes to the wrongful or negligent actions of the child, the former can be made a codefendant in the suit and can be held liable in actual and/or compensatory damages in an amount determined by his contributory part in the tort. At the same time, the parent or other person having custody of the child may be judged to have neglected the child or may be found guilty of the criminal offense of contributing to delinquency. In addition, the child may be found to be delinquent or may be handled in other ways by the youth court. However, in either instance, the fact that a crime may have been committed would generally have no real bearing on the tort issue.

Since tort law is very confusing to some, perhaps some factual examples will be useful. Little George is 13 years old, and for 3 months his father has been trying to teach George how to drive an automobile in preparation for the driver education course George will take at school when he becomes old enough. Almost every Sunday afternoon, the father has taken George out in the country to an open pasture where the lessons take place. After 3 months of practice, George has become a fairly good driver, and his father decides to allow George to drive from the pasture, on the highway, to their home in the city. On the way home, a police officer stops George and his father at a driver's license checkpoint. George receives a traffic ticket for operating a vehicle without a license and the father is issued one for allowing an unauthorized person to operate a motor vehicle.

It is fall now, and the pasture is too wet and muddy to practice driving. Besides, it's football season and the Sunday afternoon games have captured the father's attention. On this particular Sunday, the television game of the week is not too interesting, so the father decides to take a nap. George decides to have a Coke but he can't find any in the house. He goes to the kitchen cabinet and reaches to the top shelf, where all the keys are kept in a bowl, takes the family car keys, gets into the car, and heads toward a drive-in grocery approximately 6 blocks away. As he approaches a traffic light which is just turning to red, he gets excited and presses hard on the accelerator instead of applying the brakes. George runs the red light and hits another vehicle which is passing through the intersection on the green light, killing three occupants of the other vehicle.

Notwithstanding the fact that liability insurance might have some bearing on the case, depending on the jurisdiction in which the accident occurred, who would be liable for the wrongful deaths of the three people—George or his father? Could both of them be held jointly liable? Did the father contribute by his past actions of trying to teach George how to drive? Were the parents negligent in leaving the keys in a bowl on the top shelf of the kitchen cabinet? What effect would the two previous tickets have on a suit against George and his father? Certainly the answers to these and other questions are difficult to determine. However, the task may be made easier by changing some of the facts of the case.

Let us assume that everything has happened just as described previously, except that on this Sunday afternoon the game is very interesting, and both George and his father are watching attentively. The father suddenly realizes that he is out of cigarettes, and he tells George, "Jump in the car and run down to the drive in grocery for me." He hands George the car keys, gives him some money, and tells him to get the cigarettes and something for himself. George does as he is told, runs the same red light, and kills the same three people. Who is liable for the wrongful death of the three now? Did the father contribute to George's actions this time?

The answers are more obvious in this example. There is no doubt that the father did contribute to George's actions in the second case by directing George to take the car and drive to the grocery. In the second case, both George and his father may be held liable. However, in the first case, it is doubtful that the father's actions would be deemed to have been contributory or neglectful. As far as the two previous tickets are concerned, they probably would not carry a great deal of weight in either case. A father's teaching his son to drive a motor vehicle is not wrongful or negligent per se, and therefore that fact would not be of much value to the plaintiff's case either.

At this point, the officer should realize that finding absolute and irrefutable answers to these questions is not possible and should not be attempted. As any attorney would agree, arguments could be made for both plaintiff and defendant. It is enough that the reader recognize the issues involved and have some basic concept of the applicable theory. If these hypothetical situations were to happen in real life, the answers to these questions would be left to the finder of fact, the jury.

Again, it should be stressed that the issues and theory discussed here may not be applicable in all jurisdictions. The officer should attempt to find and study the applicable statutes and rules in his jurisdiction before embarking on a course of conduct that may prove to be unwise or unlawful. For as will be seen in the next chapter, he may be held liable for his own wrongful actions.

CAN POLICE HELP CHILDREN IN TROUBLE?

At least one writer feels that law enforcement officers can help children who are in trouble in many different ways. Howard James, staff correspondent of *The Christian Science Monitor,* has listed at least 24 ways in which police might, in addition to their regular duties, assist the child:[11]

> 1. Carefully test all officers on attitudes toward adolescents and minority groups. Screen out those with bad attitudes.
> 2. Give classes to all new officers in adolescent behavior. Require a high mark to pass.
> 3. Hold frequent in-service training sessions on teen-agers and how to deal with them for officers already on the force.
> 4. Return officers to neighborhood beats.
> 5. Increase police salaries so standards for policemen can be raised.
> 6. Sponsor Boys Clubs, Boy Scouts Troops, and other similar groups.

7. Sponsor automobile clubs, drag races, and other auto-oriented activities.

8. Sponsor a Police Athletic League, a program run by volunteer officers and aimed at those young people on the edge of trouble.

9. Start a big-brother-in-blue program. This would be related to the traditional Big Brother program, with individual officers taking a personal interest in boys who need adult guidance and friendship.

10. Sponsor summer camp programs, with policemen acting as counselors.

11. Start police clubs in local schools for youngsters interested in police work.

12. Start a youth patrol, where older children interested in police work are trained by veteran officers to do specialized jobs. In some communities these groups have helped ease tensions and prevent violence. In other communities youngsters serve as information aides in neighborhoods. Still others do clerical work and other routine jobs.

13. Open neighborhood store-front offices for easy, non-threatening citizen access to police.

14. Hold regular discussion sessions where individual policemen either serve as leaders or become involved in give and take.

15. Sponsor drum and bugle corps, drill teams, and other similar groups.

16. Collect and distribute data on alternatives to jail or detention homes for children in trouble. Prepare a manual listing all community agencies and their services for children.

17. Urge local schools to adopt the University of Cincinnati school program to encourage understanding of law and law enforcement.

18. Take youngsters on patrol, as is done in St. Louis.

19. Have officers make regular visits to schools for assembly programs and to talk to individual classes.

20. Demonstrate police equipment and the positive side of the profession on elementary school playgrounds. Give children a ride in police cars. Hold first-aid classes.

21. Assign officers to schools full-time to teach and counsel.

22. Give officers working in ethnic neighborhoods special courses to help them understand the group's culture, problems, and needs. Require language training for those working among non-English-speaking groups.

23. Lock officers in jail or prison overnight, as a California chief does, and take steps to sensitize policemen.

24. Avoid bluster, unnecessary violence, cockiness, or displays of bravado. Follow advice given in the King County, Washington, Sheriff's department manual: "It is of the utmost importance that officer attitude, demeanor, and speech toward juveniles be civil and respectful, but at the same time firm."*

---

*Reprinted by permission from The Christian Science Monitor.

It is not known exactly how many of these suggestions are being followed today in different areas of the United States. Likewise, it is not known if all of them would work successfully in every department. It seems likely, however, that if officers took it upon themselves to initiate such programs as are suggested here, it would help to decrease juvenile delinquency. Another way in which each individual officer might help is to insure that he does not add to the problem by raising a juvenile delinquent of his own. In this regard, consider the following:

HOW TO RAISE A JUVENILE DELINQUENT
(IN TWELVE EASY LESSONS)

1. Begin in infancy to give the child everything he wants. In this way, he will grow up believing the world owes him a living.

2. When he picks up "bad" words or "dirty" words, laugh at him. That will make him think he is "cute."

3. Never give him any spiritual training until he is twenty-one, and then let him decide for himself. By the same logic, never teach him the English language. Maybe when he is old enough, he will want to speak Bantu.

4. Praise him in his presence to all the neighbors; show how much smarter he is than the neighbors' children.

5. Avoid the use of the word "wrong." It may develop in the child a "guilt complex." This will prepare him to believe that when he is punished later on for stealing cars or assaulting women that society is "against him" and that he is being "persecuted."

6. Pick up everything after him; his shoes, his books, his clothes. Do everything for him, so that he will be experienced in throwing burdens on others.

7. Let him read anything he wants. Have no concern whatever for what goes into his mind. Provide him with Lilly cups for his lips, but let his brain drink out of any dirty container for words and ideas.

8. Quarrel frequently in the presence of your children. In this way, they will be prepared for broken homes later on.

9. Give him all the spending money he wants; never let him earn his own.

10. Satisfy every craving of the child for food, drinks and everything that has to do with the senses of taste and touch, gratifying every sensual desire.

11. Take his part against policemen, teachers and neighbors. They are all "prejudiced" against your child.

12. When he gets into real trouble, always defend yourself and say, "I never could do anything with him."[12]

SUMMARY AND APPLICATION

Again the hypothetical situation will be used in summarizing this chapter. The problems presented here will deal with all the theory presented in earlier chapters as it applies to the juvenile.

PROBLEM I

Sam has a very good relationship with both his parents. He is only 15 years old, but his parents are aware of his problems and are generally able to cope with them. Sam has been stopped while operating a motor vehicle, and the officer finds that he has no operator's license. There is no one else in the vehicle and Sam is very upset about being stopped. The officer proceeds to issue Sam a ticket, but Sam argues that he shouldn't receive a ticket, since he is driving because his father sent him on an errand. The officer feels that Sam is being arrogant and, in fact, considers placing Sam in jail for the offense. What would you do—put Sam in jail, or turn Sam over to his parents? Why?

PROBLEM II

Later the same day and after the officer has dealt with Sam, he stops Sam's friend, Albert, who is in possession of a stolen motor vehicle. Albert is only 14 years old, and he is known to have a previous record of several minor infractions of the law. What should you do with him? Should Albert be put in jail, or should he be turned over to his parents? How much difference is there between this situation and that in Problem I? If there is a difference, what bearing would it have?

PROBLEM III

A police officer stops Sammy Green, who is 12½ years old, while Sammy is driving a motor vehicle under the influence of alcohol. There is no one else in the vehicle with Sammy, and the officer cannot get any information as to who his parents are, his address, or to whom the motor vehicle belongs. In fact, the officer is unable to gain any information at all from Sammy because of his incoherent state. What should be done with Sammy? Should he be put in a jail to sober up? Should he be turned over to the youth authorities? Should he be given a medical examination? What reasoning should be applied here?

PROBLEM IV

Joe Warmblood, aged 15, was arrested, tried, and convicted of rape and was sentenced to serve 30 years in the state penal institution for adult offenders. Since only adults can serve time in this particular penal institution and Joe is only 15, how was this legally accomplished?

PROBLEM V

A police officer picks up James Fleetfeet, aged 17, and detains him as a runaway. When the officer arrives at the local jail, the jailer tells him that there are no empty cells and that each one is occupied by at least one adult offender. However, there is one cell for three people that has only one occupant. The jailer tells the officer that James may be put in this cell, since he will just be held overnight. Is the jailer correct or incorrect? Why did you answer this way?

PROBLEM VI

Frank Blackstone, aged 10, is arrested on an outstanding felony warrant. He is taken by uniformed officers to police headquarters where he is questioned about the alleged crime by five plainclothes detectives. He is not advised of his rights according to the guidelines set down in *Miranda* v. *Arizona,* nor are his parents or attorney present during the questioning. Are the officers' actions right or wrong? What procedure should be followed in this situation?

PROBLEM VII

An attorney requests that two officers meet him at their headquarters. When he arrives, he requests that he be allowed to see the identification files of Sally Brown, a juvenile. The two officers had previously investigated a traffic accident in which Sally was the driver of one of the vehicles. The attorney represents the driver of the other vehicle. What would be the officers' correct legal response to the attorney's request? Why should he be answered in this way?

PROBLEM VIII

Bruce Toughboy, aged 15, is arrested for speeding and possession of marijuana. He is advised of his rights according to *Miranda* and states that he wants an attorney. An attorney is contacted, and he tells the officer, "just hold Bruce at the jail. I will meet you there within the hour." While waiting for the attorney to arrive, the officers book, fingerprint, and photograph Bruce. Three hours later the attorney arrives. He now claims the officers have violated Bruce's 5th and 6th Amendment rights, because they did not wait for his arrival before doing the aforementioned acts. Is the attorney right or wrong? What reasoning should be applied in arriving at the answer?

PROBLEM IX

While a burglary was being committed at John's Men Shop at 6:00 P.M., a city police officer saw three males emerge from the shop with their arms full of clothing. He gave chase, but they got away. During the subsequent investigation, a pair of pants was found in one of the dressing rooms, which contained probation papers for one I. B. Sharpe, aged 14. I. B. apparently had changed into a blue suit and left wearing the suit. The police, after checking juvenile records, found a photo and the address of I. B. They immediately went to the address, but I. B. was not at home. The father told them that he was away somewhere with his mother and gave the officers a full and complete description of the family car. An arrest warrant was immediately issued and broadcast via the local police radio network. At about 11:00 P.M., the car, occupied by the mother, is stopped. I. B. is not with her, and she tells the officers that she had just let him out at a movie. The officers ask to search the car, and they are allowed to without argument from the mother. They find a blue suit, which has a John's Men Shop label. Is the suit likely to be admissible evidence against I. B. at his trial? What reasoning should be applied in arriving at the correct answer?

PROBLEM X

James Davis, aged 17, met Joan Smith, aged 16, on the street in front of the soda parlor. James asked Joan to go to a country swimming hole with him to go skinnydipping. She said yes and they did! James had known Joan ever since they were small tots, and when they were 2 years old, their mothers had caught them nude together, playing in the yard. Since James had known Joan for so long, he knew that she was a hemophiliac, and that she had to take great pains not to get a small cut or tear in her skin. It was spring at "ye olde swimmin' hole." The flowers were blooming and the birds were singing. Being young and full of vim, vigor, and vitality, the pressure was just too great and they entered into intercourse, at which time Joan began bleeding and subsequently died. Could James be tried for murder? Should he be tried for rape? Would he likely be tried in juvenile court? Could James use his age as a defense for the crime of rape? Do you think Joan might have been negligent in her acts? What is the probable outcome of this situation?

PROBLEM XI

You are the officer and are called to investigate a traffic accident which has occurred on a two-lane street in a very congested area. There is a speed zone (45 m.p.h.) and there are houses along both sides of the street. When you arrive, you see Little Joe Blow, aged 13, lying at the edge of the pavement with both arms broken. A Corvette is parked about 10 feet from Joe and there is blood on the hood of the car. The driver of the Corvette is Julius Caesar, aged 99, and his 19-year-old bride is sitting beside him. Mr. Brown, Joe's neighbor, is standing beside Joe with a shotgun in his hand. Several other people who have witnessed the accident are also present. After medical assistance arrives, you begin an investigation and the following statements are elicited from the persons involved:

Mr. Brown: "Joe was throwing rocks in my yard. I came to my front door and told him to stop and go home. He did not do as I told him, but instead picked up a big stick and threw it at my house. It hit an electrical wire, knocking it loose and causing a short circuit, which caught the house on fire. I got the fire put out and then picked up my shotgun, which was loaded with rock salt, and shot above Joe's head. However, one of the pieces of salt went wild and hit Joe in the eye. Joe put his hands to his eyes and ran into the street, not looking where he was going. Mr. Caesar was approximately 4 feet from Joe at the time when he entered the street. He seemed to try to stop the car but he hit Joe anyway."

First Witness: "I was following Mr. Caesar, and if my speedometer is correct, he was doing about 55 miles per hour just before the boy ran into the street."

Second Witness: "I was walking along the street and saw Mr. Caesar hit that little boy, and he couldn't have been more than 4 or 5 feet from the boy when he ran into the street."

What crime or crimes could Joe possibly be charged with? What about Mr. Brown? Who is liable for Joe's injuries? Did Mr. Caesar's speeding constitute negligence per se? Who is liable for the damages to Mr. Brown's house?

REFERENCES

1. Black's Law Dictionary, rev. 4th ed., St. Paul, West Publishing Co., 1968, p. 1269.
2. Mississippi Code of 1972, Revised and Annotated, Sec. 7185-02.
3. *Kent* v. *United States,* 383 U.S. 541 (1966).
4. *In re Gault,* 387 U.S. 1 (1967).

5. *In re Winship,* 397 U.S. 358 (1970).
6. *Ivan* v. *City of New York,* 407 U.S. 203 (1972).
7. *McKeiver* v. *Pennsylvania,* 403 U.S. 528 (1971).
8. The Congressional Record, Vol. 120, No. 127, August, 1974, pp. 1–12.
9. Report on Police, National Advisory Commission on Criminal Justice Standards and Goals, Foreword.
10. Ibid., pp. 221–223.
11. James, Howard: "Children in Trouble: A National Scandal," The Christian Science Monitor, July 5, 1970.
12. Joe McGuire, Chief of Police. Crime Prevention Bureau, Tulsa Police Department, Tulsa, Oklahoma.

J.C. FUZZ FACE
ATTORNEY
AT LAW

CHAPTER VII

PERSONAL LIABILITY OF THE LAW ENFORCEMENT OFFICER

Tort law, which deals with civil liability for personal wrongs, is a complicated and broad field of the law of which the law enforcement officer must possess some basic knowledge. *Black's Law Dictionary* gives the following definition of a tort:

> A private or civil wrong or injury. A wrong independent of contract. . . . A violation of a duty imposed by general law or otherwise upon all persons occupying the relation to each other which is involved in a given transaction. . . . There must always be a violation of some duty owing to plaintiff, and generally such duty must arise by operation of law and not by mere agreement of the parties. . . .
>
> Three elements of every tort action are: Existence of a legal duty from defendant to plaintiff, breach of duty, and damage as proximate result. . . . A legal wrong committed upon the person or property independent of contract. It may be either (1) a direct invasion of some legal right of the individual; (2) the infraction of some public duty by which special damage accrues to the individual; (3) the violation of some private obligation by which like damage accrues to the individual. In the former case, no special damage is necessary to entitle the party to recover. In the two latter cases, such damage is necessary.[1]

Black's Law Dictionary defines a personal tort as:

> One involving or consisting in an injury to the person or to the reputation or feelings, as distinguished from an injury or damage to real or personal property, called a "property tort."[2]

The officer must realize that a tort is based on fault. The mere fact that harm is caused to another is not a basis for liability. Generally speaking, in order to hold a person liable for harm caused, there must be negligence involved in the act causing harm. However, an officer is only required to guard against those things which an "ordinarily prudent man" would believe, under the existing circumstances, might happen or are likely to happen. He is not required to guard against those things that *are not* likely to happen.

As an example, consider the sudden emergency doctrine. When someone is confronted with an emergency not of his own making, he is not required to act as sensibly as he would if he had time for consideration and reflection. However, he is required to act as a reasonable and prudent man would if confronted by the same emergency.

Another example is the voluntary assumption of duty rule:

> . . . a volunteer or a stranger is liable for an injury negligently inflicted on the person or property of another. The law imposes an obligation upon everyone who attempts to do anything, even gratuitously, of what he has undertaken . . . . A person who assumes to protect others against injury which may result to them from the exercise by him of a legal right in a legal manner is under no obligation to continue that protection indefinitely, and a self-imposed precaution may be pretermitted without necessarily incurring liability for negligence, but a duty voluntarily assumed cannot be carelessly abandoned without incurring liability for injury resulting from the abandonment.
>
> One who, being under no duty to do so, takes charge of another who is helpless adequately to aid or protect himself is liable for personal injuries to such other through failure to exercise reasonable care for such other's safety, or if by discontinuing his aid or protection he has left the other in a worse position than when he took charge. A person who voluntarily assumes the care of an injured person is charged with the duty of common or ordinary humanity to provide proper care and attention and may be held liable for a breach of that duty. The good Samaritan incurs a responsibility avoided by those who "pass by on the other side." One person seeing another in distress may or may not be under legal obligation to afford him relief, but if he does undertake it he is bound to act with reasonable prudence and care. . . . One who volunteers to help another who is unable to take care of himself does not become an insurer of the person he seeks to aid. No liability attaches to one who has assumed the care of an injured person where the evidence discloses that the duty to provide proper care and attention has been performed, or, assuming some neglect in performance, that the condition of the injured person was not made worse thereby. Generally speaking, the duty is fully performed by placing the injured person in the hands of a physician who is competent to treat him, providing the physician is procured without unnecessary delay.[3]

The foreseeability of harm resulting from a particular act is also at question in dealing with police liability. Acts which may be considered negligent when performed in one circumstance may not be negligent in others. If an officer's conduct is a substantial factor in causing harm to another, the fact that the officer did not foresee that harm would result or the extent of harm that would result would not always prevent him from being liable. In order for an officer's acts to be found dangerous or reckless, it is not always necessary that he himself recognize them as being so. His inability to recognize the danger could be due to his own reckless temperament or some other reason. However, these individual factors are largely irrelevant, since the officer is required to recognize as dangerous what a reasonable and prudent man would recognize as being dangerous conduct. The fact that he knows that someone might be within range of such dangerous conduct may show negligence, and it may be enough that he knows only that there is a strong probability that others are within this zone. In any case, it is within the jury's discretion to determine if an officer's actions were the proximate cause of another's injury.

The law enforcement officer should understand that the law of torts is a branch of the law that deals with civil wrongs against another person. While the criminal law protects society as a whole, tort law protects the individual. Our criminal law punishes the wrongdoer by imposing a fine, imprisonment, or both. In tort law, the wrongdoer is required to compensate his victim for the wrong done by payment of money damages. To say the least, it is the nature of a law enforcement officer's duties to expose him to the possibility of committing various kinds of torts. Some of the most common are assault and battery, deprivation of civil rights, malicious prosecution, and false arrest.

ASSAULT AND BATTERY

> Where the basis of an action is Assault and Battery, the intention with which the injury was done is immaterial so far as the maintenance of the action is concerned, provided the act causing the injury was wrongful, for if the act was wrongful, the intent must necessarily have been wrongful. The fact that the act was done with good intention, cannot change that which, by reason of its unlawfulness is essentially an assault and battery, into a lawful act, thereby releasing the aggressor from liability.[4]

> The American Law Institute's Restatement of the Law of Torts states that an act, other than the mere speaking of words, which directly or indirectly is a legal cause of putting another in apprehension of an immediate and harmful or offensive contact renders the actor civilly liable, if he intends thereby to inflict a harmful or offensive contact upon the other or a third person or to put the other or a third person in apprehension thereof, and the act is not consented to by the other, and the act is not otherwise privileged. This is the prevailing view taken in most jurisdictions.

> The Restatement further states that an act that is not done with the required intention to inflict a harmful or offensive contact does not make the actor liable to the other for an apprehen-

sion caused thereby, although the act involves an unreasonable risk of causing it and therefore would be negligent or reckless if the risk threatened bodily harm. And if the act is done with intention of putting a third person in apprehension of a harmful or offensive contact, but puts another person in such apprehension the actor is liable to such other person as though he had intended so to affect him.

To make the actor liable for an assault it is not necessary that he have, or believe that he has, the ability to inflict the harmful or bodily contact which his act apparently threatens. Nor is it necessary that the actor be inspired by personal hostility or a desire to offend.

An attempt to inflict a harmful or offensive contact, or to cause apprehension thereof, does not make an actor liable for an assault if the attempt is abandoned or frustrated before the other party knows it. But if the actor has so acted as to put another in such apprehension, he is liable for an assault even though he thereafter abandons his purpose or his purpose is frustrated. If a person intentionally puts another in apprehension of an immediate and harmful offensive contact, he is liable for an assault, although he gives to the other the option to escape the contact by obedience to a command given by the actor, unless the command is one which the actor is privileged to enforce by the infliction of the threatened contact or by a threat to inflict it.

To make the actor liable for an assault, he must have done an act other than the mere speaking of words that puts the other in apprehension of an immediate and harmful or offensive contact.[5]

The Restatement states that an act which, directly or indirectly, is the legal cause of a harmful contact with another's person makes the actor liable to the other, if the act is done with intention of bringing about a harmful or offensive contact or an apprehension thereof to the other or a third person, and the contact is not consented to by the other or the other's consent thereto is procured by fraud or duress, and the contact is not otherwise privileged. If an act is done with the intention of inflicting upon another an offensive but not a harmful bodily contact or of putting another in apprehension of either a harmful or offensive bodily contact, and such act causes a bodily contact to the other, the actor is liable for a battery although the act was not done with the intention of bringing about the resulting bodily harm. If an act is done with the intention of bringing about a harmful or offensive contact or apprehension thereof to a third person, but causes an offensive bodily contact to another person, the actor is liable to such other person as fully as though he intended so to affect him.[6]

A peace officer acting within his prescribed powers has the duty to use such force as may reasonably be necessary in the enforcement of law and the preservation of order, and he is not civilly liable for such force exerted on the person of another.

Although a peace officer who has lawful custody of a person is entitled to use such reasonable force as is necessary to carry out

> his duty to put the prisoner in jail he is liable for assault and battery if on that occasion he inflicts physical injury by using force not necessary to subdue the prisoner or to effect his incarceration, or unnecessarily subjects the prisoner to indignities of a physical nature. A peace officer may, of course, justify his act on the ground of self-defense.[7]
>
> It is the duty of peace officers acting within their prescribed powers to use such force as appears reasonably necessary in the enforcement of law and the preservation of order, and they cannot be held liable in an action for assault and battery for the use of such force on the person of another.
>
> The protection afforded to a peace officer in the use of force lawfully exercised in the performance of his duties extends to any person who comes to his aid. Therefore, ordinarily, a person aiding an officer is not liable for assault and battery on account of force used by him in rendering such lawful aid.
>
> An officer has the right to use such force as is reasonably necessary to prevent escape of a person who is in custody.[8]

The following cases are illustrative of the possible consequences to the officer if he uses excessive force in making an arrest or commits an assault and battery on the person of another.

A journeyman printer, who became a quadraplegic after he was struck with a nightstick by a Transit Authority officer and who allegedly received poor medical treatment at a city hospital, was awarded $3 million in damages by a New York state court. In addition, the man's wife received $135,000 for loss of marital services. The Transit Authority was held liable for 60 per cent of the damage award, and the New York Health and Hospitals Corporation, for the remainder. The victim, Robert Savaterre, became paralyzed as a result of his arrest in a subway station. Officer Reinhart responded to the screams of Savaterre's girlfriend, who was hysterical at the time. Savaterre was then arrested for harassment and for resisting arrest. Savaterre, who weighed 130 pounds, was handcuffed with his hands behind his back and was lying face down when the 260-pound officer allegedly beat him with his nightstick. The injured plaintiff was taken to a hospital emergency room where a resident physician allegedly manipulated his neck and spine, which resulted in a partially severed spinal cord. The projected cost of his annual hospitalization was computed to be $125,000 and his life expectancy as a result of his treatment after arrest to be 30 years.[9]

In a highly unusual settlement, the city of Newark, New Jersey, paid $135,000 in damages to Elmer Dunning after a 5-year court battle. Dunning, who was 49 years old, alleged that in 1969 he had been beaten by several Newark policemen after refusing to pay them for safe passage through the city.

In a recent case, the mother of a diabetic black man, who died 10 days after he was allegedly slapped several times while unconscious and hit repeatedly in the testicles by a city policeman, accepted a $12,000 settlement from the city. The incident occurred when Timothy O'Brien, aged 38, became unconscious in his home, and the police were called. Officer Frank Motyka accused the man of drunkenness and struck him at his home and later at the hospital. After a thorough investigation, Officer Motyka was dismissed from the police force. The mother, dissatisfied with the investigation, filed suit against the city. The litigation challenged the treatment he had received from a municipal employee. The $12,000 settlement was awarded by the court for the mother's "pain and suffering."[10]

In another case, a South Carolina sheriff was held liable for an assault committed by members of his posse. Sheriff Harold Vandiver of Abbeyville County, South Carolina, received a police report that a woman had been shot. The sheriff requested two county employees, James Hunter and Tay McMahan, to go along and help in the investigation. Traveling in a separate car from the sheriff, the two stopped Luther Scott, Jr., while he was walking along the side of a road near the scene of the shooting. The two did not identify themselves or explain their authority in any way, but commanded Scott to stop. When Scott saw that the two were armed, he fled. Hunter and McMahan gave chase and fired at Scott. He fell and injured his shoulder before reaching his brother's home, where he remained until the sheriff arrived.

Scott filed suit in federal district court against the sheriff, the two county posse-men, and the county supervisor. The court ruled that the sheriff was liable for the assault committed by Hunter and McMahan, since they were acting as his subordinates, but held that the supervisor was not liable. On appeal, the United States Court of Appeals awarded Scott $22,933.44 and found that Hunter and McMahan had used "excessive force . . . in the unlawful apprehension and arrest of Scott." The defense argued that the two were private citizens and were not acting "under color of law," as required under the Civil Rights Act. However, the court found that, under common law, the sheriff had the power to call out a *posse comitatus* to assist him, and thus Hunter and McMahan became temporary state law enforcement officers.[11]

What do these cases mean to the law enforcement officer? They should make him aware that he must never abuse the duties, privileges, and obligations bestowed upon him when he pinned on his badge and took the oath to uphold our laws. He must always be mindful that he is entitled to use only what force is necessary to make a lawful arrest and is never permitted to use unnecessary force. It might help him to imagine himself in the position of the offender and treat him as he would want to be treated himself. He owes an obligation to himself and to the people he serves to obey as well as enforce the laws. He can never allow himself to be controlled by personal spite or animosity toward an offender and must remember that under our legal system, each man is presumed innocent until proven guilty in a court of law. If the officer remembers that it is his duty to apprehend and the court's responsibility to punish, he will certainly be in a better position to do his job effectively. As some unknown author has said, "We, who, at best, know only in part, sometimes judge as if we were omniscient. May God grant us the ability to understand and help rather than to judge and hurt."

MALICIOUS PROSECUTION

A malicious prosecution is a suit "begun in malice without probable cause to believe the charges can be sustained . . . instituted with intention of injuring [the] defendant and without probable cause, and which terminates in favor of the person prosecuted."[12] A malicious prosecution may or may not be construed as a deprivation of a person's civil rights. Although it is closely akin to false arrest or false imprisonment, discussed in the next section, it will be treated separately here. If an officer is found to have acted wilfully or maliciously, out of personal revenge or spite, in prosecuting the defendant, the defendant may ask for punitive damages in addition to compensatory damages. Punitive damages are not awarded to compensate the victim for the wrong done to him but are imposed to punish the wrongdoer for his malicious or wilfull act and to deter him and others from engaging in such conduct in the future. As with most damage cases, the question of whether to award punitive damages and in what amount is generally left to a jury. When punitive damages are assessed, the amount is usually substantial.

Although suits for malicious prosecution are uncommon, the officer should be aware of the tort and should take precautions so that he does not become involved in such circumstances.

FALSE ARREST OR IMPRISONMENT

Generally, a false arrest or false imprisonment is an intentional, unlawful, and unprivileged restraint of a person's liberty, either in prison or elsewhere, whereby harm is caused to the person so confined. For example, an officer who makes an arrest, having the proper legal authority to so do, is privileged, and therefore, he may not be held liable in damages for false arrest or imprisonment, even if the person is later found to be innocent of the alleged crime for which he was arrested by the officer. The fact that one is acting under real or assumed authority distinguishes an arrest from other acts which might be unlawful. Therefore, the legality of the arrest or imprisonment depends upon the existence of that privilege, and hence, if an officer acts without proper legal authority he is not privileged and may be held liable for damages, even if the arrested person is found guilty.

> The police officer will be acting without proper legal authority, and therefore in an unprivileged manner, in any of the following situations:
>
> 1. If he arrests a person under an obviously invalid arrest warrant;

2. If he improperly executes a valid arrest warrant, as, for example, by arresting the wrong person;

3. If he arrests a person without an arrest warrant in a situation where the law says he must have one, as, for example, where he arrests a person for a misdemeanor not committed within his presence;

4. If he arrests a person without an arrest warrant where he lacks reasonable grounds for making the arrest;

5. If, after a valid arrest, he unreasonably detains the prisoner before bringing him before a magistrate; or

6. If he fails to release a prisoner from custody after the release is ordered by a court or other proper official.[13]

Our laws seek to strike a balance between the harm done to an individual and the overall good of society. They do so by protecting an officer if he acts within the limits of the legal authority vested in him, even though the person he arrests later turns out to be innocent. However, when the officer acts improperly or without authority, he loses that immunity, regardless of whether the person he arrests is actually guilty of the crime charged. This, like the operation of the exclusionary rule in evidence, is the penalty an officer must pay if he acts improperly.

The Florida Supreme Court held the city of Miami liable for $5000 in damages for false arrest when an injured man with a fractured skull was arrested and treated as a drunk. Two officers found Alton Exson, who was suffering from a head injury, in the front seat of a taxi in a dazed, incoherent condition. They stated that they smelled no alcohol on his breath. Exson was then taken to a hospital where he was examined by an intern who stated that he "felt he had been drinking" but had "no opinion as to whether he was drunk." After being booked on a drunk charge, Exson was kept in a cell. When his condition worsened, he was returned to the hospital where he died of a fractured skull. Thereafter, Exson's estate filed suit against the city for false arrest and imprisonment and won the suit. The city appealed. The Florida Supreme Court, in sustaining the damage award, said that the officers could not make a bad arrest good by relying on the doctor's finding, which was made afterwards. "The arresting officer must exercise his judgment at the time of the arrest, not later," the court commented, in finding that there had been no reasonable cause for the arrest or imprisonment.[14]

A United States district court held Police Commissioner J. F. O'Neill and Inspector George Francl in contempt of court for violating a temporary restraining order which had been issued on the day of President Nixon's visit to Philadelphia, enjoining police from interfering with a planned protest. Forty-five demonstrators had been forcibly removed from the Independence Hall area, and nine protesters had been arrested outside Mrs. Nixon's hotel. The United States Supreme Court refused to hear the appeal of the lower court's decision that found 13 police officers in contempt. In addition, the 45 protesters filed a false arrest suit in federal court and received a $45,300 settlement from the city. The settlement between the city and the demonstrators, in effect, affirmed the right of citizens to peacefully demonstrate against the President in public places.

In another case, Clyde C. Fye was driving through Andalusa, Illinois, when he was stopped by the police chief for speeding. Chief Ralph Woeckener charged Fye with disorderly conduct, but Fye was later acquitted on the charge. In a suit for $25,000, Fye alleged that he had been falsely arrested. A jury awarded Fye $1,500 for the false arrest and $500 for the violation of his civil rights, to be paid by both the town and the chief of police.[15]

A Detroit man accepted a $30,000 settlement in a civil suit against the city, in which he alleged that he was falsely imprisoned and brutally beaten by Detroit police. B. X. Tines, aged 20, claimed that police burst into his apartment and began beating him about the head with a shotgun and chair. Tines lapsed into unconsciousness and spent 2 days in and out of a coma in a hospital while being held for a robbery charge. Police testified that they had received an anonymous telephone call identifying Tines as the man who had robbed a drugstore. The department later conceded that he was not the man and released Tines without charging him. After 3 days of testimony, during which several witnesses stated that they had heard sounds of the struggle and saw police drag the bleeding Tines from his apartment, the city offered the $30,000 out-of-court settlement, which Tines accepted, even though he had originally sought a much higher amount in damages.[16]

In another case, a shopper filed suit against a department store that had temporarily detained him for alleged shoplifting. The shopper later received a $155,000 judgment. Store detectives had become suspicious of a male shopper who had a faltering gait, nervous appearance, and bruises and needle marks on his arm when he selected a shirt and cufflinks and put them in a shopping bag. While the shopper contended that he had merely moved to another counter in the men's department, the detectives claimed that he had been heading for an escalator when they stopped him. He was detained for 1½ hours and signed a form releasing the store from civil liability before leaving. He was not booked or prosecuted in any way for the alleged offense.

The irate shopper filed suit against the May Department Store for false imprisonment. He stated that his physical condition was caused by kidney dialysis treatment, and that he signed the release form only because the store detective refused to release him until it was executed. He also claimed that the detectives denied him the right to make a phone call, verbally abused him, and toyed with a revolver while questioning him. The jury awarded him $25,000 compensatory and $50,000 punitive damages for false imprisonment, $40,000 compensatory and $40,000 punitive damages for assault, and $10,000 for "insulting words." In affirming on appeal, the District of Columbia Court of Appeals left standing all damage awards, except the $10,000 for insulting words, reasoning that the language used in the questioning by the detective was properly related to the legitimate suspicion of the plaintiff's possible use of drugs.[17]

DEPRIVATION OF CIVIL RIGHTS

Many times, in cases in which the plaintiff claims a deprivation of his civil rights, the question narrows to the issue of whether or not the officer was acting in his official capacity or under color of law. To answer this question, it is often necessary to examine the provisions of certain sections of the United States Code in order to arrive at an equitable solution.

Title 42, United States Code, Section 1983, states:

> Every person who, under color of any statute, ordinance, regulation, custom, or usage, of any State or Territory, subjects, or causes to be subjected, any citizen of the United States or other person within the jurisdiction thereof to the deprivation of any rights, privileges, or immunities secured by the Constitution and laws, shall be liable to the party injured in an action at law, suit in equity, or other proper proceeding for redress.

A suit under this section may be filed in the United States district courts under the provisions of Title 28, United States Code, Section 1343, and in addition, may also be tried in state courts. An officer may also be criminally prosecuted for violating constitutional rights in addition to being required to respond in damages to the injured victim. The two principal federal criminal statutes available for the prosecution of cases involving police abuse are Sections 241 and 242 of the United States Criminal Code. Section 242 makes the wilful deprivation of federal constitutional or statutory rights by those acting *under color of state law* a criminal offense punishable by as much as a $1,000 fine, one year imprisonment, or both. The language of Section 242 closely parallels that of Section 1983, the civil rights damage statute, previously cited. It should be noted that the fact that an officer's conduct is also a crime under local law would not insulate him from federal prosecution, since he can be tried and convicted by both jurisdictions.

Section 241, a conspiracy statute, provides:

> If two or more persons conspire to injure, oppress, threaten, or intimidate any citizen in the free exercise or enjoyment of any right or privilege secured to him by the Constitution or laws of the United States, or because of his having so exercised the same; or if two or more persons go in disguise on the highway, or on the premises of another, with intent to prevent or hinder his free exercise or enjoyment of any right or privilege so secured . . . they shall be fined not more than $5,000 or imprisoned not more than ten years, or both.

This statute remained rather dormant until 1966, when the Supreme Court in *United States* v. *Price*[18] took what was for all practical purposes a dead statute and remodeled it into a potent civil rights law. The *Price* case grew out of the highly publicized deaths of three civil rights workers near Philadelphia, Mississippi. Eighteen persons were indicted under Section 241, but the district court dismissed the indictment on the ground that Section 241 did not embrace conspiracies to deprive an individual of due process of law as provided for in the Fourteenth Amendment. The government appealed, and the issue of the proper interpretation of Section 241 was brought squarely before the United States Supreme Court. The Court ruled that Section 241 did embrace conspiracies to interfere with Fourteenth Amendment rights, at least when state officers and agents participated in them.

To understand the scope of Sections 242 and 1983, it is necessary to understand how the courts have interpreted the phrase "under color of" state law.

> Misuse of power, possessed by virtue of state law and made possible only because the wrongdoer is clothed with authority of state law, is action taken 'under color of state law.'[19]

> Under the construction of *Classic* it is irrelevant that the officer may be exceeding his authority or even that he is violating a positive directive. State law empowered him to act when it entrusted him with the responsibilities of a peace officer. Everything he does in his official capacity from this point on is considered to be action taken under color of State law.[20]

> A law enforcement officer cannot divorce himself from liability under Section 1983 by removing his badge before embarking on a course of unconstitutional conduct.[21]

> The responsibilities that inhere in the office accompany the officer whenever he acts in the line of duty. He is no less accountable for his conduct because he was dressed in plainclothes and riding in an unmarked car when the incident occurred, or because he was motivated by personal spite or animosity toward the victim.[22]

> The cause of action created by Section 1983 is against the wrongdoer only and the department that hired him cannot be held answerable in damages to the injured party for the officer's misconduct.[23]

The following remarks were made in a lecture presented by Special Agent John A. Mintz of the Federal Bureau of Investigation, Training Division, at the Law Enforcement Institute, Memphis State University, Memphis, Tennessee, on May 23, 1968, and later were reprinted in the *F.B.I. Law*

Enforcement Bulletin. The excerpts reprinted here present an excellent explanation of Section 1983 and how it is applied today.

This federally created right was largely ignored until the late 1930's when the first notable test of its effectiveness came in a Supreme Court decision (*Hague* v. *CIO,* 307 U.S. 496 [1939]) that the language of 1983 was adequate to remedy an alleged interference with the right to free speech and peaceful assembly. Since that time, the statute has slowly but steadily assumed greater importance for the law enforcement officer. Significant cases concerning policemen, sued under this statute, found their way to the Supreme Court in 1961 and in 1967. There is reason to believe that such suits will be filed with increasing frequency in the future.

This estimate of the situation seems dire, but there is no need for despair—at least, not yet. However, we cannot simply ignore this problem in the hope that it will retreat to the obscurity of the statute books whence it came. Experience and good judgment dictate that we respond in some affirmative fashion. The purpose of this study is to equip officers with the information necessary to understand the present and potential significance of 1983 and to suggest alternatives that may be used to limit its impact. The rest will be up to the officer, his department, and the community being served.

Officers generally are acquainted with the basic mechanics of criminal procedure, and it may be useful to begin by comparing this familiar framework with that upon which civil liability depends. In the criminal context, the State accuses a person of having failed in his duty to obey the law. If the charge is proven beyond a reasonable doubt, the person may be liable for a fine, imprisonment, loss of certain rights, or the death sentence. In a civil suit, one person (plaintiff) accuses another (defendant) of having failed in some duty he owed the plaintiff. If the evidence presented to support the charge is more convincing than that offered to the contrary, the plaintiff wins. The defendant may be liable to pay a sum of money determined by the case as necessary to compensate the plaintiff for his damages. If the defendant has been shown to be a particularly bad actor who needs to be taught a lesson, he may be ordered to pay an additional amount as a penalty.

Under both systems, if the defendant owed no duty to the complainant, he should not be penalized even if the plaintiff in fact suffered some damage. The defendant will be liable only where it is shown that (1) he was obliged to do or refrain from doing something and (2) the complainant was damaged because of the defendant's failure to comply with his obligation.

One of the heavy responsibilities of each law enforcement officer is to recognize and protect the rights, privileges, and immunities of persons within the jurisdiction he serves. 1983 crystallizes the officer's duty in this respect where *constitutional* or *Federal* rights are concerned. It declares that persons injured by a deprivation of rights, privileges, and immunities secured by the

Constitution and laws of the United States may sue for redress. Thus the statute implies that an officer has a specific duty to avoid depriving others of the enjoyment of these guarantees and that, by his failure to comply with that duty, he may incur personal liability for the resulting injuries.

But why identify this statute with police officers when it uses the words "every person" to describe those who may be liable? Two limitations on the applicability of 1983 provide the answer. First, the defendant must have been acting under color of any statute, ordinance, regulation, custom, or usage of any State or Territory. This eliminates all those persons, including Federal agents, who have no official connection with and do not assume to act under any sort of State authority. (*Sheridan* v. *Williams,* 333 F.2d 581 [1964] [FBI Agents not liable under 1983]; *Bryant* v. *Donnell,* 239 F. Supp. 681 [1965] [private person making citizen's arrest is not acting as a public officer under color of law].)

Second, many persons who do act under the authority of the State are protected against suit by special immunity, long recognized under the common law. For example, judges cannot be sued personally for having rendered an unpopular or unconstitutional decision or for issuing a judicial order that has the effect of depriving the plaintiff of his rights. (*Carmack* v. *Gibson,* 363 F.2d 862 [1966] [plaintiff's conviction was set aside and further prosecution declined, his suit against the State judge under 1983 dismissed]; *Gaito* v. *Strauss,* 249 F. Supp. 923 [1966] [judges have absolute immunity without regard to their motives].) Generally the prosecutor enjoys the same immunity in deciding which cases should be prosecuted and in what manner. (*Bauers* v. *Heisl,* 361 F.2d 58 [1966].)

Private attorneys are "officers of the court," but, for purposes of 1983, they are not "acting under color of" law whether they are appointed or retained. (*Kregger* v. *Posner,* 248 F. Supp. 804 [1966] [private attorney]; *Reinke* v. *Richardson,* 279 F. Supp. 155 [1968] [court-appointed attorney is immune].)

Government officials, required to make decisions necessary for the continued functioning of the government, also are protected from personal liability for executing the duties of their respective offices. Such officials are described as having a "discretionary function," and, to get the business of government done, it is necessary for them, like judges, to work free of the harassment of civil suits. Other government officers such as policemen, whose decisions are more routine, have a "ministerial function." They do not enjoy official immunity because it is not essential for the perpetuation of government that they be protected from personal civil liability. Thus the officer stands alone. His police department cannot be liable. It is not a "person" under 1983. (*Burmeister* v. *NYCPD,* 275 F. Supp. 690 [1967].) And, private citizens who obey a police order to assist are not considered as acting under color of State law for purposes of the statute. Finally, "sovereign immunity" protects the unit of government from suit unless it consents to assume responsibility for the actions of its officers.

With all of these exemptions, it is obvious that the law enforcement officer has little competition insofar as qualifying as a defendant in a 1983 suit is concerned. It is true that others such as election officials, school authorities, and hospital administrators have been sued under this statute. But the problem is particularly acute for the officer, who is expected to enforce the law as well as administer it. The frequency of his confrontations with potential plaintiffs is unequalled by any other class of persons who could be liable under 1983.

One thing should be made clear. It is not because a man is a police officer that he is liable. Rather, liability is imposed where a man uses his official authority to deprive the plaintiff of the protections described above. Acting "under color of" law does not require that the officer must have been enforcing a statute or ordinance at the time, nor is it necessary that his actions be within the authority granted him as a police officer. Acts may be "under color of" State law even where they are clearly in violation of the State constitution and statutes. In short, if the defendant was acting as an officer at the time of the alleged deprivation, then he was acting "under color of" law for purposes of personal liability under 1983. (*Monroe* v. *Pape* 365 U.S. 167 [1961]; *U.S.* v. *Price,* 383 U.S. 787 [1966]; *Stringer* v. *Dilger,* 313 F.2d 536 [1963].)

The statute provides for cases in which an officer is alleged to have been directly responsible for the injury, as well as instances where the officer allegedly caused the deprivation by some indirect means. Thus, the defendant officer might be liable for ordering another person to act in such a way as to bring about the alleged injury. The existence of the officer's responsibility has been measured in terms of cause and effect. In brief, the question has been: Did the officer's acts or his orders result in the alleged deprivation of rights? The plaintiff has not had to prove that the officer actually intended to deprive him of constitutional or Federal rights. (*Cohen* v. *Norris,* 300 F.2d 24 [1962]; *Stringer* v. *Dilger,* 313 F.2d 536 [1963].) For a sufficient complaint, he has been required to show only that the *effect* of the officer's conduct was to deprive him of such rights.

On the contrary, an officer may be able to defend himself in such a civil suit by showing that he did not *intend* to deprive the plaintiff of constitutional rights, that he was acting in good faith, and that his actions were based on what reasonably appeared to him at the time to have been valid authority. Such a case was *Pierson* v. *Ray* (386 U.S. 547 [1967]) in which it was held a sufficient defense for the officer to show that, in making an arrest, he acted in good faith and on probable cause while enforcing a statute that had not been declared invalid at the time of arrest, though it was later declared unconstitutional in an unrelated case. (See, also, *Notaras* v. *Ramon,* 383 F.2d 403 [1967] [case dismissed against officers where they ". . . reasonably and in good faith believed that their conduct was lawful, even though it was not"].)

Other defenses may be available to the officer. For example, he might claim that he violated no legal duty to the plaintiff under the facts alleged in the case. In *Striker* v. *Pancher* (317 F.2d 780 [1963]) the plaintiff sued the officer for failure to furnish legal counsel and for failure to advise him of his right to counsel in a State criminal trial. The officer was exonerated as he had no duty to furnish counsel or to advise concerning the availability of counsel. "The failure to inform him and the failure to furnish counsel was a failure in the judicial process." (317 F.2d at 783.) Of course, the result in this case should not be confused with the requirements flowing from *Miranda* v. *Arizona* (384 U.S. 436 [1966]) that advice of the right to counsel must be given prior to custodial interrogation. *Miranda* is concerned with the admissibility of evidence while *Striker* is concerned with the positive duty an officer owes to any person. If there is to be no interrogation, the officer has no constitutional obligation to give the pertinent warning or to obtain counsel for anyone. In *Huey* v. *Barloga* (277 F. Supp. 864 [1967]) a father sued officers for failure to provide protection to his son who was beaten to death on the street. The court ruled that the public officers are not guarantors of the individual safety of citizens.

Another available defense is the statute of limitations. Generally, civil actions must be begun within a specified period of time after the injury or they are barred. Since the Federal law does not provide a time limitation on actions filed under 1983, the period is determined by reference to the law of the State in which the Federal court having jurisdiction over the case is located. This is ordinarily done by selecting the State statute of limitations that applies in circumstances most like those which exist in the Federal suit (*Mulligan* v. *Schlachter,* 389 F.2d 231 [1968]) or by following the statute which sets limitations for cases not specifically provided for. (*McIver* v. *Russell,* 264 F. Supp. 22 [1967].) There, if the plaintiff files suit after the time period has elapsed during which he should have begun the action, the officer need only claim the statute of limitations for his defense.

At one time, the officer had available, as defensive ammunition, the abstention doctrine and the requirement of exhaustion of administrative remedies. (*Stefanelli* v. *Minard,* 342 U.S. 117 [1951].) It was thought that the plaintiff could be required to look first to his own State and exhaust the possibilities that local machinery would give relief against the alleged wrongs committed by the State officer before coming to the Federal court. Moreover, the Federal court would sometimes decline to hear a case where it appeared that abstention was called for to maintain the balance between Federal authority and State authority. These efforts were aimed, in part, at avoiding Federal direction of State and local law enforcement policies. Then came *Monroe* v. *Pape* (365 U.S. 167 [1961]), in which the Supreme Court clearly established the principle that the right to sue police officers under 1983 was completely independent of any State remedies that might be available. The Court said, "It is no answer that the State has a law which if enforced would give relief. The Federal remedy is supplementary to the State remedy, and the latter need not first be sought and refused before the Federal one is invoked." (365 U.S. at 183.) So, with the basis for abstention crumbling, the officer should not regard abstention or exhaustion of local remedies as useful avenues of defense. (*Marshall* v. *Sawyer,* 301 F.2d 639 [1962].) (The abstention doctrine does not permit the Federal district courts to defer to the State courts for the decision of Federal constitutional questions, and whether there is "color of" State law is a Federal, not a State, question.)

However, *Monroe* v. *Pape* provided good reason to believe that the officer will be permitted to raise other defenses that are familiar in civil suits. The Court said that 1983 ". . . should be read against the background of tort liability that makes a man responsible for the natural consequences of his actions." (365 U.S. at 187.) That background includes such defenses as self-defense, unforeseeability, and good faith. (*Cohen* v. *Norris,* 300 F.2d 24 [1962].)

The allegations of misconduct in 1983 suits are drawn from a broad spectrum of rights, privileges, and immunities afforded protection by the Federal Constitution and laws of the United States. But mere conclusory allegations of what otherwise would be State-law claims against the officer, as for false imprisonment, malicious prosecution, assault, and battery, have not been enough to satisfy most Federal courts that a constitutional violation was involved. The courts have been ". . . very strict in requiring that a complaint set forth *facts* showing a denial of the protected rights and not merely "factually unsupported characterizations of the complained of acts of the defendants, as 'malicious, depriving plaintiffs of their constitutional rights.' " (*Hornsby* v. *Allen,* 326 F.2d 605, 611 [1964].) Moreover, it has been said that "No one has a *constitutional* right to be free from a law officer's honest misunderstanding of law or facts in making an arrest." (*Agnew* v. *City of Compton,* 239 F.2d 226 [1956]; *Gabbard* v. *Rose,* 359 F.2d 182 [1966].)

Yet the trend of recent cases has been to open the Federal courts to an increasing number of suits filed under 1983. The current volumes of the Federal Supplement and of the Federal Reporter, Second Series, which publish decisions of the U. S. District Courts and the Courts of Appeals, respectively, now show a substantial number of 1983 cases being handled in the Federal system.

This increasing emphasis on 1983 may escalate its significance to the officer, but emphasis alone cannot broaden the scope of its authority. For example, in *Ream* v. *Handley* (359 F.2d 738 [1966]), the court declared that the statute does not ". . . confer jurisdiction where a person seeks only to protect property or monetary rights." It is clear that there must be a deprivation of *constitutional* or *Federal law* protection to support a claim under 1983.

The most common approach is for the complainant to allege a violation of the 14th amendment, section 1 of which contains the following language:

> "No State shall make or enforce any law which shall abridge the privileges or immunities of citizens of the United States; nor shall any State deprive any person of life, liberty, or property, without due process of law; nor deny to any person within its jurisdiction the equal protection of the laws."

The key words, "privileges and immunities," "due process of law," and "equal protection of the law," are the vehicles by which 1983 protections are usually identified. For example, the guarantee against unreasonable searches and seizures contained in the fourth amendment is applicable to State officers by reason of the "due process" language of the 14th. Thus, an officer acting contrary to the fourth amendment might be held liable for denying a citizen his constitutional right to due process of law.

The "equal protection" language has been used largely in 1983 suits against public officers other than policemen. This trend is demonstrated by the numerous school desegregation cases following the Supreme Court's decision in *Brown* v. *Board of Education* (347 U.S. 483 [1959]), which have cited the statute as authority for suit. A few "equal protection" cases have concerned law enforcement problems which seem to engender equal treatment of individuals. (*Butler* v. *Crumlish,* 229 F. Supp. 565 [1964] [prisoner's inability to furnish bail resulted in continued detention and subjection to lineup procedures]; *Marshall* v. *Sawyer,* 301 F.2d 639 [1962] [plaintiff alleged his name was listed as an undesirable in a "black book" used by casino operators to deny him privileges enjoyed by others]. See, also, *Rivers* v. *Royster,* 360 F.2d 592 [1962] [inmate claimed that, unlike other prisoners, he was denied opportunity to receive newspaper of his choice.].)

Alleged deprivations of "privileges and immunities" have been even less evident in suits against officers under 1983. The law has not provided the necessary background for such guarantees to be readily identified; therefore, this part of the 14th amendment has achieved no real significance in the area of civil liability of police officers.

Two decisions of the Supreme Court have provided the major guidelines for application of 1983. The facts in both cases are basically simple and familiar to all officers who have worked on the street. In many ways, the defendant officers in these cases represent the plight of policemen everywhere, as the problems they faced are not unlike those being faced daily in all jurisdictions. The distinction is that *their* responses to the challenges of the law enforcement profession were characterized as causing deprivations of somebody's constitutional rights. One case arose in Illinois and the other in Mississippi, but they could well have been produced in any other State. When this fact is added to the expanding application of 1983, little more should be required to convince officers of the need to be aware of the problem of potential liability and to do something about it.

Monroe v. *Pape* grew out of a murder investigation in Chicago. The facts alleged by the plaintiff were that 2 days after the murder, at 5:45 A.M., 13 police officers led by the deputy chief of detectives broke through two doors of an apartment, woke the complainant and his wife with flashlights, forced them at gunpoint to leave their bed and stand naked in the center of their living room, and then aroused their six children and herded them into the living room. One detective struck the father several times with his flashlight and called him offensive names and another officer pushed the mother. Other officers hit and kicked several of the children and pushed them to the floor. The officers ransacked every room, throwing clothing from closets to the floor, dumping drawers, and ripping mattress covers.

The father then was taken to the police station and detained on "open" charges for 10 hours, during which time he was interrogated about the murder and exhibited in lineups. He was not advised of his procedural rights. He was not permitted to call his family or an attorney. He was subsequently released without criminal charges having been filed against him.

The officers acted without warrants.

In the 1983 suit filed against the officers and the City of Chicago, the plaintiffs were the father and mother and the children. Their complaint alleged that the officers, acting under color of law and as agents of the city, were liable for invasion of the home, search without a warrant, and arrest and detention which deprived rights, privileges, and immunities secured by the Constitution.

The City claimed it was not liable under the statute. The individual officers moved to dismiss on the ground that the plaintiffs failed to state a claim on which relief could be given because the activities alleged also violated the laws of the State of Illinois and therefore the officers could not have been acting "under color of" law.

The Supreme Court examined the legislative history of the statute and held that "persons" in the statute did not include municipalities. However, officers *are* "persons," and the fact that the Illinois constitution and laws prohibit unreasonable searches and seizures is no barrier to a 1983 suit. The Court said, "Misuse of power, possessed by virtue of State law and made possible only because the wrongdoer is clothed with the authority of State law, is action taken under color of State law." Moreover, the plaintiffs did not have to show that the officers specifically intended to violate their constitutional rights; the ". . . statute should be read against the background of tort liability that makes a man responsible for the natural consequences of his actions." (365 U.S. at 187.) Therefore, the complaint stated a cause of action against the officers but not the city.

The facts alleged in *Pierson* v. *Ray* were that clergymen, dressed in clerical attire, participated in a prayer pilgrimage commencing at New Orleans and continuing through Mississippi to Michigan. When they got to Jackson, Miss., fifteen of them went to the bus terminal. They had bus tickets for transportation to Chattanooga, Tenn.

Arriving at the station about 40 minutes before the bus was due to depart, they started toward the coffee shop but were stopped by two city police officers. They were directed to "move on." The clergymen remained where they were. Soon a captain of police arrived, and he ordered them to "move on." There was testimony at the trial that a crowd had gathered and they were "mumbling in a very ugly mood."

The clergymen were arrested and the police captain charged them with disorderly conduct under a Mississippi statute. They were tried before a municipal police justice and given the maximum sentence. On appeal to the State court, one of them was found not guilty and the charges against the rest were dropped.

The clergymen sued the officers and the police justice, under 1983, claiming $11,001 damages. In the District Court the jury verdict was for the officers, and the clergymen appealed. In the Court of Appeals, the court said:

1. The police justice was immune from suit.
2. The officers were immune from liability under general tort law because they had probable cause to make the arrest, and because the statute on which they based their authority had not at that time been declared unconstitutional.

But the Court of Appeals held that the officers could be liable under the Federal Civil Rights Statue, because in *Monroe* v. *Pape* the Supreme Court indicated that good faith and reliance upon a statute, subsequently declared invalid, are not good defenses for the officers. The court ordered a new trial on the Civil Rights Statute liability.

At the new trial the court held that the ministers could not recover if it were proved they went to Mississippi anticipating that they would be illegally arrested because such action would constitute *consent* to the arrest, and there is a principle in tort law that "he who consents to a wrong cannot be injured."

This case eventually went to the Supreme Court to resolve three questions:

1. Is a local judge liable for an unconstitutional conviction?
2. Should the clergymen be denied recovery where they acted with the anticipation they would be illegally arrested?
3. Can the officers defend their case on the grounds they acted in good faith and had probable cause when they made the unconstitutional arrest?

The Supreme Court held:

1. A judge is not liable under 1983 as long as he is acting within his judicial discretion.
2. The clergymen did not consent to the arrest. There was no proof they tricked or goaded the officers into arresting them. They exercised their right to enter the premises and the fact that they expected they might be arrested for so doing does not prevent them from suing.
3. There is a general common law rule that an officer who arrests someone with probable cause is not liable for false arrest simply because the innocence of the suspect is later proved. A police officer does not have to choose between being charged with dereliction of duty if he does not arrest

when he has probable cause, and being sued for damages if he does. The same reasons would excuse the officer from liability for acting under a statute that he reasonably believes to be valid but which is later held unconstitutional.

Section 1983 should be read against the background of tort liability that makes a man responsible for the natural consequences of his actions. Included in that background are the defenses of good faith and probable cause.

Drawing from both *Monroe* v. *Pape* and *Pierson* v. *Ray,* there are some broad general guidelines that can be ascertained. As an officer, you may be liable under 1983:

1. If you are enforcing a valid statute in such a way as to deprive an individual of constitutional rights.
2. If you are enforcing a statute you know or reasonably should know to be unconstitutional in such a way as to deprive such rights.
3. If you violate the State constitution and laws, as well as the Federal, in depriving rights (you are still acting "under color of" law).
4. If you do not have the specific intent to deprive of a known constitutional right.

In contrast, you should not be held liable under 1983:

1. If you act in good faith and on reasonable grounds, assuming that the law you are enforcing is constitutional. The fact that some court decides at a later time that the statute is unconstitutional should not deny you this defense.
2. If you fail or refuse to act and you had no legal duty to act in regard to the complainant, there is no basis for liability.[24]

RECENT DECISIONS RELATED TO SECTION 1983

The officer can gain better insight into the application of Section 1983 by comparing the following decisions with the material previously discussed.

A civil rights action under Title 42, United States Code, Section 1983 was brought against Officer Joseph Ziedonis after he fired a 12-gauge shotgun twice at three fleeing youths, who had attempted a burglary of a residence. Ziedonis testified that he "reasonably believed" that one of the three youths who turned on him as they fled the scene was armed. One youth was carrying a 12-inch steel-blue file which he pointed at the pursuing officer. Two of the teenagers were wounded when the officer fired. The federal court held that the officer's use of deadly force was unreasonable, since Ziedonis knew that his partner was covering the only exit of escape. One boy received \$1,500 in damages and \$279.83 for medical expenses. His companion was awarded \$5,000 and an additional \$1,767.31 for medical expenses. Officer Ziedonis has appealed the decision to the Seventh Circuit Court.[25]

In Long Island, after four years of legal arguments, George Roache, Jr., a 24-year-old black student, was awarded \$22,000 under the Civil Rights Act against the Suffolk County Police. Roache had been arrested in September,

1970, at a gas station near the college which he attended. His parents did not hear from him for 11 days and were outraged to find him bruised with swollen eyes, a beaten prisoner in jail.

Five persons arrested in a Dekalb, Illinois, drug raid were awarded $22,000 by a federal jury which found that three policemen had violated the plaintiffs' civil rights. The former Northern Illinois University students and their wives were among 12 persons who sued the police for $1.2 million in damages. The suit alleged that three law enforcement officers planned and executed the raid without search or arrest warrants. One Northern Illinois University security officer, a Dekalb city police officer, and a Dekalb County sheriff's deputy were held liable for false arrest, false imprisonment, and assault and battery.[26]

Three vice officers broke up an open house at the home of a university professor where the guests were protesting anti-ballistic missiles. David Lykken was selling beer, coffee, and soda, but no hard liquor, for a 50¢ donation. Detective Kenneth Tidgewell and two officers purchased beer at the "cash bar" and then announced that all 17 guests and the Lykkens were under arrest. A search of the house was then made. All of Professor Lykken's personal papers were seized, and everyone was taken to jail. Fifteen guests were booked at the county jail and two received citations; periods of detention ranged from 37 minutes to 5 hours. All the charges against the guests for patronizing a disorderly house were dropped, and the charge of selling liquor without a license was also dropped against the Lykkens.

Bringing suit under Section 1983 in federal court, the Lykkens and their guests alleged false arrest and illegal search. The court found that the search incident to the arrest exceeded the scope delineated in *Chimel* v. *California,* and, noting that there was no evidence to support a belief that the police were engaging in political surveillance, the court found inescapable the inference that the raid was a harassment tactic against the Lykkens because of their political beliefs. Damages of $19,000 were awarded against the three detectives: the 17 guests were awarded $500 each, totaling $8,500; the three Lykkens were each awarded $1,000 compensatory and $2,500 punitive damages.[27]

A Detroit waitress challenged the hiring procedures of the Detroit Police Department in federal court and obtained a summary judgment and preliminary injunction against the police commissioner and other defendants. The Civil Rights Act suit was brought in behalf of all women who were applicants for police positions, but had been denied employment. The court noted that (1) only 1.56 to 2.15 per cent of the force were women; (2) separate eligibility lists were maintained; (3) entrance exams were offered less often for women; and (4) females were not given usual police assignments. Alleging violations of Title 42, United States Code, Sections 1983 and 1000(e), the plaintiff class put the burden on the defendants to show a rational basis for sexual discimination. The department's lawyers maintained that past quota practices were "necessary to safe and efficient operation" of the department; however, no evidence was brought forth to justify this statement. The terms of the injunction were:

1. All future exams must be given to men and women together.

2. No later than June 1, 1974, a special entrance exam must be given to all women whose applications have been held on file and who have never been tested.

3. At least one qualified female must be hired for every male hired until further order of the court.

4. All assignments are to be made without regard to sex.

5. Recruiting materials must stress the equal role of men and women in the department.

6. A press release was ordered, outlining the provisions of the injunction and informing the public that henceforth the police department would hire officers without regard to sex.

It is believed that the Detroit Police Department does not plan to appeal the decision but hopes to obtain a temporary stay of the injunction in order to better prepare for its implementation.[28]

In another case, an Illinois woman, who was considered qualified enough to work as a clerk in the DuPage County Sheriff's Department but not as a deputy sheriff, also brought suit. Ms. O'Brien took and passed the written and physical examinations for county deputy sheriff and was placed on an eligibility list. She was not hired, however, and was informed that it was because of her sex. She filed a civil rights action against the sheriff under Section 1983, alleging discrimination. Furthermore, when the department found out about her suit, she was fired from her clerk's job; and she therefore also sought damages for wrongful discharge.

The United States district court ruled that the would-be deputy had a triable action against the sheriff under state law. As to her loss of her job as a clerk, the court noted that the plaintiff had stated a good cause of action for wrongful discharge and the claim was maintainable under Section 1983. In view of the court's decision, the DuPage County Board of Supervisors offered the plaintiff a $9,000 settlement, which she accepted.[29]

OTHER RELATED DECISIONS

The family of a Whittier, California, man, killed in a bizarre, accidental police shooting, received a $900,000 settlement. Heyward Dyer was holding his infant son in his arms when a bullet smashed through the apartment ceiling, grazed the baby's head, and fatally wounded the father in the head. The apartment directly above the Dyers' had been the scene of a narcotics raid by six state, county, and Vernon, California, officers. While they were questioning suspects, a detective lowered his AR-15 rifle toward the floor and was trying to put on the safety catch when it discharged the fatal bullet. Dyer's death was witnessed by his pregnant wife and three other family members, who subsequently filed a $4.25 million suit. A compromise was worked out by a superior court judge who estimated that a jury verdict would range between $600,000 and $1.5 million. The costs of the stipulated judgment were divided among the state ($373,500), county ($193,500), and the city of Vernon ($333,000). All six officers were disciplined by being suspended from duty without pay.[30]

In another case, Duane Marusa sought to recover damages for a bullet wound he suffered when he was shot by an allegedly "grossly intoxicated" off-duty District of Columbia police officer. In his negligence suit, Marusa named as defendants Officer Delbert Clark, Police Chief Jerry Wilson, and the District of Columbia. Marusa contended that Wilson was negligent in hiring Clark and in failing to properly train and supervise him. The District of Columbia was also named as being liable for negligence on the same grounds as Chief Wilson. Chief Judge Bazelon stated, "Officer Clark's tort was made possible only through the use of his service revolver, which he carried by authority of the city government. Policemen are not only authorized but required to carry their service revolvers, as well as their badges and identification cards, 'at all times' . . . thus if the officer misuses his weapon, a judge or jury might reasonably find that misuse to have been proximately caused by the government's negligence in hiring, training or supervising the policeman."[31]

Sheriff Robert Carroll of Blount County, Tennessee, unsuccessfully appealed a United States district court judgment that held him liable for punitive as well as compensatory damages for personal injuries caused by his deputy in a shootout. At the time of the shooting, the deputy was attempting to serve an arrest warrant, which was in the performance of his official duty. The shooting was decreed by the court to have been entirely unjustified. On appeal, the sheriff did not question the award of compensatory damages, but he argued that punitive damages should not have been assessed against him, because he was not present at the shooting and did not authorize it. In his defense, he contended that under federal law, damages may not be assessed against a principal for acts committed by an agent that were not participated in or ratified by the principal. However, under Tennessee law, punitive damages are allowable in such situations, and the court affirmed the assessment of punitive damages.[32]

OBSERVATION

The current trend toward more civil rights lawsuits began in 1961 when the United States Supreme Court ruled in favor of a plaintiff who claimed that Chicago police officers had brutalized him and his family in their home. Since that date, a more than welcome number of lawsuits, based on alleged "police brutality" or "deprivation of civil rights," have been decided against the individual officer, his department, his superiors, or even the governmental entity that employed him. At present, federal courts are flooded with civil rights lawsuits, and it would seem that this trend will not end in the near future. It would appear, to any intelligent person who is cognizant of his environment, that in many instances, law enforcement officers throughout the nation are being harassed and persecuted by spite suits filed against them in the name of "civil rights" merely for doing their duty to preserve law and order.

In every city and state, it is becoming increasingly difficult, if not impossible, for the various law enforcement agencies to recruit and retain qualified and capable enforcement personnel. Job risks and the danger of loss of life or serious injury, at the hands of "non-violent demonstrators" as well as "regular criminals," are becoming more serious, possibly because some of our courts increasingly tend to sympathize with those who cry "police brutality" and file liability suits without just cause.

With the exception of some few who will probably never change, law enforcement officers today realize that brute force is not the answer to our problems. Officers must be educated and trained to comply with the standards expected for maximum performance. Yet, many departments are still hiring personnel with emotional, intellectual, and physical handicaps, which will, eventually, help to deteriorate the professional status so many have devoted their entire lives to attaining. Minimum standards are lowered almost daily by judicial decisions in the name of "discrimination." Yet the very people who would force the various law enforcement departments to hire just anyone who walks in off the street are the same ones who award damages against those officers who abuse their authority

CONCLUSION

The material in this chapter is offered to help the law enforcement officer to become aware of some of the problems he may face if he is not cautious or uses poor judgment in the performance of his duties. He must realize that anyone can be sued, including police officers. The officer is responsible for foreseeing the consequences of his actions, and he must, to protect himself, do so before any harm is done and before he embarks on a course of unprofessional or improper conduct. The officer must remember that he cannot hold another liable for his own negligent conduct, even if he is injured thereby. If an officer is sued and found guilty of negligence, the probability is that a judgment will be levied against him, which may result in garnishment of his pay. And how many law enforcement officers could afford anything less than what they already earn? Even if the officer is covered by a surety bond and it pays the assessed damages, he would be required to repay the amount at a later date. The officer would also be required to hire his own attorney for his defense, because very few departments, if any, furnish legal counsel for their employees in civil suits against the employee.

How can law enforcement agencies and their employees protect themselves against the problems of civil liability? Certainly everyone agrees that in hiring capable officers, a person's race or sex is not a factor. Good law enforcement officers come from all races and both sexes, as do bad ones. One of the best safeguards against civil liability is the fostering of an attitude and environment of professionalism at every level of law enforcement. This will, of course, require heart-felt dedication by officers who are educated and well-trained, as well as the support and respect of the community in which they serve. In order to gain and keep the respect so essential today, an officer should never abuse the confidence expressed in him by his fellow citizens when he was entrusted with the power and authority of his position. There is no substitute for reasoned judgment and good faith.

The law enforcement officer can offer only one thing, and that is service to others. He does not deal with a product as the butcher, grocer, and others do. It bears repeating that all officers should treat every citizen with courtesy and respect in their associations or confrontations, no matter how he may personally feel at the moment. It is in this way that law enforcement shall gain the standing it has strived for for so long.

REFERENCES

1. Black's Law Dictionary, rev. 4th ed., St. Paul, West Publishing Co., 1968, pp. 1660–1661.
2. Ibid., p. 1661.
3. 57 Am. Jur. 2d 357–359, Negligence, Sec. 17.
4. 6 Am. Jur. 2d 8–14, Assault and Battery, Sec. 1.
5. 6 Am. Jur. 2d 95–96, Assault and Battery, Sec. 110.
6. 6 Am. Jur. 2d 96–97, Assault and Battery, Sec. 111.
7. 6 Am. Jur. 2d 105–106, Assault and Battery, Sec. 125.
8. 6 Am. Jur. 2d 126, Assault and Battery, Sec. 148.
9. *Savaterre* v. *New York Transit Authority.*
10. *Brown* v. *City of Philadelphia* (Common Pleas Court 1974).
11. *Scott* v. *Vandiver,* 476 F.2d 238 (1973).
12. Black's Law Dictionary, rev. 4th ed., St. Paul, West Publishing Co., 1968, p. 1111.
13. Police Law Reporter, March, 1969, pp. 7–9.
14. *Spicy* v. *City of Miami,* 280 So.2d 419 (1973).
15. *Fye* v. *Woeckener* (Rock Island County Circuit Court 1974).
16. *Tines* v. *Beebe* (Wayne County Circuit Court 1972).
17. *May Department Stores, Inc.* v. *Devercelli,* 314 A.2d 767 (1974).
18. *United States* v. *Price,* 383 U.S. 787 (1966).
19. *United States* v. *Classic,* 313 U.S. 299 (1941).
20. *Monroe* v. *Pape,* 365 U.S. 167 (1961).
21. *Catlette* v. *United States,* 132 F.2d 902 (1943).

22. *State ex rel. Smith* v. *Heil,* 308 F. Supp. 1063 (1970).
23. *Nugent* v. *Sheppard,* 318 F. Supp. 314 (1970).
24. F.B.I. Law Enforcement Bulletin, August, 1960, pp. [illegible]
25. *Clark and Travis* v. *Ziedonis,* 368 F. Supp. 544 (1973).
26. *Richards* v. *Busby.*
27. *Lykken* v. *Vavreck,* 366 F. Supp. 585 (1973).
28. *Schaeffer* v. *Tannian filed sub nom. Wright* v. *Nichols.*
29. *O'Brien* v. *Shimp,* 356 F. Supp. 1259 (1973).
30. *Dyer* v. *Sweeney* (Los Angeles Superior Court 1973).
31. *Marusa* v. *District of Columbia,* 484 F.2d 828 (1973).
32. *McDaniel* v. *Carroll,* 457 F.2d 968 (1972).

GLOSSARY OF LEGAL TERMS

Abet: To encourage another to commit a crime. This encouragement may be by advice, inducement, command, etc. The abettor of a crime is, under most state laws, equally guilty with the one who actually commits the crime.

Accessory after the Fact: One who harbors, assists, or protects another person, although he knows that person has committed a crime.

Accessory before the Fact: One who helps another to commit a crime, even though he is absent when the crime is committed.

Accomplice: One who is involved in the commission of a crime with others, whether he actually commits the crime or abets others. The term *principal* means the same thing, except that one may be a principal if he commits a crime without the aid of others.

Accumulative Sentence: A sentence, additional to others, imposed at the same time for several distinct offenses; one sentence to begin at the expiration of another.

Acquit: To free a person legally from an accusation of criminal guilt.

Adjournment: Postponing a session or a hearing to some other time or place.

Adult: Any person who is 21 years of age or older.

Adultery: Voluntary and unlawful sexual intercourse or cohabitation on the part of a married person with a person of the opposite sex.

Affidavit: A written declaration of facts, made voluntarily under oath or affirmation and taken before an officer who has authority to administer the oath.

Affirmation: To swear on one's conscience that what he says is true. An *oath* means that one calls upon God to witness the truth of what he says.

Alias: Any name by which one is known other than his true name. *Alias dictus* is the more technically correct term but it is rarely used.

Alibi: A claim that one was in a place different from that charged. If the person proves his alibi, he proves that he could not have committed the crime charged.

Alienist: A physician or psychiatrist qualified as an expert to testify before the court upon the insanity or mental condition of persons.

Allegation: The declaration of a party to a lawsuit made in a pleading, that states what he expects to prove.

Amnesia: Loss of memory.

Appeal: A case carried to a higher court, that seeks to have the decision of the lower court altered or overruled completely.

Appellant: The party appealing a decision or judgment to a higher court.

Appellate Court: A court that has jurisdiction to hear cases on appeal; not a trial court.

Appellee: The party against whom the appeal is taken.

Arraign: To bring the accused before the judge, in open court, to plead to the charges against him.

Arrest: To take a person into custody that he may be held to answer for a crime.

Arson: Setting fire to or burning any building or other property, wilfully and maliciously or with intent to defraud.

Asportation: The moving of an object from its original position.

Assault: An unlawful attempt to hurt another person physically. Should the other actually be beaten, the act is called *Battery* (see).

Attestation: Witnessing an instrument in writing and recording that act in writing on the instrument.

Attorney of Record: Attorney whose name appears on the permanent records or files of a case.

Bail: To free a person who has been arrested or imprisoned, on his giving some security for his appearance at a specified date and place.

Bail Bond: An obligation signed by the accused and his sureties, that insures his presence in court.

Bailiff: A court attendant whose duties are to keep order in the courtroom and to have custody of the jury.

Barratry: The practice of bringing unnecessary lawsuits to vex and annoy others. If done three or more times, it is often made a crime. If a suit is legitimate, there is no barratry.

Battery: Wrongful physical force inflicted on another without his consent. It is associated with an *Assault* (see), and the two terms are usually applied together as "assault and battery."

Bench Warrant: Process issued from the bench, or court, for the arrest of one named or described therein.

Bigamy: Marriage to another person while having a legal husband or wife who is living and from whom one has not been divorced.

Bind Over: To hold on bail for trial.

Blackmail: To extort money or goods from another by the threat of accusation or exposure. Sometimes known as *extortion* or *robbery* by threatening letter demanding goods or money.

Bona Fide: In good faith.

Brief: A summary of the law relating to a case, which is prepared by the attorneys for both parties to a case and handed to the judge.

Burden of Proof: The duty of affirmatively proving a fact or facts in dispute.

Burglary: Breaking and entering with intent to commit a crime within.

Calling a Docket: The public calling of the docket (list of cases) at the beginning of a term of court for setting a date for trial or entering orders.

Capias: "That you take." The general name of writs issued by a judge from the bench that order the arrest of the defendant. Often appears in the same document with a *Search Warrant* (see), appearing as "Search Warrant and Capias."

Capital Crime: Any crime that may be punishable by death.

Chambers: Private office or room of a judge.

Change of Venue: The removal of a suit from one jurisdiction to another or from one court to another within the same jurisdiction. See also *Venue.*

Circumstantial Evidence: Indirect evidence; evidence from which the principal fact can be proved or disproved by inference.

Civil Rights: Rights guaranteed to every person by the United States Constitution, the Congress, and the state legislature.

Code: A compilation, compendium, or revision of laws, arranged into chapters, having a table of contents and index, and promulgated by legislative authority.

Codicil: An addition to a will.

Coercion: The compelling of a person to do that which he is not obliged to do, or to omit doing what he may legally do, by some illegal threat, force, or intimidation.

Cohabit: To live together as man and wife.

Commit: To place a person in custody in a prison or other institution by lawful order.

Common Law: Law that derives its authority from usage and custom or court decisions. Also known as *case law.*

Commutation: To change the punishment meted out to a criminal to one less severe.

Competency: The capacity to give testimony.

Complainant: See *Plaintiff.*

Complaint: A sworn written allegation stating that a specified person committed a crime. Sometimes called an *information.* When issued from a *Grand Jury* (see) it is called an *indictment* (see).

Compulsion: An irresistible impulse to commit some act, such as stealing, setting a fire, or an illegal sexual act.

Consanguinity: Blood relationship. Those who descend from a common ancestor are related by consanguinity. Marriage or sexual intercourse between close blood relatives is forbidden and is termed *incest.*

Conspiracy: A secret combination of two or more persons who plan for the purpose of committing a crime or any unlawful act or a lawful act by unlawful or criminal means.

Contempt of Court: Behavior that impugns the authority of a court or obstructs the execution of court orders.

Contralegem: Against the law.

Corporal: Relating to the body. Corporal punishment is force used against the body of another.

Corpus Delicti: The material substance upon which a crime has been committed.

Corroborating Evidence: Supplementary evidence that tends to strengthen or confirm other evidence given previously.

Court of Record: A court obligated to keep records of the proceeding. The statutes specify which courts are of record.

Court Reporter: A person who, by shorthand or stenographically, takes down testimony during court proceedings and transcribes it.

Crime against Nature: Unnatural sexual act or unnatural sexual intercourse. The crime of sodomy is a crime against nature.

Criminal Insanity: Lack of mental capacity to do or refrain from doing a criminal act; inability to distinguish right from wrong.

Criminology: The scientific study of crime and criminals.

Cross-Examination: The questioning of a witness by the party who did not produce the witness.

Cumulative Sentence: See *Accumulative Sentence.*

De Facto: In fact; actually.

Defendant: The party against whom an action at law or in equity is brought; party denying, opposing, resisting, or contesting the action.

Defraud: To withhold from another what is justly due him or to deprive him of the right by artifice or deception; to cheat.

Degenerate: A term applied to a person who has intense impulses and satisfies them by unnatural acts; sometimes called a *pervert.*

De Jure: Lawfully.

Dementia: Loss of sanity or weakness of mind. Not to be confused with *amentia,* which is feeblemindedness due to a lack of mental development from birth.

Demurrer: In court procedure, a statement that the claim of the opposing party has no sufficient basis in law, despite the truth of the facts alleged.

Deposition: The testimony of a witness not taken in open court but taken in pursuance of authority given by statute or rule of court to take such testimony elsewhere.

Dipsomania: Abnormal desire for alcoholic beverages.

Directed Verdict: An instruction by the judge to the jury to return a specific verdict.

Direct Evidence: Proof of facts by witnesses who actually saw acts or heard words, as distinguished from *Circumstantial Evidence* (see).

Direct Examination: The first questioning of a witness by the party who produced him. See also *Redirect Examination.*

Domicile: The place where a person has established permanent residence.

Double Jeopardy: To be prosecuted twice for the same offense. See also *Jeopardy.*

Due Process: Law in its regular course of administration through the courts of justice.

Ejusdem Generis: Of the same kind, class, or nature.

Embezzlement: The fraudulent appropriation of the property of another after a fiduciary relationship has been established.

Embracery: An attempt to influence a jury, or a member thereof, in their verdict by any improper means. If something of value is offered, the crime is *bribery.*

Eminent Domain: The power of the state to take private property for public use.

Entrapment: The instigation of a crime by officers or agents of a government who induce a person to commit a crime that he did not originally contemplate in order to institute a criminal prosecution against him.

Erotic: Pertaining to sexual conduct. That which arouses sexual desire or passion.

Et Al.: And others. Used after the names of plaintiffs and defendants to indicate that others are involved besides those specifically mentioned.

Euthanasia: Putting a person to death by painless means when that person has an incurable disease or disability and is living in great pain and suffering.

Evidence: All the means used to prove or disprove the fact at issue.

Examination: An investigation of a witness by counsel in the form of questions, for the purpose of bringing before the court knowledge possessed by the witness.

Exception: A formal objection to the action of the court during a trial. The indication is that the excepting party will seek to reverse the court's action at some future proceeding. See also *Objection.*

Ex Officio: By virtue of office. A mayor is often an ex officio magistrate.

Ex Parte: Done by or for one side only and without notice to, or consideration by, any person adversely interested.

Expert Evidence: Testimony by one qualified to speak authoritatively on a technical matter because of his special training or skill.

Ex Post Facto: After the fact. An ex post facto law is a criminal law that makes an act unlawful although it was committed prior to the passage of that law.

Extradition: The surrender by one state to another of an individual accused or convicted of an offense who is outside the receiving state's own territory and within the territorial jurisdiction of the surrendering state.

False Arrest: Any unlawful physical restraint of another's freedom of movement.

False Pretense: A knowing misrepresentation of an existing fact or condition by which a person obtains another's money or goods with intent to defraud.

Feasance: The doing of something. *Nonfeasance* is a term applied to neglect of duty by a public officer. *Malfeasance* is the act of a public officer in committing a crime in relation to his office. *Misfeasance* is the act of a public officer who, as such, does a lawful act but in an unlawful or wrongful way.

Felonious: Evil, malicious, or criminal. A felonious act is not necessarily a felony, but is criminal in some degree.

Felony: Generally, an offense punishable by death or imprisonment in a penitentiary. Those offenses of a more serious nature than *Misdemeanors* (see).

Fence: A term applied to a professional receiver of stolen or embezzled goods.

Fetishism: A type of sexual perversion in which a person is desirous of possessing some object belonging to another who is the object of the sexual perversion.

Fetus: An unborn child. Sometimes referred to as an unborn quick child.

Forensic: Relating to the court. Thus, forensic medicine would refer to medicine in relation to court proceedings and the law in general.

Fratricide: The killing of one's brother or sister. The killing of one's self is *suicide;* of one's father, *patricide;* of one's mother, *matricide;* and of one's wife, *uxoricide.*

Fraud: An intentional misrepresentation or deception employed to deprive another of property or a legal right or to otherwise do him harm.

Grand Jury: A jury of inquiry whose duty is to hear *Complaints* (see) or accusations in criminal cases and return *Indictments* (see) against the accused when the evidence so warrants.

Habeas Corpus: A writ of habeas corpus is an order from the court to the one holding the prisoner to produce him in court so that the legality of the detention may be decided.

Hearsay: Evidence not originating from the witness' personal knowledge.

Homicide: The killing of one human being by another.

Illicit: Illegal. *Licit* means legal.

Impeach: To discredit. To question the truthfulness of a witness.

In Articulo Mortis: At the point of death. See also *In Extremis.*

In Camera: Behind closed doors. A case is tried in camera when the general public is excluded.

Incest: See *Consanguinity.*

Inculpate: Tending to accuse of or implicate in a crime. To *exculpate* is to wipe out a charge of crime.

Indictment: An accusation of crime, in writing, by a grand jury. Also called a *true bill.* See also *Complaint; Grand Jury.*

In Extremis: The state of a person who is near death and beyond hope of recovery.

Infant: One who is under the statutory age of adulthood.

Infanticide: The killing of a newborn child.

Inference: A conclusion one draws about something based on proof of certain facts.

Inferior Court: A court subordinate to the chief appellate court in a particular judicial system.

Injunction: An order by a court prohibiting a defendant from committing an act that is injurious to the plaintiff.

In Pari Delicto: Equally guilty or at fault.

Intent: A design or determination of the mind to do or not do a certain thing. Intent may be determined from the nature of one's acts.

Introvert: A person occupied with his own thoughts and not interested in other persons or activities. The opposite of *extrovert.*

Jeopardy: The danger of conviction and punishment that a defendant faces upon being indicted. See also *Double Jeopardy.*

Judicial Notice: The rule that a court will accept certain things as common knowledge without proof.

Jurisdiction: The power of a court to hear and determine a matter.

Jurisprudence: The philosophy of law. The science that deals with legal principles and legal relations.

Jury: A certain number of persons who are sworn to examine the evidence and determine the truth on the basis of that evidence.

Kidnapping: The carrying away or secreting of a person against his will.

Kleptomania: An insane desire to steal an object regardless of its value or use.

Larceny: The taking and carrying away of the personal property of another with intent to steal.

Latent: Lying dormant.

Libel: A type of defamation expressed in writing, pictures, or other permanent form. In general, any publication that is injurious to the reputation of another. See also *Slander.*

License: Permission accorded by competent authority allowing one to do something that would otherwise be illegal.

Locus Delicti: The place where a crime occurred.

Lucri Causa: For sake of gain.

Mala Fide: In bad faith.

Mala In Se: Evil in itself. Acts that are made crimes because they are, by their nature, evil and morally wrong..

Mala Prohibita: Evil because they are prohibited. Acts that are not wrong in themselves but which, to protect the general welfare, are made crimes by statute.

Malfeasance: See *Feasance.*

Malice: An evil intent to vex, annoy, or injure another; intentional evil.

Malicious Prosecution: An action instituted in bad faith with the intention of injuring the defendant.

Mandamus: A writ that issues from a superior court, directed to any person, corporation, or inferior court, requiring it to do some particular thing.

Manslaughter: The unlawful killing of one human being by another without *Malice* (see). It may be either voluntary, done in the heat of passion; or involuntary, done while committing some unlawful act without due regard for others.

Masochism: A type of sexual perversion in which one person derives pleasure from having another cause physical pain to him. See also *Sadism.*

Matter of Fact in Issue: The question of fact to be decided at the trial.

Mens Rea: A guilty intent.

Misdemeanor: Any crime not a *Felony* (see). Usually, a crime punishable by a fine or imprisonment in the county or other local jail.

Misprision: Failing to reveal a crime.

Mistrial: A false or erroneous trial.

Mittimus: A writ, issued from a court, directing an officer to convey the person named therein to jail or other place of confinement.

Modus Operandi: Method of operation by criminals.

Motive: The reason for doing a certain thing; the motivating influence.

Municipal Court: A court whose territorial authority is confined to the city or municipality.

Murder: Generally, the unlawful killing of a human being by another with *Malice* (see) aforethought. It is defined statutorily in most states.

Negligence: Failure to exercise the degree of care that the circumstances require or the care that a reasonable and prudent man would have used under the same circumstances.

Night Season (Night Time): The period of time from the termination of daylight in the evening to the earliest dawn in the morning.

No Bill: A phrase used by a *Grand Jury* (see) when they fail to indict.

Nolle Prosequi: A declaration to a court, by the plaintiff, that he does not wish to further prosecute the case.

Nolo Contendere: A pleading, usually used by a defendant in a criminal case, that literally means "I will not contest."

Non Compos Mentis: Of unsound mind; insane.

Objection: The act of taking exception to some statement or procedure in a trial. Used to call the court's attention to some improper evidence or procedure. See also *Exception.*

Opinion Evidence: A witness' belief or opinion about a fact in dispute, as distinguished from personal knowledge of the fact.

Ordinance: A statute enacted by the city or municipal government.

Overt Act: An open or physical act, as opposed to a thought or mere intention.

Paranoia: A mental abnormality in which a person has a persecution complex. Such persons suspect that everyone hates them, desires their death, or is doing something to cause them harm.

Paresis: A brain disorder caused by syphilis. The brain deteriorates as a result of the disease.

Parole: A conditional release from prison.

Parol Evidence: Oral or spoken *Testimony* (see).

Peremptory Challenge: The act of objecting to a certain number of jurors without assigning a cause for their dismissal. Used during the *voir dire* examination.

Perjury: Lying or falsely swearing under oath.

Petit Jury: The ordinary jury composed of 12 persons who hear criminal and civil cases.

Phobia: A fixed, morbid fear of some object or person for which normal persons lack fear. *Acrophobia* is fear of high places; *agoraphobia,* of open places; *claustrophobia,* of closed places; *hematophobia,* of blood; *ochlophobia,* of crowds; and *zoophobia,* of animals.

Plaintiff: The person who brings suit against another.

Police Power: The authority of the legislature to make laws in the interest of the general public, even at the risk of placing some hardship on individuals. This power has nothing to do with a police department.

Post Mortem: After death. Commonly applied to examination of a dead body. An autopsy is a post mortem examination to determine the cause of death.

Preliminary Hearing: A hearing held before a magistrate to decide if there is sufficient evidence to warrant holding the accused for further action.

Presumption of Fact: An inference as to the truth or falsity of any proposition or fact, made in the absence of actual certainty of its truth or falsity or until such certainty can be attained.

Presumption of Law: A rule of law that courts and judges must draw a particular inference from a particular fact or evidence, unless the inference can be disproved.

Prima Facie: So far as can be judged from the first appearance or at first sight.

Probation: A type of penalty whereby a convicted person is put under the jurisdiction and supervision of a probation officer for a stated time, instead of being confined.

Prosecutor: One who initiates a criminal prosecution against an accused. One who acts as a trial attorney for the government as the representative of the people.

Psychiatry: The branch of medicine that deals with the kinds, causes and cures of mental disorders.

Psychosis: General term that covers many forms of insanity. It generally refers to the more serious types of mental disorders.

Pyromania: An insane desire to set fires.

Quasi: Best defined as "almost." It serves to distinguish between two or more approximately identical things.

Rapine: Robbery.

Reasonable Doubt: That state of mind of jurors when they do not feel a moral certainty about the truth of the charge and when the evidence does not exclude every other reasonable hypothesis except that the defendant is guilty as charged.

Rebut: To contradict.

Rebuttal: The introduction of contradicting testimony; the showing that statements made by a witness are not true; the point in the trial at which such evidence may be introduced.

Recidivist: A repeater in crime; a habitual offender.

Recognizance: When a person binds himself to do a certain act or else suffer a penalty, as, for example, with a recognizance bond.

Redirect Examination: Follows *Cross-Examination* (see), and is done by the party who first examined the witness.

Relevant: Applying to the issue in question; related to the issue; useful in determining the truth or falsity of an alleged fact.

Remand: To send back. To remand a case for new trial or sentencing.

Replevin: A civil action to recover property wrongfully held by someone.

Res: A thing; an object.

Res Gestae: The thing done. The whole of the transaction; every part of it.

Rigor Mortis: The stiffening of the muscles after death.

Sadism: Sexual gratification derived from inflicting pain upon another. The opposite of *Masochism* (see).

Schizophrenic: A psychotic person who lives in a mental world of unreality, and who frequently suffers from delusions of greatness or persecution, and who exhibits no interest in activities taking place outside his own environment.

Search Warrant: A written order, issued by judicial authority in the name of the state, directing a law enforcement officer to search for personal property and, if found, to bring it before the court.

Self-Defense: The protection of one's own person (on occasion, property) against an attempted injury by another. There must be some reasonable belief of immediate danger.

Separation of Witnesses: A rule of a court requiring all witnesses to be separated, the defense from the prosecution, and remain outside of the courtroom until each is called. It does not apply to a plaintiff or defendant, however.

Sexual Perversion: Sexual practices that are considered abnormal or deviant. *Homosexuality* is a desire to commit sexual acts with a person of one's own sex. *Satyriasis* is an abnormal sexual appetite in a man. *Nymphomania* is an abnormal sexual appetite in a female. *Pedophilia* is a desire to have sexual relations with children. *Bestiality* is a desire to have sexual relations with animals. *Exhibitionism* is a tendency to expose or show the sex organs to members of the opposite sex. *Pederasty* is the commission of abnormal sexual acts between males or by an adult male upon a young boy.

Slander: Defamatory spoken words tending to prejudice another in his reputation, business, or means of livelihood. See also *Libel.*

Stare Decisis: To abide by, or adhere to, decided cases. The doctrine that once a court has laid down a principle of law as applicable to certain facts, it will apply it to all future cases when the facts are substantially the same.

State's Evidence: Testimony given by an accomplice or participant in a crime, tending to convict others.

Statute: A written law passed by the legislature.

Stay: A stopping of a judicial proceeding by a court order.

Subpoena: A process that obliges a witness or other person to appear in court at a specified time and place.

Substantiate: To verify; to establish the truth of a matter by adequate evidence.

Summons: A signed request directing a person to appear in court at a stated time and place.

Testimony: Evidence given by a competent witness, under oath, as distinguished from evidence from writings and other sources.

Tort: A legal wrong committed against a person or property for which reparation may be obtained in a suit at law.

Toxicology: The science of poisons.

Transcript: A copy of the original writing.

True Bill: See *Indictment.*

Usury: Excessive interest charges on loans.

Venue: The geographical area in which a court with jurisdiction sits. The power of a court to compel the presence of the parties to a litigation. See also *Change of Venue.*

Verdict: The decision of a court.

Waive: To give up a personal right.

Ward: A person under the care or charge of a guardian or court.

Warrant: See *Bench Warrant; Search Warrant.*

Wilful: Done intentionally; done without justifiable cause.

With Prejudice: As applied to judgment or dismissal, it means that it is as conclusive of rights of parties as if the action had been finally adjudicated against the plaintiff.

Without Prejudice: A dismissal without prejudice allows a new suit to be brought on the same cause of action.

Writ: An instrument in writing, ordering a person to perform some specific duty.

INDEX